In praise of
Mark Kitto

Mini media mogul... A genuinely fascinating insight into life in China, written with humour and nerve.
Daily Telegraph

A fantastic old-school, three-piece suited adventure from a man who knows China far better than most.
Geographical Magazine

Career went from metal trading to building a multi-million magazine publishing business that was seized by the government.
Prospect

Mark Kitto beat the odds...building a business in a boom town, in the most vaguely regulated yet tightly controlled industry in China was stressful.
Sunday Times

A fascinating and often hilarious insight into China and the Chinese.
Good Book Guide

Evocative and lyrical.
Irish Times

A funny and surprisingly fond memoir.
The Canberra Times

Under The Tuscan Sun China-style.
Straits Times

Resonates with gentle echoes of Peter Mayle's A Year in Provence… A charming adventure… Liberally peppered with intriguing history… Kitto's writing style is always self-deprecating, occasionally wide-eyed and sometimes uplifting.
South China Morning Post

(An) autobiographical love-letter to Moganshan… brings alive the 'forgotten' European history of Moganshan…China Cuckoo is a rare bird.
Sydney Ideas Quarterly

A surprisingly easy-to-read account of a foreigner trying to fit into a Chinese community… engaging insights into the Chinese in general and past and present life in Moganshan in particular… backed by plenty of researchand some interesting parallels.
China Economic Review

That's China

by Mark Kitto

Forty-six,
New Writing from Asia,
Third Floor, 207 Regents Street,
London W1B 3HH.

English edition first published 2014.
Cover design by Mandy Wang.

ISBN 978-988-16775-7-0

Mark Kitto was a captain in the British Army before he became a metals trader in London and then China. His series of *that's* listings magazines became the most successful English language publications in China. On the verge of signing a groundbreaking deal that would make him the first authorized foreign publisher in the People's Republic of China, the Communist Party took over his business.

Variously accused of being a spy, pornographer and terrorist, he retreated to a dilapidated, beautiful Chinese mountain village. His efforts to gain a foothold, livelihood and respect on the mountaintop are recounted in his acclaimed '*China Cuckoo, How I lost a fortune and found a life*'. Mark returned to the UK in 2013. He now lives with his wife and two children in North Norfolk and runs a very small publishing business.

Acknowledgements

This book was first written for an American publisher who at the last minute changed their mind. They had sent a final, edited copy of the manuscript to their Beijing office who told them straightaway to cancel it or their attempts to develop business in China would be severely hampered, putting it mildly.

I can understand their concern. This is a story about building a foreign-backed publishing business in China, and what the government does to it when it becomes (too) successful.

My sincere thanks go to Forty-six, the publisher who is bringing the story into print at last. I've had time to think about it, and improve it, I hope. I even had time to write the sequel, which appeared as *China Cuckoo, How I lost a fortune and found a life in China*.

When I was in China, building a publishing business, I was no muck-raking journalist. I didn't set out to fight against corruption (though I had to deal with it every day) or strike a blow for press freedom (except inadvertently). I was just an entrepreneur who had an idea for a magazine which I thought people might like. We had principles though, like any media company should, and we stuck to them.

If I was to make a dedication, it would be to the young people working in mainland Chinese media, like the young journalist Ms. Wang, who interviewed me about this story. Afterwards I turned the tables on her and asked why she and her colleagues had not been firmer when they protested against government censorship and interference in their paper, and she said, 'We can't do anything. It's up to the next generation.'

Well it's not. Please don't think that. I suppose that is more a request than a dedication.

My sincere gratitude, and true dedication for this book, goes to the people who helped me. They know who they are. Most of them have no idea of what is in these pages. If they do, they were damn good actors. I'd like to list their names but they don't need that. After all, hardly any of them, according to Chinese law, ever worked for me.

To all of you: thanks. This is for you.

Contents

The Question

The Chinese official leaned towards me, looked me in the eye, and said something that made time stand still.

'Mr. Mark, would you like to co-operate?'

We were alone, the two of us, in an empty apartment on the outskirts of Beijing. It was too easy to imagine myself in an interrogation chamber, or a safe house in a spy thriller. I wondered if I'd been summoned to this remote, anonymous location so the meeting could be denied if the man opposite me, and the people he represented, changed their minds. Or was he acting on his own initiative, testing me in private, without authority from his superiors?

I was out on the very limit of Beijing's frayed, endlessly unfolding suburbs. From downtown a taxi had taken me north-west, past Beijing University and the high tech district of Haidian, and out of the city proper past the Old Summer Palace, famous for being ransacked in 1860 by British and French troops. Beyond it the Fragrant Hills cut a jagged horizon across the azure sky. A biting wind had blown away the dust and pollution and the harsh sunlight blasted the grey apartment blocks, the brown earth and skeletal trees, with an ethereal radiance. The dull colours crystallized and sparkled. On winter's days like this in northern China the air seems to disappear and all that's left is a white, cold, crisp light that burns your throat and your eyes.

In that blinding light Beijing, the 'northern capital', appears naked; as naked as its brazen, shameless ambition to become a world leader: economic, political, cultural… a leader in everything. In the 1990s it was an ambition that many people shared, not just Chinese, but foreigners like me, who set out with deliberate plans to hitch a ride on it.

In the back of the taxi I looked out of the window and lost myself in memories of 1986, when I had first lived in the city as a student. My friends and I spent our weekends roaming those 'fragrant' hills. We raced Flying Pigeon bicycles down the steep cobbled lanes and dared each other to hang by our fingertips from the chairlifts that carried tourists to the highest peak. On a stone bench beside a lake in the Old Summer Palace (I turned in the seat: just there, behind that wall!) I'd held hands with a girl who put a piece of chewing gum in my mouth and kissed me. 'To get rid of your funny foreign smell,' she said. I tried to remember her name. It was over twenty years ago.

How innocent. And how ironic, that after all the years and dreams of making a career in China, I was returning to where it started to find out how it was going to end.

The taxi driver interrupted my sweet daydreams. We were driving the wrong way down a dual carriageway, a ring road to nowhere.

'I'm lost,' he said. 'Can you call and ask for directions?'

I dialed and handed him my phone. He spoke and listened.

'Got it,' he said and handed it back.

We turned around and onto a dirt track. On our right a brown field stretched ahead to a row of three-sided shacks: an unfinished golf driving range. The ten-metre poles for the net at the far end looked like stakes outside a Mongol encampment, waiting for a defeated enemies' heads. To our left was a white wall. Stencils of a tennis player, a horse-rider and a golfer in mid swing had been spray-painted onto it at regular intervals. Chinese characters in between them repeated: 'Villa style living in an apartment complex!'

We drove through a gateway and pulled up outside a drab Soviet style block.

'Here you are,' the driver said.

I took his name card, asked him to hang around in the area, and climbed a dark concrete stairwell to the sixth floor. I knocked on a metal door.

I had arrived to hear my fate. I was ready.

I didn't expect a question. Least of all that question: 'Mr. Mark, would you like to co-operate?'

For the past seven years, Chinese government officials like the man opposite me had been anything but co-operative. They had raided my offices, confiscated my computers and financial records, fined me millions of yuan, and deported my staff. That was the everyday, straightforward stuff. Then there was the blackmail, the threats, bullying, humiliation, and the libelous yet undocumented accusations — impossible to dispute. I had come close, so close, to giving up, but I had hung on with a desperate hope that one day it would all be worth it, that it would all be all right.

In my heart of hearts I knew that was far from guaranteed. At least, that's what my friends implied, with sympathy and a pat on the shoulder. 'How stupid are you, to think you can build a business in the most restricted industry in the most powerful one-party state in the world?' they asked. Sometimes I noticed a guarded look of concern in their eyes.

'Pretty damn stupid.' I replied. 'But it might work.'

It was worth trying.

The industry was media. Magazines. English language city listings magazines. By January 2004 we were the biggest and best in the business in China. Turnover was in the millions of US dollars, profits more than ample to support constant expansion, 120 staff, four offices across the country, monthly distribution just shy of 100,000, a travel magazine on the side, popular websites, annual guides, and all of it self-funded, organically grown.

It had been one hell of a ride. The world's most populous country had emerged from decades of isolation. The zeitgeist was bold experimentation — economic, social and sexual. The usual rules didn't apply. By luck as much as good judgment — or good editing — our magazines had hit the spot for an emerging generation of Chinese as they embraced individualism and the outside world, and at the same time shepherded the vast flock of foreigners pouring into the China in search of adventure, the wild life and the sense of unlimited potential.

I hadn't held back from the wild life myself. As the publisher I had thrown myself into the craziness with abandon, partying all night with artists, writers and foreign adventurers, drinking myself under the table with government officials and Party members, living the high life yet always fighting a constant and desperate battle to keep my business alive.

My magazines, while successful beyond my wildest expectations, were never safe. There was an enormous catch, one never-ending conundrum I woke up to every hung-over morning.

Since the Communist takeover of the country in 1948, the media had been China's most tightly controlled sector. No private company or individual — let alone a foreigner — can own a media business in China. You can't even own a part of a media business, not one single tiny point something of one per cent.

The reason is simple.

The declared aim of the Chinese media is: 'To promote the leadership of the Chinese Communist Party'.

To the Party, media is state-owned propaganda. No individuals, let alone foreigners, will ever have a stake in it.

That was the rule.

As with all rules, especially those laid down by a rigid yet practical political system, there are ways round them. To enter the Chinese media industry you asked the Party to help you break its rules, in return for a fee. There were other costs too, non-monetary, which I'll come to. Suffice to say: building a media business in China was difficult and expensive. But I seemed to have been pretty good at it, so far, and I was playing the game for keeps. I'd pulled off corporate and political manoeuvres I am proud of, and some I am not so proud of but will own up to. I'd fought competitors to protect my partners, and my partners to protect my dream. I would make it up to them later.

My plan was to hang on to control of my business until it was possible to own a stake in it.

(That sentence will make no sense to anyone with knowledge or experience of business. But *that's China*. Don't expect logic.)

That was the obsession that drove me for all those years. The door to the Chinese media industry would open one day, I was sure it would.

If it didn't? If I lost everything?

I wasn't going to think about that. I couldn't because I had put everything, my heart and soul, my every cent, every living breath and waking minute into my dream, my creation. I had neglected friends and family, I had spurned relationships, and I had earned myself a reputation as an arrogant, driven, selfish bastard. But one day I would put that right. I had another reputation too, a good one, and public supporters, loyal colleagues and long-suffering friends. I'd prove myself for them, and the others. It would all turn out all right.

On that cold January Sunday morning in 2004, in the empty

apartment out near the Old Summer Palace and the Fragrant Hills, a man who represented the highest authority in the Chinese media industry told me he could make it possible for me to own a stake in the magazines I had created.

I hadn't been that stupid. I was right to have held out hope. It was going to be all right.

'Mark,' he repeated. I was still staring at him. 'Mark, do you want to co-operate with us? Do you want to form a joint stock publishing company?'

I took a deep, silent breath and looked away for a few seconds, to give the impression that I was weighing up the pros and cons, wondering whether I should even talk about the idea.

A drowning man would more likely think twice about a lifebelt because it didn't match his swimming trunks.

I set my face into the inscrutable blank that is vital for a business meeting in China. The man opposite me would have his terms ready and expect me to negotiate right away, before I was ready. It's an old trick. I was about to get lost in a thick fog of terms and conditions, and diversions and impossible constraints, yet through it all, as harsh as the winter sun outside the window, shone the blinding light at the end of the tunnel.

I turned back to him, put my elbows on the table, and with a lump in my throat I said, 'Yes please.'

Chapter One
Clueless

Machines were clacking and grinding inside the factory. A worker in ink-spattered overalls wheeled a trolley stacked with paper into place at one end of a four-colour printing press. It was a Heidelberg, imported from Germany. Mr. Wang, the print factory manager, was explaining how it worked, but my mind was elsewhere.

The worker fed the sheets into the machine. It clunked like a train leaving the station. Mr. Wang walked me to the other end and took one off the first sheets to come out. On it were eight pages of a magazine: pictures and text and titles, 'standfirsts', bylines and page numbers in neat little orange boxes, and advertisements for ice cream and wine and airlines, upside down and back to front. I had just learnt this is called a 'signature'.

Mr. Wang took it to a sloping desk against the wall, laid it flat and stood back.

'What do you think?'

I tried to look knowledgeable, experienced, and demanding, but I was thinking: 'This is bloody amazing. Someone pinch me and tell me it's true. My first real magazine on real paper and in colour too. I'm a bloody publisher!'

Eight months ago I'd been an ex-soldier who'd resigned from his first proper job and set out to become a China-based freelance journalist, an amateur hack. Today I was the publisher of two magazines, one a rough and ready community rag in Guangzhou, and this — brand new, the real thing — in Shanghai.

'Yes!' I screamed inside my head.

I leaned over the desk.

'Very good,' I said.

'The colours are OK?'

I pretended to study a photograph. I'd taken it myself. It was a portrait of a nightclub lavatory attendant. It looked brilliant. My own photograph, in my own magazine.

'They're fine.'

Mr. Wang took me back to the machine.

'Press that button.' He pointed to a yellow, mushroom-shaped knob.

It gave like a piston. The clunk of the Heidelberg sped and blurred into a deep whir and thump, accompanied by the snap and crack of the sheets being snatched from the feeder tray.

I pulled out my mobile and dialed my business partner's number. She was a couple of thousand miles away, looking after the first magazine, back in Guangzhou.

'Hey, Kathleen!' I shouted. 'Can you hear this?' I held the phone to the press and brought it back to my ear.

'What's that?' she asked, I think.

'You'll have to speak up.' I shouted.

'What — is — that?'

'It's our Shanghai magazine going to print.'

'Cool!' she shouted back. 'Can't wait to see it. Keep me a copy!'

I hung up and grinned at Mr. Wang. 'Do you mind if I keep it?' I pointed at the inspection desk.

'Of course.'

I folded the sheet three times and slipped it into a folder. I shook his hand. 'See you in a few days, when it's ready.'

My taxi had waited. As I walked towards it I waved at Mr. Wang and pulled my mobile back out of my pocket. I called up a bar on

Fuxing Road and booked it for a staff party the day the magazine would hit the streets. We were off.

Eight short months before that day in June 1998, I'd been a metal trader in Guangzhou, the unofficial capital of southern China. I had been sent there from Beijing where I had worked for the Chinese boss of the Beijing branch of my British-owned company. He had done everything he could to get rid of me. I was the only foreigner in his office and he suspected me of being a spy sent from the London one.

My chairman, George Wilson, had told me over a farewell pint in London that I was to spend two years learning the ropes in Beijing and then move on, perhaps to Hong Kong, or Shanghai. My Beijing boss, who used the English name Norman, told me on my first day: 'Don't unpack.'

He had an idea to set up an office in Ulan Bataar, capital of Mongolia, and said I was the man to do it. There is not much metal in Mongolia, apart from some copper and a few thousand rusting Ladas.

On my second day in Beijing I was offered a job running the office of one of our biggest rivals, a Swiss commodity trader. The meeting took place in the presidential suite of a hotel next door to our office. It was the most charming job interview I have ever experienced. I put it down to coincidence. I also turned down the offer.

Stuck with me, Norman made every effort to ensure I screwed up. I was sent on a commercial suicide mission to recover a hundred thousand dollars from a state-owned company in Shijiazhuang, a day's trip from Beijing. They had shipped us shavings from the factory floor instead of the alloy we had paid for, which was rocketing in price.

The evening I arrived my hosts threw a banquet, the standard business welcome and warm-up session. They told me the full story with unabashed pride and delight at their trickery. I struggled to write a report in my room and faxed it to London before I passed out from mild alcohol poisoning. The next morning, in the official meeting, I told my opponents that my head office knew the full story and would be suing them.

'But that was just chitchat!' they shouted. 'We are now going to give you our official statement of the facts. Last night's conversation does not count!'

'I'm sorry,' I said, my head throbbing. 'I thought it did. That's why I sent the report already. And it's with our lawyers.'

They agreed to pay back the hundred thousand.

Norman was furious.

A trader from the London office came to Beijing and Norman organized a major in-house meeting. He went round the Chinese staff one by one, and the table of elements from A to Z. He had everyone recite which metals they were sourcing or selling and give an account of their progress. It was a classic show, carefully prepared for the London visitor.

I was left until last. Norman turned to me with a smirk. He'd set me up. But someone had blundered. There had been no mention of Antimony. It should have been at the top of the list.

'I'll do everything left then,' I announced. 'Oh, and Antimony.'

Fresh out from London myself, I knew we were keen to buy up stocks of the metal.

Norman's face was a picture. The guy from London, wise to Norman's game, smiled.

As everyone dispersed, Norman pulled me aside. 'Of course, the person who knows antimony suppliers best is so-and-so, so you should really just help him out,' he said.

'And then,' he continued, fudging his argument, 'Antimony

comes mostly from South China, so I think you should spend some time down there in our Guangzhou office.'

I started running it. I got my own office. Norman got me out of his hair.

Also known as Canton, Guangzhou in the 1970s and 80s had established itself as the trading hub of modern China thanks to the biannual Canton Trade Fair. In 1992 Deng Xiaoping, architect of modern China, made a speech declaring wealth respectable. The location of the speech was significant. It was the new city of Shenzhen, on the border with Hong Kong, down the road from Guangzhou. Deng said, 'To get rich is glorious,' or something like that, and, he added, 'It does not matter what colour the cat is, black or white, so long as it catches mice.'

It became the catchphrase of the new generation.

With characteristic political cunning, Deng was only jumping on a bandwagon. The Cantonese are renowned for getting on with life, and business. The unofficial motto of the city is 'Heaven is high above, and the Emperor is far away.' In other words: 'No one is looking so let's get on with our own thing.'

The Cantonese had been getting rich and trading black cats for white ones for years.

There is an energy and entrepreneurial spirit to Guangdong Province that sets it apart from the rest of China. It is also the ancestral home of most of the Chinese diaspora. Thanks to family connections across the globe and down the Pearl River in Hong Kong, Guangzhou-based businesses began to thrive the minute they were given the chance. It helped that in 1956 the government had decreed that Communist China's trade with the outside world could only be carried out at the Trade Fair. The month-long event, held once in April and again in October, attracted foreign traders like an oriental El Dorado. Those who got in early made fortunes.

One of them was George Wilson, my UK boss. He told me how the traders spent one month at the fair on a single-entry visa and contrary to expectation were free to roam everywhere. Sometimes the best business was done at the end of the fair or even after it had finished.

At the end of one long month, George got onto the train to Hong Kong with his friends and competitors and just before it pulled out of the station announced he'd forgotten his passport and would follow the next day. The bottom was falling out of the world Aluminium market and he realised the surest way to save money was sell to the Chinese for a modest loss, rather than take a bigger one back in London. He stayed behind and completed his business while one of his closest competitors, who couldn't wait to get home, found he'd been fired by the time he got there. He turned around again, went back East, and ended up running a bar in Bangkok.

With the Cantonese enthusiasm to race ahead came chaotic development. In their rush the city and its people overlooked some of the basic requirements for a commercial centre, such as roads, buildings even. By the 1990s the place was a mess. Every other building in the city was under construction. Rows of half-built apartment and office towers dominated complete blocks. Their concrete skeletons gaped like giant crossword puzzles waiting for the glass and cladding to fill the blanks. In between them, muddy tracks led to more, brand new, smaller office buildings. Power and telephone cables hung like washing lines from telegraph poles to the eaves of buildings. The noise of construction crashed and banged around the clock. At night arc lights shone through the darkness up the sides of the towers like searchlights, sparks from welders' torches cascaded from the heights in vivid orange showers. In every apartment block, every office tower, someone was setting up anew or ripping out the old and renovating. The hammer blows echoed from every corner, every ceiling, every waking minute.

From my office high in a new tower block I used to slip into the empty room next door for a cigarette. I stood by the window and watched the mayhem at the road junction below. From my bird's eye view the traffic jams were works of art. Traffic lights were ignored. The concept of a right of way did not exist. Everyone was rushing to get to the market, get to work, get ahead. Drivers cut sharper and still sharper corners, forcing the oncoming traffic to sweep around into the wrong lane until the system was completely back to front, or gridlocked. No one reversed or gave way. The only way was forward, pushing, nudging, and squeezing.

In the summer the air was heavy with humidity. The atmospheric pressure sat on the pollution from traffic and factories and plastered it to the streets. On bad days you could see the brown clouds of exhaust fumes rolling off the overpasses like a blanket slipping off a bed. No one cared. The pollution was not a price of progress, it was part of it.

Guangzhou was a happening city, a supercharged boomtown, and a perfect place to start a business, a new life.

The excitement of buying antimony began to wear off. The metal's main use is in its oxide form as a flame retardant. Your computer is full of it. So are sofas and planes. While I enjoyed my trips through beautiful parts of southern China to inspect mines, factories and slag heaps, the drinking competitions with suppliers, and wild weekends in Hong Kong, I had begun to wonder if this was the career for me. I was a couple of months short of thirty, working for people I liked and admired — with one exception. The company had given me a crash course in business, taught me how to buy and sell, and thrown in a lesson in office politics, China style.

But there had to be more to life than flame retardant.

According to Confucius: 'A man stands up at thirty.' In plain English: it's time to get your shit together.

I had a secret ambition: to be a journalist. My girlfriend was one, and she was generous with her advice, which amounted to: it's all about knowing people, and having something to show them. She was also in London, and I was beginning to think I'd had enough of a long distance relationship.

We came up with a plan.

I needed some experience, a CV and press cuttings. Those could be acquired in China, or maybe Hong Kong. Then I could return to the UK and try my luck, with her connections.

I sent an apologetic resignation to George Wilson and flew back to London for a formal farewell. He had been good to me and taught me everything I knew about business. After a final pint in the pub across from the office, I rode a hired Triumph motorbike to the offices of the *London Metal Bulletin* in Waterloo. I walked in, dressed in black leather, and offered my services as a China-based stringer, special subject: the antimony market. I had written to them beforehand.

I walked out an ex-metal merchant and a rookie journalist.

For another 'string', back in Guangzhou I replied to an advertisement in the *South China Morning Post*, Hong Kong's English language newspaper. *Action Asia*, an adventure sports and travel magazine was looking for an editor. With shameless re-invention of a CV that highlighted my Action filled past in the British army, and my familiarity with Asia, the magazine put me on their list of freelancers. They said it was my cheek that did it.

I spent my second week as a metals correspondent writing a story about the beaches of Hainan Island, China's 'Hawaii'. On the strength of that, *Action Asia* sent me to Vietnam for twelve days to write a ten-page adventure travel feature, the most formative experience of my brief career as a bluffing journalist: I was a rank amateur searching for X Factor excitement in a country where all they wanted was peace and quiet after decades of turmoil.

I found two diving centres, a paraglider, and a mountain bike rental shop. My tight schedule left no time to visit the north of the country around Sapa, a former hill station where there was some trekking. On my last day in Hanoi I walked into a travellers' café and shouted as if I was on a parade ground: 'Anyone been to Sapa and want a beer?'

The cuttings collection had started. I had two travel articles and five reports about antimony.

My first month as a freelance journalist taught me a harsh truth about the profession. It's lonely. When you are not out and about you sit at home and stare at the walls. Nor will you earn much money if you don't work at the endless task of developing contacts and getting onto — and staying on — editors' lists of who to call.

I didn't know enough editors. I'd had a lucky start. Now I was staring at walls and outside them a city was racing past on its way to becoming an 'economic miracle', as the western press called it. I was missing out.

Then my future fell into my lap.

In Guangzhou in 1997 there was a ramshackle bar at the dead end of a twisted alley. It was called Kathleen's, after its owner.

Kathleen's was furnished with mismatching plastic chairs, folding tables, and a bar. Garish art hung on the bright orange walls. In an alcove beside the door a couple of threadbare sofas were flanked by stacks of dog-eared American magazines such as Cosmo and People. The floor was polished concrete, the ceiling high and the alley-facing frontage all glass. The place was light, airy and welcoming. The clientele were foreigners almost without exception, mostly American: quality supervisors, teachers, general managers of joint ventures, long stay traders. Half the regulars were from the American soap makers Proctor and Gamble. The Hash House Harriers, the club that called itself 'the drinking club with a running problem', met there before and after their gambols through the paddy fields. Kathleen's was the only place that served decent western food and drink other than the few expensive state-owned hotels or the infamous Hill Bar, best known for San Miguel beer on tap and Mongolian prostitutes.

The other reason Kathleen's was popular was Kathleen.

Kathleen Lau was an American-Chinese in her early forties. She looked and acted younger. She wore slip-like summer dresses, with low fronts and no bra; a most un-Chinese habit that could be distracting when she leant over a table to give you a cup of coffee. Her round face was framed by long black hair, which she screwed up sometimes into a spiky bun and fixed in place with a chopstick. She wore oversized glasses that gave her the look of a schoolteacher, yet could switch in a flash to teary-eyed little girl if it suited her purpose.

Kathleen was born in Guangzhou in 1954 and raised in Hong Kong, then America. In 1995 she'd returned to the city to look for her roots, only to find she didn't have any. She would have to put down new ones. She started out as an English teacher and then set up her restaurant. She invited a cousin from Shanghai, whose English name was Shirley, to help her. Shirley was the official owner of the business, those being the days when it was prohibitively expensive to establish a foreign-owned small business in China.

On my return from Vietnam I dropped by the bar and found Kathleen handing out copies of an English language magazine. She thrust one into my hands. 'Look what I did,' she said.

The cover photograph was of Kathleen and two friends dancing, in matching summer-slip dresses. Kathleen was to the front, her blond wig slipping back to reveal a black hairline.

'That's you?' I asked.

'Yuh, right.' Kathleen spoke with a Brooklyn accent. 'We had a lip synching contest. But what about the name? You like it?'

'*Clueless in Guangzhou*,' I read out loud. 'Because?'

'Because we're clueless, all us foreigners in Guangzhou,' Kathleen's voice rose with excitement. 'You get it? Uhuh? There's this massive number of foreigners coming into town and they don't know the first thing about China. They don't know how to eat Chinese food, how to behave at a banquet, where to buy stuff, you know, uhuh? They're clueless! We're all clueless!' She looked at me. 'So I thought, why not make a magazine, a free one!' she stressed the third syllable of the word, 'a magazeeene, uhuh, that can help them understand China, and Guangzhou. Take a look at my *Lao Pengyou* page. You like the name?'

The words mean 'old friend'. Kathleen was talking fast. I opened the cover and saw the column running across the foot of the first page

'I wrote about falling off my bike and my Chinese friend laughing at me because she didn't know how else to react. That's what Chinese do in those situations, but foreigners think they're being rude. I explain why.'

I murmured approval and swept my eye over the rest of the spread, then flicked through all eight pages.

The layout of the first issue of *Clueless in Guangzhou* gave the impression it had been designed by a committee that never met. There was no hint of consistency. The only section with any semblance of order was an alphabetic list of restaurants and the few bars in town. It began at the letter K before starting again at A. Six out of the month's eleven events were at Kathleen's.

Yet for all its chaos, American grammar, spelling mistakes and bias towards her own restaurant, Kathleen had produced a magazine. I was impressed, and said so. I asked her how she'd done it.

'A friend, a client here, whose name I'm not gonna to tell anybody, he's a big business guy and I told him my idea for a community paper and he agreed to fund the first issue. He gave me two thousand *kuai*,' she used the colloquial 'buck' word for Chinese yuan that foreigners automatically adopt. 'That's all it cost. I did it on my kitchen table. Peter Logue was a great help. He's my chief consultant.'

Everyone knew Peter. He sat at the bar in Kathleen's and told anyone who would listen about his journalist friends across South East Asia, the stories they had written, and the crazy times they'd had. Despite the heat he wore tweed jackets, corduroy trousers and heavy brogue shoes. His craggy, bespectacled face never showed a drop of perspiration. The input of cold beer and output of hot air must have kept him cool. Logue was a charming rogue.

'Is it going to be a regular magazine?' I asked Kathleen. 'I mean, you're coming out with another issue?' Despite the first one being a brochure for Kathleen's bar and restaurant with some vague information about other venues thrown in, I liked the concept, and to have something to read in English about Guangzhou on a regular basis would be a major improvement to my dislocated life.

'Yeah, that's the idea. There's lots of people I know who wanna write. Hey, what about you? You told me you wanted to do stuff like that.'

'Well actually,' I said, 'I'm already doing it. I resigned from my job and I've started up as a freelance journalist.' I tried to look confident.

'Wow,' Kathleen moved into the chair across from me. 'So you're a journalist now? You want to write for *Clueless*?'

'Sure, love to.'

'You can help out with the editing too. Why don't you come down to the office when you're not busy with your other stuff and help out a bit?'

'I could do Wednesdays to Fridays if you want, no problem.'

'Hey, I could even pay you. Come by my new office soon as you can.'

In return for an advertisement Kathleen had acquired a tiny, glass-walled retail space at the Gitic Hotel, known locally as '63' after its number of floors. Inside this goldfish bowl Kathleen had crammed three desks, a desktop computer and a coffee machine.

When I arrived on the Wednesday morning she cleared a plastic chair and invited me to sit down. It was a broken one from her restaurant. I made space for my notebook amongst the floppy discs and scraps of paper on the desk and once Kathleen had poured coffee she talked me through the process of magazine making.

Putting together an issue of *Clueless in Guangzhou* was a shambolic labour of love. As Kathleen admitted, she was making it up as she went along, with Peter Logue's guidance.

Starting with the content, she told me how articles were sourced by cajoling her friends and customers to knock something together that she considered instructive for the readers, who were pretty much the same people as the writers. Everyone wrote for free.

My job was to be to commission articles and edit them, so we started by discussing ideas for features and regular columns.

After lunch at her bar Kathleen took me to meet her designer, a slick Cantonese called Ah Bo. His office was round the corner from 63.

Ah Bo could barely speak Mandarin so Kathleen translated. She explained she gave Ah Bo a hand-drawn sketch of how she wanted the pages, annotated with the file names on the floppy discs where she had stored the text and pictures, and let him get on with it. He chose the fonts and how to lay out each page. After a few rounds of to and fro the pages were finalized, saved on more floppy discs and taken to an 'output centre'.

'I'll show you all that when we go to print with the next issue,' Kathleen said.

We walked back to the office. On the way I offered to help with advertising sales. Metal trading had taught me a few tricks for persuading people to buy things.

'Sure,' said Kathleen. So we went through advertising rates and potential clients.

I never wrote another word about antimony. My new career had begun.

It was a tumultuous, chaotic, seat-of-the-pants beginning, no little thanks to my employer. To be a friend or a regular customer of Kathleen's was one thing. To work with her was something else.

Kathleen had passion and she believed in herself and her ideas. She was creative, no question, and she loved hard work. She also understood the rudiments of design, a key skill for the business. Another characteristic useful for a novice magazine publisher was her utter lack of modesty and inability to register embarrassment. Sometimes that could go too far, but she always got away with it, thanks no little to the confusion she caused.

'I am an alien, sent to make the earth a better place,' she told me, with sincerity.

She also had a temper. The fridge in her restaurant kitchen was dented by the toasters she had thrown at her chef.

I was hardly a paragon of peace and harmony myself. I was young, ambitious and still learning the art of getting along with people. I had no experience of working with a woman. Metal trading is a blokeish business and so is the army. Questions that I thought should be answered with a simple 'yes' or 'no', to Kathleen required hours of in depth analysis, much of that a long detour through her own or my personality. I cut the discussions short. I should have shut up and listened. My attempts to break ideas down and rebuild them to see how they worked commercially were taken by Kathleen as personal attacks on her competence. My cool, collected British manner of dealing with her outbursts only made them worse. If I had screamed back at her we'd probably have sorted the problem out and got back to work. Instead, Kathleen disappeared for a day or two of sulking and toaster throwing, and I grimly pursued what I believed to be the right course of action.

Yet out of that small glass cubicle in the back alley of 63's shopping mall, more like a fiery crucible, *Clueless in Guangzhou* grew into a magazine.

By my second issue as Managing Editor, the title I had chosen for myself, I persuaded Kathleen to insert her restaurant's listing in the correct place in the alphabet, and to remove her subjective description, which was: 'The Best!'. Regular advertisers appeared. *Clueless* went from eight pages to twelve and an incredible sixteen for the 'Christmas Bumper Issue'. Circulation increased from two to ten thousand. Monthly advertising revenue reached an astounding hundred thousand yuan, about eight thousand pounds. We recruited a designer, an office manager, and a part time sub-editor and staff writer, who soon went full time.

I worked long days and in the evenings met advertising clients or reviewed a restaurant, or went back to the office to edit the medical advice column sent in by the French doctor at the only foreign speaking medical clinic in the city. If I hadn't seen Kathleen during the day I dropped into her bar for a beer and a chat. I might see Peter Logue, ask him a technical question, and get a story in return. It was a pleasant way to learn. My writing began to improve with the practice. Hints from my journalist girlfriend helped, such as 'Keep yourself out of the story. No one is interested in you, unless you're famous, which you aren't'.

There was one part of the publishing however, that would frustrate me every time it came around until I could pay someone to stand in for me. That was the dark art of 'going to film', also known as 'output'. Four sheets of transparent plastic film, one each for cyan, magenta, yellow and black, were what the printer needed to print the magazine; and a 'colour proof'.

An output centre, as Kathleen described it, is supposed to be cleaner than an operating theatre. She explained that a speck of dirt on a sheet of film can ruin a page. The computers and other machines should be the best money can buy. Smoking or drinking is taboo. The software should be one step short of a space shuttle's.

The output centre we used in Guangzhou in 1997 was not like that. The machine that produced the sheets of film was sealed in a glass box that doubled as a dusty storeroom. Tattered colour proofs of posters and scraps of magazines littered the desks and floor. The hard drives of the Macintosh computers lined up against a wall were missing their side panels. They looked like cadavers with multi-coloured wires for intestines. Overflowing ashtrays sat beside the keyboards, along with Nescafe jars full of tea. Staff waiting for the next job watched kung fu movies on the Mac with the biggest screen.

The process took all night, and we had to be there. All too often the frantic tapping of return keys was brought to an end by the ominous chime that announces the crash of a Macintosh. That was the signal for the manager, an elf-like Cantonese with a ponytail called Ah Hai, to reach for his screwdriver and push himself on his backless broken chair along the row of computers, cigarette clamped in his teeth, until he found what he was looking for. He would attack a main frame like an evil sprite, rip out its hard drive and swing his chair back up the line, holding up the black box and its connecting wires in triumph, like the beating heart ripped from a human sacrifice. Once he'd swapped the drives, we'd restart and try again.

A few hours later the colour proofs of each page would arrive at Kathleen's restaurant. We pumped ourselves with coffee, spread them across the biggest table and went over them like art experts searching for a forger's brushstroke.

Next came the most satisfying, simple, physical job: distribution.

We did it ourselves in an old van with broken air conditioning and it was a blessed break from the office, advertising sales, and output centres. When I threw a bundle of magazines through a doorway I felt fantastic.

In January 1998, Kathleen and I threw a New Year banquet for our staff and freelancers. We filled two tables in a private room at our favourite Sichuan restaurant. Ah Hai from the output centre was there.

The previous day, Kathleen had signed a lease for an office around the corner from 63. Our new home had windows, real ones that looked onto a street. We meant to decorate it ourselves over the New Year holiday. With the profits from the bumper Christmas special issue we had purchased a Macintosh computer to put in the partitioned area that was going to be the 'Design Department'. The other side was going to be 'Editorial'. The reception area would be everything else.

Kathleen and I sat beside each other at the head of one table.

'Congratulations,' I said.

'Couldn't have done it without you,' she replied.

We chinked glasses.

'So what's next?'

'I've been thinking.'

Ah Hai stood up and swayed over the table, reaching towards us with his tiny glass. 'Happy New Year!'

'We make a good team,' Kathleen said as we sat down. 'I have the passion, you have the cool head.'

'You can say that again.'

She laughed.

'How about we take off, go somewhere quiet over the New Year break, brainstorm… you know?'

There was a look in her eyes I hadn't seen before. It was asking something. I couldn't tell what.

'Good idea.' I said. 'Where?'

Ah Hai was on his feet again. 'Happy New Year! Let's all get rich!' He shouted and knocked back another shot.

'…Hong Kong. Lamma Island. A small hotel…'

'When?'

'Once the renovations are done on the new office?'

Ah Hai half rose again, made as if to speak, and projectile-vomited over the table.

'OK,' I said. 'Let's go.'

Chapter Two

The Big City

Kathleen and I went to Hong Kong, not to start a magazine but to talk about it.

I had visited Hong Kong many times since moving to Guangzhou. It was an easy two-hour train ride. Friends, many ex-Army, had stayed on after the handover in 1997. They worked in banks, as stockbrokers, or for the trading companies like Swires or Jardines.

The Hong Kong I knew was the business district in Central, the bars of Lan Kwai Fong and Wan Chai, the top floor 'mess' of the HSBC and the bank's staff apartments in the mid-levels where I used to crash overnight in small spare rooms. It was the Hong Kong of tailored suits, weekends on junks and catamarans in Tai Tam bay, water skiing, starched linen jackets and pints of cold lager served in dew-beaded pewter tankards at the Captain's Bar in the Mandarin Oriental, dinners at the Curry Club, limos to the airport.

As a metal trader I had boasted to Guangzhou acquaintances how I could catch the through-train to Kowloon, cross over to Lan Kwai Fong, sit outside a bar and when a friend walked past and asked where I was staying reply: 'With you if you don't mind,' and get myself a bed for the night. I set out to prove it one weekend and it worked. On the night of the handover I'd been at a party on the Peak, the highest point on Hong Kong Island and home to the top executives of the top companies.

So I thought I knew Hong Kong.

That was before Kathleen introduced me to Lamma Island. While I waited for her outside the guesthouse in the sea-breezed sunshine, smoking a cigarette, I observed the scene.

There was no traffic on the narrow main street because cars were banned. Everyone walked or rode bicycles. The pedestrians were almost all Caucasian, dressed as if they had just stepped off the set of '*Withnail and I*'. People wore pink trousers and bead necklaces and shouted 'Darling!' and 'Righty ho!' at each other. Lamma Island seemed to be stuck in a cross-cultural time warp.

Kathleen and I had checked into a cheap guesthouse up a side street. She suggested we share a room to save money. I replied that I was happy to pay the extra, and noticed a fleeting look of doe-eyed disappointment. It was so fleeting I ignored it.

She came downstairs after me. 'Let's get lunch' she said.

I stamped on my cigarette and followed her, past a coffee shop where a lady leaned on the counter with bangled forearms, past a bar where a British bed-head in shades was drinking San Miguel Beer from the bottle, past a bookshop where a grey-haired woman in a tie-died skirt and mismatching blouse was fanning herself with the classified ads of the *South China Morning Post*, back to the strip of seafood restaurants by the ferry. The owners waved crabs and lobsters in the air like tickets touts outside a rock concert. 'Come in, come in!' they shouted in Cantonese.

My surprise at finding this carefree, creative hideaway in Hong Kong, the fresh seafood and the chilled beer that was so much tastier than any in mainland China, the sunshine, the blue sky and the boats in the harbour, the sound of the water beneath us... I felt a surge of excitement, a sense of freshness and energy like the first day of a summer holiday.

It was time to calm down and talk. While we ate, we did.

We considered ourselves successful amateur publishers. We had passed our first test. We had taken Kathleen's in-house newssheet and turned it into a popular free monthly magazine for the expat community in Guangzhou. We had lived up to our name. We had answered the questions readers were 'clueless' about and once we'd done that we'd answered the questions they hadn't thought of, we'd given them more than they expected. It's the oldest trick in the media and entertainment industries, not that we knew it or had anyone teach us. It seemed obvious, common sense. And it had worked. We had also made a small profit, even after Kathleen had paid me my salary of a thousand pounds a month.

Now we wanted to turn professional. We already considered ourselves business partners, and — despite the fights — good friends. We needed a bigger, more sophisticated market. We had to get away from being clueless. No disrespect to the foreigners in Guangzhou, but they came, they worked for two years, they lived in villa compounds, and they left for their next posting. They did not come to China because it was China, as I liked to think I had, or as Kathleen had, to find her roots. They were, in a word: expats.

Kathleen and I wanted to make a magazine for people like us. Or if they weren't like us, if they did insist on calling themselves expats, we'd show them that there was more to life in China than sitting in a sports bar watching the Premier League on satellite TV. We wanted to our readers to be involved, and we wanted a magazine that was involved too, that made a difference.

As to how it would make that difference, our ideas began to diverge.

Kathleen had bold plans for a magazine that would tackle serious issues, social problems, the arts in the highest sense, everything but politics and economics. She wanted interviews with high profile people, to invite famous commentators to contribute with long, in-depth, intellectual articles. She wanted deep and meaningful.

She was the world-changing alien again.

I dreamed of a listings magazine like *Time Out*, packed with information, from the newest bars and restaurants to the cinema schedules and the sports fixtures, even the football. We had to make the magazine indispensable, a bible for the people who lived in the city we would cover, who read English. Only then would they pick it up and read the serious articles Kathleen wanted which, of course, I hurried to say as I saw her eyes water with frustration, there was a need for.

We had been talking hard and fast but now Kathleen fell silent. She stared out to sea. I sensed one of our fights coming on. I'd been on the point of saying we wouldn't be able to afford the writers and the pages for the content she was dreaming of, at least not until we had earned some money, and the surest and proven way to do that was a listings magazine. I wanted to ram home my point. But I kept silent.

We paid the bill for lunch and wandered up the street to the coffee shop opposite the alley to our hotel. Kathleen brightened up again. We moved on to the biggest question: where?

We needed a large, preferably growing community of English language readers — we discounted a Chinese language magazine for the simple reason that neither of us wrote good enough Chinese — and we wanted to be in China, or a Chinese environment, because that was the country and culture we knew and loved. The city we chose had to be growing and there should be no well-established competition. We might be successful amateurs but we were still amateurs. We needed leeway.

We went through the options: Hong Kong; two established English language listing magazines, expensive place to live, Singapore; too small and well-developed, Taipei, capital of Taiwan; Chinese but we didn't know anything about Taiwan, Beijing; too far north, and I'd moved from there a year ago, I wanted to go forwards not back, Shanghai; mainland China, developing, growing foreign community, one English language publication we'd heard of.

Shanghai ticked the boxes.

The stories had just begun to spread around China, the Far East and the world. They were little more than rumours, but they seemed to be self-fulfilling: everyone was moving to Shanghai. It was the next big thing. In the days before Communist China it had been a true metropolis, an international city. Now they wanted us back. The foreign community was said to be growing by the day, by the planeload, as fast as they could fly them in.

An international city would need media in the international language, and that was English.

I think we meant to agree on Shanghai all along. Our discussion was a formality, a pretense at a rational assessment. Other than Beijing, Shanghai was the obvious choice inside mainland China, and it was closer to Guangzhou than the capital, which made it a step rather than a leap, and a forward one still for me.

There was also the reputation of the locals, said to be sophisticated, cosmopolitan, open to the outside world, unlike the notoriously inward-looking Chinese across the rest of the country. They spoke English better than any other Chinese too.

We'd finished our coffees and changed venue again, back to a bar. The talking made us thirsty, and we had reached a decision. We had a cause for celebration. We ordered pints of cold San Miguel and sat back to watch the world go by, Lamma residents heading home from a day in the city and visitors coming for the seafood.

We took out our notebooks again, opened them at a fresh page and each of us wrote down one word: Shanghai.

We discussed timing. We were both free to move from Guangzhou at a moment's notice. No families, no partners. We rented cheap apartments. Kathleen had recruited a manager for her restaurant and was confident in her staff. For *Clueless*, which we'd keep going, we had recruited a young Scot as editor. We'd be back to look after him as often as we could. We penciled in a spring move to Shanghai, first issue to appear in July.

We went back a step. We should go and take a look at Shanghai, do some market research. I had visited once from Beijing. Kathleen had also been there once, to ask her cousin Shirley to come help at her restaurant. Neither of us had paid much attention to the city's make-up. I'd done the tourist traps and Kathleen had gone local. We agreed on a reconnaissance trip straight after the distribution of the next issue of *Clueless*.

Next, the serious part: money. Here we should have got out our laptops, opened up Excel, made spreadsheets and profit and loss forecasts.

We didn't have a calculator, let alone a laptop.

'How much have you got?' Kathleen asked me.

'Ten thousand U.S.,' I replied. It was all I had saved from three years as a metal trader. 'Can you match it?'

'Should be no problem.'

'Do you think twenty will be enough?'

'Should be to start with. If we need more we'll find it somehow.'

'I think we'll be OK. Let's keep costs right down. You want a salary?'

'No need, I've got the restaurant.'

'Good. Nor do I. So long as I have enough to eat and live. I'm sure we can find friends' sofas to crash on.'

I realized I was about to become an entrepreneur, with a business partner and a plan, which was four words long: Shanghai, July, twenty thousand. We hadn't even thought of a name for the magazine. It certainly wasn't going to be *Clueless in Shanghai*.

'Let's go for it.' We raised our glasses.

'One last thing,' Kathleen said, her voice serious.

'What's that?'

'Will this affect your other work?'

'What other work?'

'You know, the other stuff you do, on the side.' Kathleen seemed embarrassed.

'I really don't know what you're talking about.'

'But Mark, everyone knows you work for the British government, doing... you know... stuff on the side.'

'You serious?'

'Yuh, for real.' She named a British lawyer in Guangzhou.

'Oh God. Kathleen, he's pulling your leg. It's a joke. Just because I used to wear tailor-made suits, was in the army for a bit and speak like the BBC doesn't make me a spy! That's exactly why that guy made the story up. He's taking the piss!'

'He was angry with you?' Her Brooklyn accent came on strong when she got excited or confused.

'Angry?'

'You said pissed.'

'Taking the piss, the Mick, joking. English sense'

'Oh I get it. But you're sure he didn't mean it?'

'Of course I am! In fact the army used to worry about my China connection. A friend in Military Intelligence told me they had a file inches thick on me. I'm the last person they would ask to be a spy. Please. It's a joke.'

How ironic, I thought: we're about to set out for Shanghai, a city once famous for attracting Walter Mitties. And here I was having someone make up my past for me.

There was a significant part of my past life in the UK that I had to face up to however: my girlfriend. It had been a difficult keeping the relationship going for the eighteen months I had been in China. We had recently split and I had dashed back to the UK to patch things up. She was a fantastic girl and had been a selfless supporter. She was also smart, and taking off on a career in the tough London media world. I could not ask her to throw that in. And now I wanted to make a go of it in China. My original plan to head back to the UK had suddenly become the fall-back option, the last resort. If I was honest, I had no intention of using it.

Then there was the complication that I had met a beautiful and similarly bright Chinese girl, Joanna, in Guangzhou. What had begun as a straightforward and well-intentioned introduction by a mutual friend was turning into a mutual attraction. The appeal of staying in China had increased.

I had tried to be honest with both of them. That only made matters worse. So I took the big step and broke off with my girlfriend in a letter I'm ashamed to even remember. When Kathleen and I got back to Guangzhou I rushed round to see Joanna and tell her the plans for Shanghai, and that I was hers for the taking. I was staying in China.

'Too late,' she said. 'You kept me waiting, and you were a bastard in the meantime.' She looked at me and added. 'So I am seeing someone else.'

So I didn't have any ties, anywhere.

The rebirth of Shanghai as a modern, international metropolis has filled newspaper reports and columns, pages of magazines and special supplements, it's been filmed for documentaries and talk shows, books have been written about it. The name of the city has become all but synonymous with super-charged growth. You will doubtless have read or heard the stories.

The basic one, in a nutshell, is this: the Communist Party of China, pandering on the one hand to westerners' fondness for old buildings, and their own history in China, and on the other to their desperate impatience to get into the 'China Market', set up Shanghai as the main entry point — call it re-entry if you want — for western business into China.

You could also call it a honey trap, if you insist.

The nostalgia was a gift, for the Party. Here was a city built by foreigners, that still looked foreign and held an almost mythical appeal thanks to the fortunes foreigners had made there pre 1949. The place was its own PR machine, its own postcard — just look at all the pictures of the Bund that go with the articles in the magazines.

Pre-1949 there had even been a thriving English language media industry, dominated by H.E Morris who built the *North-China Daily News* and with its profits a greyhound track across the road from his sprawling mock Tudor mansion, now the Ruijin State Guesthouse.

In the late 1990s, there were thousands, tens of thousands, hundreds of thousands, of businessmen and businesses ready to take Morris's place. Some of them were in fact returnees, although they found the terms and conditions very different from their forbears.

The American insurance giant AIG, for example, had been founded in Shanghai in 1919. After some delicate negotiations, all the trickier since foreign insurance companies were banned from selling insurance policies, they recovered their original building. The Hong Kong Shanghai Bank took half its name from the city. They couldn't move back into their old showpiece home on the Bund. It had become the headquarters of the Pudong Development Bank. So they took over the smartest building in Pudong, the new suburb across the river, and changed its name to HSBC Tower.

Then there were the newcomers, the new generation, some like me and Kathleen who were already in China and gravitated towards

Shanghai, others who were pulled straight in, who hadn't studied Chinese or China, who'd barely heard of the place until they read those news stories and magazine articles and thought: that is where the action is. From managers of major corporations to interns fresh out of college, they all wanted to be in Shanghai, the modern China launch-pad. It could make your career for you, or your fortune.

On our reconnaissance trip from Guangzhou Kathleen and I sat in the Morrises' old garden at the Ruijin Guesthouse and argued about which of us was going to own it again, as a foreign media baron.

Quite by chance I was introduced to H.E.Morris's grandson on a visit back to England, not long after that particular Shanghai recce. I boasted how I saw myself following in his grandfather's footsteps. He frowned.

'Have you ever been to see your house?' I asked, trying to make up for my cockiness. I described how well preserved it was.

'Never,' he replied. 'They stole the lot, didn't they? I never had any interest in going to Shanghai, never will.'

I sometimes wish I'd paid more attention to that conversation.

When Kathleen and I weren't fantasizing in Morris's old garden we wandered the streets looking through the windows of bars and restaurants, and tracked down friends and acquaintances.

There was only one English language magazine in the market called *Shanghai Talk*. We knew the people behind it. Ismay, the Hong Kong based publishers, had a magazine in Guangzhou and one in Beijing, but the series was infused with a patronizing attitude: 'You poor person stuck in China. Life is tough, but don't worry. We'll help you get through it.' It was all about surviving China, not making the most of it. An issue we picked up played into our hands. The editorial proclaimed the contributors as 'expats' writing for 'expats'.

We explained how different we would be to whoever we met in

the foreign community. One was an Englishman named Graham Earnshaw.

Graham had been the local Reuters correspondent and was in the process of setting up his own media company. He asked us many searching questions, as you would expect of a journalist, and soaked up our answers and enthusiasm with a wry smile. In return he gave us some encouragement and one or two tidbits of information. He made sure we knew that he knew everyone there was to know in town. He introduced us to Ron Glotzer, a young American running a business called the *Shanghai Ticket*, a book of discount vouchers.

Jamie Wilson, son of my metal trading chairman George, was in Shanghai studying Chinese. He agreed to help us get started. Together we went to call on Glotzer. We met in one of the new generation of Shanghai restaurants, a smartened up hole-in-the-wall called Grape that served foreigner-friendly Shanghainese food and was for a time the most popular venue for the Shanghai 'expats', because it was the only one of its kind.

While Graham Earnshaw had pretended to be friendly and made encouraging noises, Ron was downright hostile. His response to enquiries about production houses and printers, which he delivered with a barely suppressed sneer, was to tell us in no uncertain terms that he considered his contacts a commercial secret.

Jamie and I pressed on regardless, assuming that a contact of a contact would offer some sign of friendliness and support. As we walked out of the restaurant, I turned to Jamie and remarked, 'What a waste of time that was,' and added a British epithet.

The final Earnshaw introduction was another American called Willy Brent. Willy also fancied himself as the next Shanghai media mogul. Jamie and I found him in his office in the basement of an apartment block. He talked of his plans for TV, advertising agencies and print media, dropping hints of movies and other big projects. Once we had made our presentation and invited his comments, he was brief and to the point.

'If you want to do anything in media in Shanghai, you will only succeed if you partner with me. Otherwise you have no hope. Now, what kind of share can you offer me?'

It seemed our first foreign contacts in the city were not going to be much help. We turned to the Chinese ones.

There is a common misapprehension: that you can't do anything in China unless you 'know someone'. The word in Chinese is '*guanxi*'. It translates as 'connections' but means more than that. *Guanxi* implies that as well as just knowing someone, they are obliged, due to an ulterior motive, or perhaps to repay a debt to the person who introduces you, to help you. And you would be obliged in due course to help them.

We arrived in Shanghai with no *guanxi*. So we tried to make them, without much success. We met friends of friends, some foreign, some local, some Chinese married to foreigners who were friends of friends, with grand sounding contacts in government bureaus who turned out to be less than grand and long since retired. Most of them wanted to see if they could benefit from our project. The people they introduced us to all did, want to benefit that is. The routine became repetitive. Someone would suggest we met someone else who knew someone who could help. The first someone would tell us how the second could sort things out thanks to his or her *guanxi*. That took a couple of dinners.

We were then booked in to see the second someone, the go-between. We turned up at the appointed time and place. Someone Number One was there, talking into a mobile phone. As we sat down he hung up and said, 'He/she can't make it. Got an important meeting.' We ate our third dinner with Someone Number One who repeated everything he or she had already told us about Someone Number Two and Three at the first and second dinners. And so it went on. On those preparatory trips we never met anyone who helped at all.

There were other people in Shanghai, however, who showed a keen interest and gave us support and encouragement. Not a few of them became our first advertisers. And we began to get a feel for the city.

We gave Jamie Wilson a box of name cards with no address and the name of a non-existent product and went back to Guangzhou to carry on with our own preparations. Jamie made the rounds of bars and clubs, dropping cards into managers' hands and telling them to watch out for us. They would be our prime target market for advertising. Since Jamie was one of the slackest students I had ever met and spent most of his time out drinking and partying, he was perfect for the job. And being his father's son, I knew that buying and selling ran in his veins.

As for practical details like finding an office in Shanghai, pre-launch marketing, recruitment, registration with the regulatory authorities, bank accounts and all the other important jobs to be done before entering a market to launch a product, we did not one of them.

On late afternoon before the May holiday in 1998, when I flew into Shanghai's Hongqiao Airport, the city came out to meet me. We descended over a vast plain, coated by haze and the fug of industrial pollution. The bright blue roofs of factories and warehouses appeared through the murky greyness. I made out green islands of small farming communities, centred on muddy brown ponds, linked by lanes lined by poplars. A patchwork of rice paddy, fish farms and mulberry groves filled every space between the concrete lots and the buildings. There was no waste, no empty space between them.

Then the city came into view, a brown carpet of the tiled roofs of low-rise old lane houses, the Shanghai *nong tangs,* built before 1949 and divided by leafy streets. Dirty grey building sites pock-marked the smooth brown surface like cigarette burns on a cheap carpet and in the distance sparkling new glass towers stood up like beacons, beckoning, like the hairs of a Venus fly trap.

I stepped out of the plane and onto the warm tarmac with a bag on each shoulder. One held my laptop and a change of clothes, the other a printer and two hundred brochures. The straps cut into my shoulders. On a piece of paper in my pocket was the name of the bar where I was due to meet Jamie Wilson.

Chapter Three

Pick a System

I'm afraid I'm one of those people with a hang-up about systems: political systems, education systems, corporate systems, any system. I love them. Systems are a playground for grown-ups. I'm a product of a notorious one: the British public school. Besides maths and French, it taught me how a system works, how rules could be bent, regulations twisted, how to play the game.

I learnt the hard way too. I was thrown out at the end of my penultimate year for a 'dangerous, potentially fatal, sense of humour', in the words of the headmaster. I thought I was only endangering myself. But abseiling off buildings with an old rope round my shoulder and through my legs, borrowing the school Cadet Force Land Rover and racing across the playing fields in the middle of the night, taking turns to 'surf' on the roof, might attract emulation. He had a point. The headmaster remained ignorant of a multitude of other pranks my small gang pulled off, and the black market emporium of filched rarities from the school kitchens has stayed a secret until today, along with the alcohol brewed in the watertight containers from the canoe club and the unmasked duels I organized as captain of the fencing team.

Straight after university I signed up for another notorious British system; the Army, which while strict in itself, tacitly endorses individuality, within limits and once it has knocked off the rougher edges. Besides, the main job is playing with guns and big boys' toys, at least as a junior officer. There was no urge to fight the system when the system was all about fighting. A little creativity now and then such as playing Queen's 'Another One Bites the Dust' over the P.A. system on the rifle range kept me happy. It was the local town council who weren't, which struck me as odd. Music was surely more pleasant than gunfire.

'Reacts well under pressure,' my course reports said, 'but otherwise shows a marked lack of interest'. I think I might be one of the only cadets at the Royal Military Academy Sandhurst to have been put on 'Restriction of Privileges' for paying attention during a lecture.

My platoon commander had asked politely, but pointedly: 'Kitto, I'm curious to know how the hell you stayed awake through that one?'

I had developed an acute case of narcolepsy brought on by a military education.

'I actually thought it was rather interesting, Sir.'

'Are you implying that the course has not, until now, been interesting?'

Having had it drummed into us from day one that above all else an officer must be a paragon of integrity, I answered with absolute honesty. My reward was a week of sweeping the parade ground and late night inspection parades.

China is the biggest and best system in the world. It is a playground made in heaven and supplied by Hamley's, if you like playing with systems. It is big because it is all encompassing and it is the best because it is riddled with contradictions and loopholes. The last great communist system in the world — which looked on as the Berlin Wall fell and socialist governments were tumbled by Velvet and Orange revolutions — has survived remarkably intact. The only comparable one is across the Yalu River in North Korea, but you can't get in there to muck about very easily and it is unlikely you would come out afterwards if you did.

The Chinese system governs, or thinks it does, every aspect of daily life.

I had my first taste of it as an overseas student. I had been a free and easy-living freshman at the School of Oriental and African Studies in London for one year and I enjoyed the liberty, but it was almost a relief to get back into a system. I was like a convict who prefers life on the inside.

The Beijing Language Institute in 1986 even looked like a prison camp, or a barracks. It was surrounded by a high wall and we lived in segregated blocks. In our rooms the plaster was peeling off the walls, the windows were all broken, the floor was polished concrete and we were issued a metal washbowl per person. Hot water was rationed and the heating ineffective. In winter we froze and in summer we steamed. Dust and grit from northwestern deserts worked its way into clothes drawers, food cupboards, and our ears and noses.

An old man, the *shifu*, our building superintendent, tracked our every move. We were assigned 'responsible teachers', a cross between a housemaster and a parole officer. We nicknamed our one: 'Dragon Hou'. She was short, round and wore thick glasses, and was proud to have been a Red Guard in the Cultural Revolution.

Our international band of misfits organized firework battles with foreign students at other universities during the Chinese New Year and played ten pin bowls down the long corridor of our block with a ball pinched from a local bowling alley and empty beer bottles for pins. We gatecrashed the only disco worth the name, at the Lido Hotel, by befriending the security guards and sneaking in the fire escape, or through the front in drag on one memorable occasion — transsexuals were unknown. We 'borrowed' taxis and rearranged traffic systems.

More responsibly, I produced a foreign student play, Oscar Wilde's *The Importance of Being Earnest*. It was a first for the college. The Chinese student union leader who helped us stage it told me he had never seen so many chops — also known as stamps — on a single piece of paper. I made only one slip-up when I sawed the legs off an old desk I found at the back of the Institute's theatre. I needed a tea table for a prop. Dragon Hou told me I had vandalised one of the Institute's precious Party Committee conference tables. The replacement cost ten pounds.

In due course I was thrown out. My offense was hardly exciting. It was absence from lectures. The minimum attendance required was fifty per cent. I never once made it to the first of the two lessons at 8.30 a.m.

A note was slipped under my door telling me I was expelled and to report to Dragon Hou.

'You are in serious trouble,' Dragon Hou said. A giant enameled tin mug with a lid sat between us on her desk. It was the biggest tea mug I had ever seen.

'Yes, Teacher Hou, I am very sorry,' I said, my eyes fixed on the mug. I explained I had left school under similar circumstances and a departure from university would upset my parents very much. 'Is there anything that can be done?' I asked.

'You could write a self criticism,' she suggested. 'If you apologize in writing and promise to be a better student next term, the board might allow you back in.'

'A self criticism?'

'Exactly.' Dragon Hou looked almost wistful, her mind back in the good old days of putting dunce's caps on people's heads and making them kneel in the 'aeroplane position' with a board listing their crimes hanging from their necks.

'How do I do that?' I asked. 'I'm afraid that thanks to my lack of attendance — of which I am very ashamed, Teacher Hou — I don't know enough characters.'

'So you are willing to confess?' She caught herself. 'I mean: apologize?'

'Yes, of course. I just don't know how.'

'We'll take care of that. I will have a document prepared and you can go to the admissions office tomorrow and sign it.'

'Thank you Teacher Hou.'

I was re-admitted.

Next thing I almost got thrown out of China.

In late spring the campus was dug up for new water mains. Steep-sided ditches crisscrossed the basketball courts and cut every one of the narrow laneways between classrooms and dormitory blocks. There was one right outside the door to our block and over it a bridge made of wooden railway sleepers. We frequently fell off it into the mud on our way back from the local dumpling shop.

I suggested to my friends that we relieved our frustration by setting a 'Heffalump trap'. My multinational friends asked for an explanation. They learnt about *Winnie the Pooh*. I still had a saw from the play, the one that had chopped up the Party table. In the darkness we sawed almost the complete way through a couple of the sleepers.

The next morning I was woken by Dragon Hou hammering on my door. 'Mark! Get up! And get out here! Now!' She sounded mad as a rabid Red Guard. I opened the door and Dragon Hou grabbed me by the arm and marched me to the end of the corridor where a window overlooked the bridge across the ditch. It was an ex-bridge and a highly successful heffalump trap. A light van was stuck with its front wheel in the middle. No damage. Just a very confused driver on his haunches staring at what had been a strong piece of wood the previous day.

'You did that!' Dragon Hou screeched in my ear, her spittle hitting my cheek. 'You have a saw, I know you have!' She sounded and looked so furious I decided the only course was outright denial. I asked, with genuine concern, if there had been any serious damage.

'This is sabotage of the public road system!' She really was upset. Chinese universities are mini fiefdoms. But this was not a public road. It was a plank.

A week later I was invited to the Beijing Police Department Responsible for Foreigners. I was concerned. Getting thrown out of a country would top being expelled from school. It would also deny me a university degree and have the army cancel my provisional acceptance. This was serious.

'Are you prepared to sign a statement saying that you did not sabotage the bridge over the ditch at the Foreign Languages Institute last Thursday?' asked the tired police officer.

'Yes.'

'Good.' He looked even more relieved than I felt. 'Sign here. Thank you.' I signed.

I was getting the hang of the China system. I had just discovered one of the keys to it: relieve it of responsibility. I was also coming to realize that no matter how strict the rules were, they really are made to be broken in China. Everybody does it.

In the seven years I lived in Shanghai the city government issued decrees banning car horns, hanging laundry outside to dry, spitting, satellite television, cricket fighting, sleeping on the street or in a park and men going bare-chested in summer, students kissing… the list goes on and will be twice as long today. Those were just the social issues. Then there were the campaigns against illegal activities such as pirated goods, gambling, drugs, smuggling, tax evasion and so on.

Walk down a Shanghai street in summer and you will see laundry hanging next to a satellite dish, taxi drivers honking their horns as they spit out of the window while they drive past a park where locals are preparing their deck chairs because their houses have no air conditioning, and behind them in the bushes, shock horror, students kissing. The cricket fights are seasonal so you will have to wait for autumn for those. You will be able to buy rip off Nikes and Gucci handbags, Rolexes, DVDs, you name it, from a man not wearing a shirt.

The government once made an announcement along the lines of, 'We are now mounting a campaign to enforce the country's laws'. No one paid the blindest notice.

Not only are the rules made to be broken, they are carefully designed that way because the people who make them are most likely to be the ones who want to break them.

Take publishing for instance.

To publish a magazine in China you need a periodical publication number, *kanhao* in Chinese, issued by the General Administration of Press and Publications, GAPP. *Kanhao* are only given to the government because only the government can publish, because media is information and information is power.

Kanhao cannot be rented or loaned to a third party. Yet that is exactly what the government does. *Kanhao* are a rare commodity. It is a seller's market. Anyone, Chinese or foreign, who wants to publish a magazine in China is obliged to find one. You cannot apply for a new one unless you are already a publisher, and — just to labour the point — a government official. So outsiders who want to be publishers find a government partner who has a *kanhao* available for a price, strike a deal and 'co-operate'. The 'government' publisher keeps an eye on the content because he does not want to get into trouble for something with his name on that might upset his superiors, while the actual, commercial, publisher does his best to produce something like a real magazine that people will read and advertisers will advertise in. The magazine must be given the title that came with the *kanhao* and is on record at GAPP, such as *Workers' Information Weekly*, while the people doing the work can give it a supplementary title of their choice, for example *Computer Games Monthly*.

A *kanhao* sets out everything you can do with your magazine: how many pages it may have, their size, colour and which language you can put on them. It all but tells you what to wear to the office. Make any changes, even to the number of pages, and you could be in trouble, no matter how many advertisements you have to fit in. According to the rules, if you want to make a change of any sort, you must seek approval from GAPP. When they issue a *kanhao* the administration will make a record of the editors, their address, and any other detail they can get hold of. If an editor dies on the job he stays on the masthead, with a box around his name, until GAPP approves his replacement.

Not only are the rules about *kanhao* rigid and flexible, every official publisher has his own interpretation of them. If I had a hundred dollars for everyone who told me they knew someone who had a *kanhao* for rent I would be a rich man. If I had another hundred dollars for everyone who told me that I would never find one, that I could never rent one, or there was a freeze on the issue of new *kanhao*, I would be even richer. If you add a hundred dollars for every time I heard that English language *kanhao* were easier to get hold of or more difficult than Chinese language ones, or plain impossible, and finally throw in the people who told me the freeze on new *kanhao* was about to be lifted or that you did not need one for a free magazine, or you definitely did, then I would be rich enough to have bought *Time Out* magazine in London and never left the UK in the first place.

What it boils down to, as always, is money. The government publishers were not making any with their publications, which were all, in effect, propaganda. In the entrance hall of the largest newspaper group in Shanghai, the *Wenxin Jituan*, there used to be an enormous sign. If you were dropping in to buy some advertising space or a subscription to one of their many papers, it hit you in the face. 'The purpose of media is to propagate the glorious truth about the Communist Party.'

What Kathleen and I didn't know, and could never have guessed, while we sat in the sun on Lamma Island, drinking beer and dreaming up our next magazine, was that the Chinese government had just told its 'publications', whom it had been supporting since 1949, that they had to pay their own way.

Something else was going on too. A business as yet unknown to China had barged in through Deng Xiaoping's open door — or should that be cat flap. It didn't barge in in fact so much as kick it open and leave it hanging on its hinges, because that's the brash, crude, in-your-face business it is: advertising.

The government publishers could not believe their luck. As far as they could tell, advertising was propaganda, which they knew all about, and the international advertising agencies would pay a lot more than the miserly handouts they had been getting from the government.

The advertising agencies could not believe their luck either. Here was a print media industry that had never created its own content. It printed what it was told to. The agencies snapped up cheap advertising and then, as if they were doing the publishers a favour, supplied 'free' content about their clients' products. It was a classic win-win. The readers, used to being told what to think by the media, did not notice the difference. Content and advertising became indistinguishable.

When we came out with a restaurant guide to Shanghai, I was invited to dinner by a distinguished member of the local press. The venue was a new restaurant whose décor was way over the top. A marble entrance hall was encircled by gilt statues of mermaids and Greek gods. Doric pillars towered up through the atrium round which a sweeping staircase led to the private rooms. I was ushered upstairs by a meet-and-greet girl in a ball gown.

My dinner companions were editors of local Shanghai newspapers' entertainment columns. We enjoyed a frosty relationship. The way the manager was fussing over our table made me suspicious. Sure enough, during the meal each of us was given a plain envelope, for 'expenses'. I guessed from its thickness that there was about 500 yuan inside. I did not see it, let alone feel it, but my journalist friend who had arranged the dinner for sure received a thicker one.

Soon after I sat down I pulled out a couple of copies of my new guide and passed them around. I saw genuine respect in the faces of my rivals.

'Mark, how many reviews in here?' one of them asked.

'About three hundred,' I replied.

There was a gasp of admiration.

'That's fantastic!' said another. 'Wow, three hundred! You must have minted it. How much for each?'

'Sorry, what do you mean? How much did we pay? For the food or writing?'

'No stupid! How much did the restaurants pay for each review? Three hundred of them too.'

'I'm afraid you've got it wrong.' I tried to sound contrite. 'They didn't pay a cent. In fact we reviewed anonymously, paid for the food and of course paid the writers. We made some advertising sales in the guide though and I think it will sell well at retail...'

I trailed off. The looks of admiration tinted with envy had

turned to contempt. The copies of the guide were slipped under the table. Perhaps they would be taken away and used for reference, or the good reviews copied into Chinese for a fee from whichever restaurant.

This blatant pandering to advertisers and writing glowing reviews in return for cash had one unexpected advantage. The content of the brand new magazines that started to pop up was harmless. It contained no politics, no hard news, no social commentary, nothing that could upset the authorities or be seen as negative propaganda. The publishers rarely got into trouble. If they did it was perhaps thanks to a risqué picture noticed by a bored GAPP official who, once he had admired his fill, exploited it to extract a modest fine. It was also becoming obvious there was money being made.

At the risk of sounding like one of the missionary zealots who had flooded into China in the 19th century, with Kathleen I wanted to teach the Chinese that there was a better way, that you could print honest reviews and still make money. Integrity could pay. I didn't want to write about politics, or even social commentary — I wasn't *that* naïve — but we'd do our best to stir things up.

Now I am going to sound like a missionary: we wanted to take advantage of another opportunity too. Thanks to the complete and utter novelty of anything like an independent media in China, not only had none of the good practices of 'western' media made it into the country yet, neither had any of the bad ones. We weren't going to inflate our circulation figures, pump up our advertising rates so we could give impressive discounts, disguise advertising as content, pay kickbacks, slander or copy our competitors or employ any of the other underhand tactics not unknown in the West. We didn't know the tricks anyway, because we were media virgins. Neither Kathleen nor I had worked in media outside China before *Clueless*. We were making it up as we went along and we could make up our own rules.

There was one more thing Kathleen and I knew nothing about, the *kanhao* system. In Guangzhou we had published *Clueless* under the guise of a community newsletter. It had barely been a guise even, because no one bothered us or asked. For the advertisers we issued official receipts, required by clients and the tax authorities, from Kathleen's restaurant. The advertisers somehow persuaded their auditors they did their marketing and advertising by purchasing hundreds of dollars' worth of pizzas for potential clients, every month.

As the advertising sales increased our clients began to ask for real receipts, for advertising. A wholly foreign-owned enterprise (WFOE) in our names would have required hundreds of thousands of dollars in registered capital, so Kathleen set up a domestic one. Her cousin Shirley put her name on the documents and was the nominated 'Legal Representative', the equivalent of chairman and major shareholder. Kathleen paid the registration fees and service charge to the company that lent the required capital — still not a small sum — for the required time, to satisfy the Administration of Industry and Commerce, the agency that oversees all commercial activity in China. She called it Guangzhou Kaishenglin Advertising Ltd, a rough pinyinisation of her English name, translated back into Chinese.

Shirley Li was tall and striking. In her youth she must have been a looker, a classic Shanghainese beauty. She dressed smartly and carried herself well. She was in her early forties, married with a daughter, but her family had stayed in Shanghai for the year or two she had been in Guangzhou. Shirley had worked as a bookkeeper in a state-owned factory in Shanghai and been laid off in the restructuring that came with Deng Xiaoping's 'opening up' of the early nineties. She had lost her 'iron rice bowl' — the lifetime job at a work unit and guaranteed pension. Hence she had been free to come and help Kathleen in Guangzhou.

At first I had only seen her occasionally at the restaurant, but as the advertising incomes increased so did her role at the *Clueless*. She was excited at the thought of returning home to Shanghai. She would come to play a major role in the business, and this story.

Before we set off for Shanghai, Kathleen and I put our 20,000 dollars into Guangzhou Kaishenglin Advertising Ltd. Shirley agreed to let us manage the company that was her responsibility, and we promised not to get her into trouble by not paying taxes, or giving out advertising receipts for pizzas.

Meanwhile, Kathleen and I set up a 'shelf' company in Hong Kong. We wanted something to show for our partnership. For a few a few hundred dollars in fees we had a board of directors and a company secretary. We called our company Klau and Benedict Ltd. Klau for Kathleen Lau, and Benedict after my great grandfather, founder of Benedict Kitto and Sons of St. Swithin's Lane, London, in 1901. We thought we sounded media-like in a German-American New York sort of way. One day when the regulations allowed it, we hoped to link Klau and Benedict with the magazines, and transfer whatever value we had built into it. Until then it could stay on the shelf.

Chapter Four

The Easy Part

On my second day in Shanghai I found an office in the library block of the Shanghai Music Conservatory, in the old French Concession area. Apart from an auditorium on the ground floor the building seemed to have little to do with music, the rooms mostly rented out to small businesses. I never saw any students enter it, although I did discover a room with some books on shelves.

The Conservatory had seen and heard better times. During Shanghai's heyday it was a world-class musical institute thanks to the émigré White Russians who fled to the city, many of them virtuosi.

The office was tiny, about 30 square metres. It was an old practice room. The plaster was crumbling from the pockmarked walls and the floor tiles chipped and rutted by piano wheels. Where an air conditioning unit had hung a gaping hole let in the wind and swallows, whose droppings dappled the floor.

The rent was seven hundred US dollars a month. It was all we needed and all we could afford, so I took it on the spot.

'You had better buy a padlock for the door.' The property manager gestured to the narrow double glass doors. 'We've lost the key.'

'What about furniture?' I asked.

'Come with me.' She took me across the hall to an old classroom stacked with battered school desks and wooden chairs.

'Help yourself,' she said, and departed with a final instruction:

'If you put any nails in the walls you will have to pay to have the holes fixed when you leave.'

I stuffed a scrunched up newspaper in the gaping chasm left by the air conditioner and made a rough calculation of how many desks I could fit in. Then I went back to the classroom and humped them across the corridor. They weren't big or heavy. I spread them around the walls and stood back to admire the launch pad for our new publishing business.

It looked more like the storeroom I had just raided for furniture.

I went out to buy a second-hand fax machine from an expat German's Chinese wife, and a padlock.

My first employee was Miss White, a young woman fresh from her rural town, a category the Shanghainese call *'waidiren'*: outsiders. Miss White was in charge of the toilet paper since her desk was closest to the door. Her other job was answering the phone, which she did with an officiousness that only a new immigrant to Shanghai can muster. 'I am now Shanghainese,' her tone proclaimed, 'so give me some respect.'

She was joined by Iris Zheng, a proper Shanghainese who outclassed Miss White by several generations. She was bright and ambitious, and it was tough to persuade her to take the job, which was a good sign.

The main problem with recruitment was just that, persuading people we were a real business, with prospects. To do so I had a couple of copies of *Clueless*, a four-page brochure and a promise that we would give them a full time job and once we had the money, a decent salary.

Like many a start-up business, I got myself a bunch of go-getters, adventurers and misfits.

Australian Kirk Jobsz was the first of the adventurers. Kirk had run a couple of small businesses in Melbourne, spent time as marketing and promotions manager at TNT magazine in London, and sailed charter boats around the world. When we met for a coffee he was working as a tennis coach and English teacher. He turned up in tattered trainers, jeans and a Hawaiian shirt, looking like a laid back student DJ. But Kirk was bursting with energy and ideas. Then we hit the deciding point in our conversation.

'I have to tell you one thing' he said. His tone implied that I was the one being interviewed now. 'I absolutely hate bullshit.'

Kirk agreed to help but as soon as he was ready he'd get on with his own thing. We would use each other, no bullshit. If he could sell advertising space as well as he sold himself, I'd be happy.

Mark Secchia, an American student, was a tougher catch. Although I later found out he was part inspiration for the character of Stiffler in the movie *American Pie*, on our first meeting he came across as a serious, mature young man. He knew what he wanted and he had a clear idea how to get it. Before it was caught up in a clampdown on pyramid selling schemes and banned in China — and later allowed to restart — Mark had worked for Amway, a company founded by a buddy of his father, who was an influential Michigan businessman and had served as ambassador to Italy. Mark was due to put himself through business school at the end of the year, in Shanghai. After some desperate persuasion he agreed to help set up and manage the advertising sales department.

I had Mark, Kirk, and Jamie Wilson who was hanging around for the summer before returning to the UK for university. They were joined by Faith Qu, a local girl who had been marketing French brandy. I had a sales team.

To put together the listings I found an acquaintance from Guangzhou, a Canadian Chinese called Shelley Yip, who had come to Shanghai to see what all the hype was about. We bumped into each other as I was leaving my meeting with Kirk and I was buzzing with espresso and Kirk's enthusiasm. Despite being ethnic Chinese Shelley could barely speak a word of Mandarin. But she was a punchy five foot with ideas and attitude aplenty, and at a loose end.

Someone introduced me to an out-of-work French chef called Pascale. He knew how to work a Macintosh computer and the basics of graphic design. I signed him up. An English girl called Melissa Grey, who had a proper job at an international advertising agency, agreed to drop in and give the all-important 'art direction'.

The trumpets blared across the campus and we started work.

Like with any start-up, the work was physically and mentally exhausting. I flew round the city interviewing subjects for features and recruits for jobs, researching articles, commissioning them, editing, visiting printing factories and flogging space for advertisements. I had something to discuss with everyone. If I went to eat in a restaurant I spoke to the manager about distributing and advertising in the magazine, and all that time I'd be making notes about the food and service for a review or a listing. If he turned his back I'd sneak a photograph.

Kirk was a selling machine. He recruited his own assistant, Jenny, and put her on a payroll, which he paid. He spent the days running around the city, calling in contracts as he did the deals and then moving on. Jamie and Faith went about sales in their own less frantic way. Jamie drank with his potential clients, who were mostly bar owners taking his cash, until they gave in and signed up out of admiration and gratitude for Jamie's bar tabs. Faith bargained the Shanghai way, begging me and Mark Secchia to let her cut the price just a little more. Mark created a sales commission system that survived for years after he had left for business school.

I drifted around Shanghai, living out of a suitcase, crashing for a week or so wherever I could find a place to sleep. Not that I slept much. One week found me on the floor of a sitting room in a tiny apartment downtown, the next living like a king in a borrowed flat in a brand new development on the outskirts whilst the owner was away.

I called up Angel, a Shanghainese girl I had met a year ago on a train from Guangzhou to Hong Kong. 'Look me up,' she had said, 'if you come to Shanghai and need some help.'

Angel was an interior designer. She lived with a maid in a large villa by the Botanical Gardens. She invited me over. For the home of a successful interior designer the villa lacked a lot. In fact it lacked everything. The place was empty except for a piano, a dining table and chairs and a wok on the gas stove in the kitchen. Angel was a typical enigmatic Shanghai girl: beautiful, charming, intelligent, and lived in a big house of questionable provenance. I never believed it was hers but it might have been. She had several spare en suite bedrooms, one of which I settled into for a nominal rent.

The first issue began to take shape. Kathleen and Shirley followed me up from Guangzhou and I took Kathleen through my progress. I had commissioned an article comparing the city's two best known artists, Mi Qiu, very modern, and Chen Yifei, very traditional. It was the kind of deep and meaningful feature Kathleen had dreamt of. She was happy. I got on with the listings with Shelley. The office, the team, was beginning to look real. It was June 1998.

We were due to launch the first issue of our all-new, English language city-listings — with deep and meaningful feature articles — magazine, on July the first. We had chosen its name on one of our flights to Shanghai, Kathleen and I chucking ideas over seat-backs like a ping-pong ball. It was *Ish* and stood for In Shang Hai. We didn't want to be *Clueless* in Shanghai, nor did our readers. We were going to pretend we knew what we were doing. And our readers were going to be 'In Shanghai', really in it. The name was also inspired by what we thought we could do with the suffix 'ish'.

We'd be stylish, more'ish and er... well, lots of other cool words with 'ish on the end. We'd come up with them.

We planned to start with 48 pages, far more than we had ever published in *Clueless,* and enough to look like a magazine. There was to be not one single free advertisement, not even for Kathleen's restaurant — which was in the wrong city, I know, but she still mentioned the idea. With only days to go, we still had a page to fill.

'I know,' Kathleen said, 'give it to me. 'I'll write about my thoughts and feelings and call it "My Space".'

She set to work.

Half an hour later she printed off her first column and handed it to me. I read it through. This was Oprah Winfrey doing *Wild Swans*. It was personal, very personal.

I sat down to edit. 'I was an "accident", one of those unexpected births after my parents had long thought their child-raising days were over... One of my earliest memories of family bliss was witnessing a stormy argument between my Mom and Dad...'

Kathleen was working beside me. I felt her flinch every time I touched the keyboard. I explained I was correcting grammar and spelling. She sat a while longer and then went outside. Thus was born the magazine's most popular column, the one the readers loved to hate.

We thought we had everything done when Pascale asked a question. 'Hey guys, what are we going to put on the cover?'

'Oh God,' I said. 'I'd thought the artists. But we can't put them both on because we'd need them in the same shot and Mi Qiu is out of the country, if we had time anyway to set it up. And we can't put just one, because the other will get crazy. Let's go through the photos again, see if there is one that fits.'

The feature writer, an artist himself, had taken reels of abstract shots in Mi Qiu's studio; out of focus, swirling with colours, objects clipped by the frame. I had thrown them in the bin. I retrieved them. Thank God we had no cleaner. I pressed flat a shot of Mi Qiu's paint-splattered shoes.

'How about this one?' I said. 'Maybe we can say something about "first step" or "stepping forward", tie it in with this being the launch issue?'

Pascale came over. 'Shame it is all scrunched up,' he said.

'Have a go at scanning it.'

We had our first cover by the skin of our teeth. We were ready.

Jamie returned from a sales call. 'Mark, there's something I think you should know about,' he said. 'We have some new competition.'

'New competition?' I thought there was only one, *Shanghai Talk*, and we had them beat before we'd even gone to print. 'Who?' I tried to sound calm.

'Well, I'm not sure but the bloke I just met showed me this.' Jamie handed over a fax. 'It's a rate sheet for something called *Shanghai Buzz*. A new rag.' Jamie looked away. 'Sounds like they are trying to go head-to-head with us.'

I looked at the introduction to *Shanghai Buzz* that ran across the top of the sales pitch: 'City magazine for people who speak English... by people in Shanghai for people in Shanghai ...not an 'expat' magazine...going to get involved in city life, not just observe it.'

They were the precise words I had said to Graham Earnshaw, Rob Glotzer and the TV guy, whatever his name was. They had taken our idea and were trying to beat us to it.

The bastards. The sly, cunning, deceitful bastards. I felt betrayed. I took it personally. I was still new to business, and naïve.

'Seems they are planning their first issue to appear just before ours,' Jamie added.

I took a deep breath. 'Can't expect to have things all our way, can we?' I smiled. 'We'll just have to be better. Maybe some competition will help.'

What would have helped right then was to go round and smack the conceited grins off a couple of Shanghai old-timers' faces.

There was an increased intensity to our work, as if there hadn't been in the first place. We had to come out as fast and perfect as possible. It was our idea and we had the will to make it work.

At last Kathleen and I set off for the output centre. We were late. It was the first day of July. We spent two days and nights there without a break, sleeping on sofas. Shanghai output centres were just as much a mess as Ah Hai's in Guangzhou. We took a break one evening and stumbled on a cavernous bar with waiters and waitresses dressed in tartan. We ordered a couple of beers.

'We're going make it. I'm sure of it,' Kathleen said. 'This city is ready for us. It needs a magazine like ours... You got a place to live yet?'

'No. Still crashing at friends.'

'You want to look for a place together?' Kathleen was not looking at me like I was her business partner. That made me uncomfortable.

'It's OK thanks. I'll take care of myself,' I said, and knocked back my beer. 'Shall we go and see how they're getting on?'

At last we were ready. It was the third of July. Neither *Shanghai Talk* nor *Buzz* had appeared yet.

Mr. Wang, the man at the printing factory, sent a Miss Tang to pick up the films and proofs from our office.

Miss Tang was a tiny, bouncy ball of confidence. She rolled up the sheets of film, wrapped the proofs around them and taped the lot into a massive roll. She tucked them under her arm and said: 'See you then.'

Kathleen and I went downstairs with her, walked into the sunshine, and I looked for Miss Tang's car. Somewhere above us a student was practicing the cadenza from Beethoven's violin concerto. Miss Tang walked over to a battered moped, placed the bundle across the footwell and leant on it with her knee as she started the machine up. I flinched.

'You're going to your factory on that?'

'No problem. I'm used to it,' she replied.

'But what about the films? What if they fall off? What if it rains?' They looked precarious enough before she started.

'Really, no need to worry. This is how I always collect them.'

I imagined the package falling under a lorry on the dirt roads that led though the construction belt surrounding downtown Shanghai. Two months of toil depended on a dumper truck driver who hadn't slept for 18 hours and whether he would look to his left as he drove out of a building site.

Kathleen and I went back up to the office. 'Well, we're off to print,' she declared.

'Now let's plan the distribution.' Kathleen was leaving the next day for Guangzhou. It fell to me to see our newborn baby into the light of day.

Four days after my trip to the factory to press the yellow knob, Mark Secchia, myself, and a couple of helpers went back in two vans borrowed from an American-Chinese friend of Mark's who ran an office cleaning company. The day was scorching hot, the sun blazing. Neither van had air conditioning. We backed them up to the factory ramp and four pallets stacked with 20,000 magazines wrapped in brown paper packages.

I tore a top one open and pulled out a copy. I held it and felt the weight of it in my hands. It felt solid, like a magazine. I flicked through the forty-eight pages and felt proud. A gang of amateurs and we'd delivered a magazine that was published by professionals.

Half a dozen hot sweaty foreigners in shorts and T-shirts hurling bundles of magazines through bar and restaurant doors, rushing into hotel lobbies, drew curious looks. Foreign businessmen in suits stared over their coffee cups, tourists glanced askance as we barged past to explain to the concierges what to do with the packages. If they looked uncertain we extracted copies and thrust them into the hands of the foreign guests. 'Staying in Shanghai for a while? Here, have one of these. Might come in useful.' We distributed the lot in one long day. By the end of it we were dusty, dirty and absolutely exhausted, and exhilarated.

I rushed back to Angel's to shower, put on clean clothes and stash an un-opened brown package of magazines in my cupboard. I sat on the bed and stared at it while I smoked a cigarette and drank a warm can of beer. Then I caught a taxi back downtown to the Zoo Bar on Fuxing Road. The champagne was on ice. Spirits were sky high. We slapped each other on the back and laughed at the typos. We were 'In Shanghai'. We had arrived. We partied hard.

The next day, the phone rang. It was painfully loud. I picked up.

'I'd like to speak to Mark.'

'Speaking. Who's this?' I squinted with the hangover.

'Hi Mark. It's Adam, from Henry Restaurant. I'd like an explanation.'

'What's up Adam?'

'What the hell do you think you are doing? I advertised in your magazine, invited your writer to my restaurant, and look what you print!'

Adam was a forty-something Shanghainese who had been born and lived all his life in Canada. He was one of the first of his generation, and type, to come home and jump on the bandwagon. Credit to him for that. He'd opened a restaurant called Henry and asked us to write about it. He also wanted to buy an advertisement. I'd done the deal myself. Adam had hammered the price and at the last minute switched to black and white and hammered even more.

I got him to pay in advance, at least for the first of the two issues.

He also wanted a review.

Henry, the restaurant, was one of the first in modern-day Shanghai to revive the décor of the 1930s as a crowd-puller. The food was cheap and basic. But the place had style. Everyone was talking about it. I was happy to do the review, but I did explain we'd write what we wanted.

'I am cancelling my second ad. You betrayed me!' Adam raised his voice. 'How dare you accept my invitation and write what you did, not only about my restaurant, my daughter too!'

We had sent an American, known by his nickname Puffy, to do the review. You couldn't find a sharper or more cynical young China Hand in town. He was perfect for the job. He had been briefed to be fair, highlight the positive, and go for it.

Neither Puffy nor we had known that Adam had organized an evening for the local press.

As he went from table to table, lingering beyond his welcome, Adam Chu had begun to annoy Puffy. The review started out as a sarcastic attack on dinners thrown for local press by vain restaurant owners, and continued into dangerous territory: 'Adam Zhu sat down to give us more than a bit of his life story. After all, what's a review if you don't know that the bathrooms were built first, or what Adam did in Canada.

'A salty waitress from Anhui gave us an earful of suggestions along with the bilingual menu. Adam told us he makes the staff shower in the locker room before starting work. Makes them clean, if a bit neurotic.'

Puffy had been on the point of leaving, well and truly bored by Adam's life story, but had changed his mind when Adam brought over his daughter. She was hoping to be a model, and was charming and personable. So Puffy changed his mind and stayed a while longer, and wrote about that too: 'Suddenly we liked the place a dozen times more.'

I loved the review. It was a brilliant opportunity to show what we were about. Now I had to deal with the consequences.

'Did we write anything factually incorrect Adam?' I asked.

'Yes! You did not write about me, or my brother, who was there too, or about how we came back to China from Canada, all that stuff I told everyone. You did not mention how much we invested, or... or how many staff we have. It's... it's outrageous...' he was stumbling over his words with fury. 'I want a refund!'

'Sorry Adam, but the advertisement got printed as per the contract. We can't give you a refund. And I am sorry you do not like the review but I did explain that we would be objective...' and so on. I finished off, 'I thought it was quite a good read actually and I think our readers will like it and it won't stop them coming to your restaurant. Don't worry.'

'You're the one who should worry!' he screamed. 'No magazine like yours is going to make it in Shanghai!' He hung up.

The afternoon of the next day an American called Daniel Kohler walked into the office. He was about to launch a Yellow Pages phone book. He was holding the first issue of *Ish* open at the page with the Henry Restaurant review.

'At last!' he said, addressing the entire staff. 'A real magazine! Boy have I been waiting for this. Congratulations you guys. Now how do I advertise?'

We sold him two big advertisements, full colour, full price. Henry the restaurant shut down within a year and we never heard from Adam Chu again.

While we tried to establish ourselves as a 'proper' magazine, angry advertisers who expected rave reviews were only the start of many problems. Thanks to the longstanding connection between content and cash, even getting information for our listings was difficult. The Shanghai Concert Hall was a good example.

Shelley had tried them on the phone but no one spoke English. She passed it to me.

'Hi, this is *Ish* magazine, a new English language free city magazine in Shanghai. Could you tell me what concerts you have for next month please?'

'Why should I tell you?' The tone, while not hostile, made clear the speaker would prefer that I went away, as if I had disturbed his afternoon nap, quite likely the case.

'Because we want to give the information to our readers.'

'Why do you want to do that?' Pause. 'How much does this cost? What's in it for you?'

'Err, nothing, except we are trying to help English speakers find out what's going on in Shanghai.'

'Then what do you want from us?'

'Just your programme for next month. Please.'

'It's not ready.'

'Will it be ready by the fifteenth?'

'We finalize our programme when we publish it.'

'When's that?'

'At the beginning of the month.'

'Ah, I see. Don't you think it would be good to tell people a little in advance what you are doing?'

'We never do that. Too difficult.'

'But perhaps you know which major concerts, I mean the big ones, you'll be having next month?'

'We cannot give that information.'

I went over that afternoon. The Shanghai Concert Hall is a beautiful building, erected in 1930 as a cinema. Squat and square, it is a functional concert hall with attractive rococo touches. The foyer is dominated by a double staircase that sweeps up to the circle. In 1998 the new, elevated Yan'an overpass was built right outside its doors. The thunder of traffic outside and the rattle of ancient air conditioning units inside hardly improved the acoustics. (The hall has since been dismantled, moved a hundred metres, and rebuilt.)

The office was a tiny corner one. The man I had spoken to sat at one desk, facing his female colleague at another. Both tables were covered in sheets of fax paper and old programmes. They looked up at me as if I had come to read the electricity meter. I introduced myself.

'This is the magazine I was talking about.' I pulled a copy out of my bag. 'Let me show you the bit I mentioned on the phone.' I turned to the music listings.

The man repeated his argument. His fallback was the possibility of cancellations and the concert hall being blamed by our readers. I tried to explain how a listings magazine worked. I may as well have been playing the violin to a goldfish.

'I know.' I had an idea. 'Let me show you a magazine from London that does the same thing. It's the kind of magazine we want to become for Shanghai.'

I pulled out a recent copy of *Time Out*, slapped it open on the table, and spoke to the top of his head while he looked it over.

'You see?' I said. I shuffled the pages. 'OK, so there are many more concerts and events in London, but this is the kind of thing our magazine will look like as Shanghai develops and more happens and we...' I trailed off. The man had transferred his eyes from the magazine to me, and they were full of confusion, verging on horror.

I looked down.

There on the pages of *Time Out*, my ideal and inspiration, where I had stopped my page shuffle like a cardsharp and jabbed my finger, was a close-up photograph of four testicles, human testicles.

Big, hairy ones. One pair was pulled into the shape of a boat and a sail. The other hung slack.

'Oh shit.'

A couple of Australians were touring the world, making origami out of their bollocks, on stage. Trust *Time Out.*

Switching back to Chinese, I flipped to another page. 'Now here's the classical music section, you see?'

He was still looking up at me, like a hare in a headlight.

I took advantage. 'What's this?' I said, picking up from his desk, right under his nose, a fax confirming a foreign conductor's concert. 'Mind if I make a note?'

I scribbled down the details. I moved around the room, picking up pieces of paper and looking over them as if I owned the place. I had nothing left to be ashamed of. Neither of them batted an eyelid. Now that I was helping myself, what I did was not their concern. They were relieved of responsibility. When I had all the information I could find I thanked them.

'I'll give you a call next month! And send you a copy of the magazine too of course... Er, my magazine,' I added as he looked at me and shook his head.

If the programmes of state-run concert halls were hard to come by, one source of event information was only too happy to bombard us with info: hotel PR departments.

There was a time, not long past, when international hotels were *the* centre of expatriate life in major Chinese cities.

When I had been a student in Beijing there had been no alternative if you wanted a proper drink in a bar, a burger, or a half-decent cup of coffee. Juliana's at the Lido was the only nightclub in Beijing in 1986.

Times had changed. Independent nightclubs, bars, and restaurants were popping up all over Shanghai. Starbucks were due in town. There was a choice, if not a vast one. The foreign run hotels were about to lose their monopoly on the coffee-swilling, burger-munching foreign market.

The hotel PR people did not agree. They'd had it so good for so long they refused to see the competition coming, even when it opened right across the street. They kept churning out their ladies' nights, two-for-one specials, sports evenings and Filipino bands playing cover tunes. And they asked us to write about them. The same content, month after month.

We had to be careful. Thanks to the PR managers' obsession with the expat community, they wanted to advertise. An original, let alone critical, review could lose us hundreds of dollars in advertising. Questioning whether a night at the brand new 'highest hotel in the world' qualified you for the mile high club lost us the Hyatt account for years. Corny interposition of the word 'cherry' with 'Virgin' in a feature title when the airline was about to start flights to Shanghai had a hotel PR girl, who had chosen for herself the English name Cherry, threatening to cancel all her advertisements. She had just found out, from a friend, what a cherry was in this instance. According to local gossip, she was not in the least bit ignorant of how to employ her physical charms in furthering her career. Perhaps that's why she took such offence.

We upset many people. We refused to give free trial advertisements, we refused to interview managers of real estate developments, we refused red packets of cash to write good reviews. We refused to compromise, and we did miss out on hundreds of dollars of advertising, maybe thousands.

In the meantime Kathleen and I had our fast dwindling 20,000 dollars and we had to watch every cent. The people who bore the brunt of our stinginess were the contributors.

In Guangzhou we had never paid a writer. We appealed to

community spirit and slipped them the occasional pizza. In Shanghai we had to behave like the magazine we intended to become and that meant paying, with cash. We started at one yuan per word, six pence. No western-based writer would answer the phone for that but in China where the local press paid half a yuan for a column inch it was considered decent money. We needed writers who could write plausible English, which meant foreigners — who due to their relative scarcity could command a higher price. We had our lucky breaks.

One of the talented amateurs we found was an English teacher from Northern Ireland, Paul Moclair. Short, shaven-headed and with a face that looked like an imminent head butt, Paul was the type you expect to see staggering drunk beside the high street kebab van at two in the morning, looking for a fight. He had a heart of gold and a way with words that could have earned him far more than his teacher's salary, had he been so inclined. Lucky for us those words ended up as reviews, a hilarious cooking column and many features. He even managed to get some well-hidden smutty jokes past the government censors, and Kathleen.

At the bottom of the list of poorly paid contributors, photographers, and staff, and our sales reps who would not see their commission for months, were Kathleen and I. We lived from hand to mouth. Kirk did a barter deal with a sushi restaurant on my way home from work and I ate raw fish for two months solid. It took me a year before I could look a salmon in the eye again.

One night I treated myself to hot food at the first KFC in Shanghai. I purchased a set meal for 20 yuan, no extras, and went downstairs to the seating area. It was late and almost empty. I plumped down beside a mother and child, out for a midnight feast. The boy had a mountain of food in front of him. Mother was sipping a Pepsi, gazing at him like he was a little Buddha.

As I expected, the boy grew bored with half a chicken to go. He pushed it away. And there was the coleslaw too, untouched. They got up and left their trays for the staff to clear away. But the cleaners were all upstairs. As mother and son disappeared, I leant over and tucked in.

Two days later I was invited for dinner with Richard Branson, who was in town to bid for the London–Shanghai air route. He would probably have appreciated the juxtaposition of dinner with him and my stealing leftovers a few nights beforehand, but I kept quiet because I wanted an interview and his business, not sympathy. I struck gold and got both, although the interview was one-sided. Branson didn't want to talk about himself. He wanted to know all about Shanghai and dealing with the Chinese.

Our competition were snapping at our heels by now and spurring us to work even harder. *Shanghai Talk* was putting out rumours that we were illegal. *Shanghai Buzz* was saying that a new English language city magazine for Shanghai had been their idea all along. Both were slamming us for being newcomers with no knowledge of the city and no right to be there. But we had made our entrance and people were paying attention.

In the humid heat of late August we prepared our third issue. We were about to break even, financially, on a monthly basis. A magazine in an established market normally takes two years. It helped that we were keeping costs low. We would have to start paying decent salaries, and I was dreading another month of sushi.

Miss Tang turned up on her moped. We had grown confident about her riding skills and dispensed with the ritual send-off. She wrapped her bundle up in a few cast-off proofs that were beginning to litter the office and bustled out.

'We'll be down to pick it up in four days!' we shouted and got back to work on the next issue, and the next. Shelley was creating forms to send out to event venues, Mark Secchia was planning his commission system, I had three features on the go and a photographer coming to see me in half an hour. Kirk was out selling advertising. Miss White and Iris were double-checking the distribution list for the September issue.

Forty-five minutes later Miss Tang called. She was agitated. I asked her to slow down. From her garbled Chinese I assumed the films and proofs had fallen under a truck. I asked her if she was OK.

'I'm fine,' she slowed down. 'It's not me. It's the films.'

'What's happened?'

'The Shanghai News Bureau were at the factory, waiting for me. They took the films and the proofs.'

'Why?' I gulped.

'They said your magazine is illegal and they were confiscating them. And that there was nothing I could do about it. They will be back later to speak to my manager.'

'So they're gone? The proofs, the films?' I asked, 'you can't print it?'

'No way. I'll call you later.' And she hung up.

Chapter Five
Banned

The office was empty. It was a Monday morning, the seventh of September. Shirley and I stood around like a new couple waiting for the guests to turn up for our first ever dinner party. We exchanged looks. There was nothing to say. We had been through every imaginable scenario a hundred times.

The officials could barge in through the door any minute. We had been told they were coming.

We had got the September magazine out, just. Miss Tang had been brilliant. After her last call she came over in person and explained what had happened.

The News Bureau was clamping down on all unofficial English language publications. They had traced us to her factory and caught us right before we went to press. Not to worry, she said in her chirpy way. Make another set of films. They won't come back again. And they hadn't, not to the printing factory. They caught the second set at the output centre.

So we moved output centres, and printers, and called all the contacts we had made since we first started preparing to launch *Ish*. We needed someone to look after us, to provide a legal means to publish and protect us. The first of September came and went. Finding a publisher had been impossible in the few days grace at the end of August, but one of our contacts had put us in touch with an unlikely supporter: the Dingxin Antiques Emporium.

Dingxin had high-level government connections and a vague plan to link us to a magazine in Hainan, China's southern island province, where they also had connections. Without a formal contract, merely a promise to co-operate, they agreed to put their name on the September masthead as 'sponsor'. We won our game of hide and seek with the News Bureau and got the magazine distributed in the first week of the month. The advertising income had increased by half again from August.

With Dingxin's name on the cover, we got away with it. We discovered they were linked to the State Security Bureau, China's MI5. But the publishing authorities knew the game we were playing and pounced as soon as they saw the magazine on the streets.

Now we had to face them. We had told the staff to get out of the office, not only the foreigners who were working illegally, but also the locals who were at best semi-legal. Kathleen was away in Guangzhou.

This wouldn't be the first time we'd had a 'visit' from a Shanghai government bureau. They'd started soon after our first issue, been gentle and polite, and we'd always managed to satisfy whoever came with the catch-all: 'thank you for pointing out our error, we'll deal with it as soon as we can'. They had also always tipped us off that they were coming. That gave me the chance to go round the foreign staff, the most vulnerable because of visas, and suggest they took off for a meeting, did some research, made a sales call, or took an early lunch.

This time we didn't bother. I announced to the entire staff: 'There's a big bust coming. Scram.'

I looked over mismatched school desks and chairs. By the window on a grey desk — our first piece of new furniture — a blank Macintosh screen stared at Pascale's empty chair. Wires draped from skirting boards and threaded across the tiled floor, here and there fastened to a desk leg by black tape. Piles of scrap paper surrounded the office printer. Black in- and out-trays were flooded with proposals and advertising contracts. Well-thumbed copies of our few back issues were scattered over editors' desks. One of our biggest investments so far, a second-hand air conditioning unit, rattled on its frame where the swallow's nest had been

Was this to be the end of my short career as a publisher?

I'd had almost a year pretending to be one. I'd done some free-lancing for regional papers and magazines too. Surely that would help me bluff my way into a job, at least in the Far East? Might be more difficult back in the UK, and I'd lost my introduction.

Kathleen and I had agreed from the start we were going to 'have a go'. If we didn't succeed, we'd walk away. We didn't even have an exit plan, the first thing you set up with any new business. We'd hoped one would come along.

Now it looked like we were to be shown the exit, not find it for ourselves.

Shirley seemed calm, or nervous. It was hard to tell.

The phone rang. I snatched it up and answered. '*Ish*, hello.'

'I'm calling back for Faith.' I smiled. Nice pun.

'She's out at a meeting. Can I take a message?'

'Please tell her Melody called, thanks…'

There was a knock on the door.

'Sure.' I put the phone down and turned to watch Shirley, all smiles, showing a small procession into the office. She did look like she was welcoming the first guests to a party.

The waiting was over. Despite myself I felt relieved.

The representatives of the Administration of Industry and Commerce, known as the *Gongshang*, were in blue trousers, white shirts, caps, epaulettes and gold braid. The Entry and Exit Bureau agents wore drab olive military style uniforms with peaked caps.

The only people not in uniforms were the News Bureau officials, a pair of them, and a lady who could have been from any one of the other bureaus. For good measure a couple of cops in blue uniforms with matt silver braiding completed the tri-service effect, as if China's air, land and sea forces were lined up against us. There were nine of them.

We had just enough chairs, which Shirley and I arranged in a semi circle. We pulled up two more and sat in the middle. Everyone smiled. And smiled some more.

'Have some tea!' Shirley said and got to her feet.

'No thank you,' one of the News Bureau men said. He was older and seemed at ease, as if he was familiar with the situation.

The Entry and Exit pair placed their man-bags on the edge of a desk. Polite coughs rippled around the circle.

'How can we help?' Shirley and I said, almost in unison.

'Your magazine,' the older at-ease man said. 'It's illegal.'

'Why?'

'Because it is,' he explained. 'No one can publish a magazine without permission.'

'Well,' Shirley and I took turns. 'How do we get permission?'

'You can't.'

'And you have no business licence!' one of the Gongshang spoke up. His voice was loud.

'How do we get the right business licence?'

'You can't!' he almost shouted.

'Can I see your visa and work permit?' Entry or Exit, I am not sure which, chipped in. He was looking at me.

'I am sorry, I do not have my passport on me.' I replied.

'Your name then?'

I gave it.

'Where do you live?'

'With friends. Just moving actually.'

The *Gongshang* butted in again. 'Who is behind this and why are you doing it for them?'

'It was just an idea we had, to help foreigners understand more about China. Here, let me show you, this is what we write about.' I picked up a copy of *Ish* and handed it over, synopsizing the articles and explaining the listings as I flicked through the pages. 'As you can see, it is quite harmless.'

The older, easier man in plain clothes was handed the magazine. He turned the pages with unreading eyes.

'Mark used to be a businessman,' explained Shirley. 'He is living off his savings. He was a metal trader, import export.'

That got some attention. I might be rich.

'It's true,' I said. 'I get no income from the magazine. I just want to see if we can help foreigners in China. I studied Chinese, ten years ago in Beijing, and even I don't know much but I think I can help others who know less than me.' I paused to think. 'Many foreigners are coming to China nowadays. They want to invest. They want to find things they are familiar with and our magazine can be that for them, and show them how to live their lives here and be comfortable. Then they won't go away again.' *With their money*, I left unsaid. They knew.

I had talked too long.

'This is an illegal business.' The *Gongshang* again. 'You have no licence to publish. You have no licence to print. You have no licence to sell advertising. You have no licence to rent this office. You have no licence to be here.' He looked triumphant.

'Well,' Shirley said in her sweetest voice, 'perhaps you could tell us where to get those licences?'

'You can't!'

'Of course. But if we could?' Shirley pressed on.

The *Gongshang* was stumped. Old and easy stirred in his chair. 'First you need a publisher,' he said.

It started. His name was Wang Jianhua. In a fatherly way he began to explain the process. He gave us the rules and then described how to break them. We needed a *kanhao*. Only official government backed publishers had *kanhao*. *Kanhao* could not be rented or loaned to anyone else. Perhaps he could help us find one in Shanghai.

We would need a company registered in Shanghai, added the *Gongshang*. Our advertising company was not. Either we needed to set up a branch office here or find a local one to put our business through. Maybe he could introduce us to one if we stated our requirements.

Our foreign staff needed visas. This could be arranged, said Entry and Exit, taking turns, but you need a company to employ them first. Officially the staff should leave the country and apply from overseas, but there were ways around that. A visit to their office would help sort things out.

And then, added the policeman, looking a little upset to have been left to last, don't forget to tell the foreigners to register their residence at their local police station.

The conversation became cordial. Shirley and I beamed with gratitude and contrition. Every other word was 'sorry… of course we should have known this but thank you for explaining…'

Shirley was doing most of the talking. She knew the game and played it well. It was the tried and tested one of 'seek forgiveness, not permission' and it seemed to be working. It is a standard method of getting things done in China. Ask permission for something original or out of the ordinary and you will never get it, because not one of the regulatory bureaus, if you can work out in the first place which one you should talk to, will take responsibility. Your idea becomes a shuttlecock like the ones kicked between children in the popular street game, *jianzi*. They will keep it in the air until you get bored and go away. Even if your project is run-of-the-mill, it is still quicker to get on with it while your applications are underway. So long as you can prove that you are trying to get permission, somewhere, from someone.

We had stuck to the rules. We had ignored them.

As I listened to Shirley dancing around the problems thrown up by the officials, and the ironies and contradictions of their arguments, my spirits lifted. Despite what they were saying, they didn't mean to shut us down on the spot. If that had been the case they would not have been talking to us. They would have taken our computers and financial records, pasted the door shut with an official seal — ominous long strips of white paper with a vertical line of business killing characters for all the world to see — and that would have been that.

While they were saying we were illegal, unlicensed, and in a heap of trouble, nonetheless, and steered ever so subtly by the kind Mr. Wang, they left us a slender thread of a lifeline. Shirley pursued it like a cat playing with a piece of string. Each time she touched it, an official chipped in his penny's worth of regulation and the string darted in another direction. With the combination of Shirley's persistence and Mr. Wang's gentle prodding, the string was never tugged out of reach.

But we did not have time for games. We had a deadline. As gently as we could we pushed them to help us fast, give us the introductions we needed as soon as possible. This was the tricky part. They knew they held all the cards. It would be good to make us sweat for a while. Besides, no Chinese official makes a hasty decision.

After four hours, they stood up. They were smiling.

'So, that's that,' Wang Jianhua said. 'You are banned. You may not continue your business. You may not publish, print, edit, sell advertising or distribute.' He smiled. 'Here's my number.' And he walked out of the door. Last to leave was Exit, appropriately, though he might have been Entry. With his foot on the threshold he turned to me, shook my hand and said out loud, 'Mark, if we do let you stay in the country, and you do find a way to keep producing this magazine, can my office put in some public notices for foreigners living in Shanghai? We have a real problem getting our announcements out to them.'

'But of course.' I beamed at him.

'Thanks,' he said. 'We'll keep in touch.'

Shirley and I sat in silence for a while. It had been a harrowing experience.

'Well,' I said. 'What do you think?'

'We'll work it out,' she said.

We discussed our options. There was only one: accept Mr. Wang's hint and see who he could link us up with to take care of *Ish*, and all our other problems.

We called Kathleen in Guangzhou and gave her a debrief. She promised to get back to Shanghai as soon as possible. Then we would go to see Mr. Wang together.

The staff filed back into the office in the afternoon. Shirley and I put on a show of confidence.

'We've been busted,' we said. 'Well and truly. But we have been shown a way to keep publishing. Don't worry. We'll be sorted in good time for the next issue.' Everyone went back to work.

I slipped outside to unwind, and think. It was a warm day and the students were moving between classes, lingering outside the tiny store beside the gates to buy a pot of yogurt or a can of Coke and talk about key shifts and chords. I left the campus and turned onto Fenyang Road. A few metres away I stopped at my usual hole-in-the-wall to buy a pack of contraband Marlboro Lights. The man was out of stock.

'You can't be,' I said.

'Government clampdown. The army's been banned.'

'Banned from what?'

'Smuggling cigarettes.'

'The army was running the smuggling?'

He looked at me like I was stupid.

So we weren't the only people suffering from a clampdown. I still needed cigarettes.

'Give me a pack of *Zhongnanhai* then.' It was the Chinese brand of choice for pecunious foreign smokers, at a quarter of the price of international cigarettes.

I paid and walked on, up to the park on Huaihai Road. I passed a street sweeper in his baggy brown uniform and cap, brushing leaves out of the gutter. What a wonderful, simple, straightforward job I thought. I wished, pathetic in my self-pity, I could have it.

I sat on a bench in the park and lit up one of the cheap cigarettes.

How many issues could we miss if the process of finding a publisher dragged on? One at the most, preferably none.

How long could we afford to pay staff if we missed an issue and its revenue? We were lucky to have a small team, poorly paid but dedicated. We could afford to pay them for a month of semi-idleness, but they wouldn't sit around much longer. There was too much going on in Shanghai. They'd find other jobs.

The sales team was harder to handle. Mark Secchia was in it for a challenge, but Kirk and Faith were in it for the money. Jamie had gone back to university in the UK and we'd found a young Shanghainese to replace him. I had told the replacement, 'You don't work for me. You work for yourself. I just give you a decent product to sell advertising in and you promise not to undersell it or do anything else with your time.' If I didn't have a product, the sales team had every right to leave.

And the advertisers? We had to be straight but confident. It was rare for a business in China not to fall foul of one government bureau or another at some time. Landing in the shit with five of them at once was less common. The clients would understand in principle. No need to tell them the smelly details.

So there was hope, if Mr. Wang was as good as his hint.

Kathleen arrived in Shanghai the next day and she, Shirley and I held a conference in the stairwell outside the office. It was brief. We called Mr. Wang and he agreed to meet. Shirley had dug out a list of publishers in Shanghai, hundreds of them. But we would need an English language publication number. That reduced the list to barely a dozen.

When we met the next day, Wang repeated his lecture. We still needed a *kanhao,* no matter whether we were a free magazine or not, or a community newsletter as we claimed to be in Guangzhou. In Shanghai things were different. People followed the rules. It was a law-abiding place, unlike that tear-away city in the south.

He kept repeating the need for an English language *kanhao* and how unlikely it was we would find one. He was letting us down gently. He shook his head and sighed, tutted and pouted, and then, as if he had rehearsed this moment in the mirror, his face lit up and he said, 'There is of course the *Shanghai Pictorial.*'

All that was missing from the performance was a raised finger and wide-eyed, drawn-out stare at the ceiling.

'They have a licence for a monthly magazine in English. Maybe you could start by asking them. They don't come out very regularly. I happen to know them well. Shall I introduce you?'

'Yes please.'

Wang was toying with us again.

'I can't predict what they will say, or — if they want to work with you — what they will want in return. But I do know they are having trouble producing the magazine. They get very little money from the government and do not seem to be able to sell advertising.'

I knew the *Pictorial* series. There were editions for major cities and regions and one that covered the entire country, *China Pictorial.* The city or regional editions were in English and *China Pictorial* also appeared in French, Japanese and a variety of other languages.

As students in Beijing we used to devour the *Pictorials,* just to be able to read something local and current in our native tongue. We didn't care that it was full of photo spreads of smiling workers and farmers, stunning landscapes and factories, and hand-waving Party leaders. I'd never seen the *Shanghai Pictorial* — for the very reason Wang mentioned: it wasn't being published.

Wang Jianhua arranged a meeting for us at the *Pictorial's* office for Shirley and myself.

The *Shanghai Pictorial* occupied the top floor of a 1950s block at the end of a long alley off Changle Road. On one of the pillars at the alley entrance there was a standard government office sign, black characters on white: 'Shanghai Pictorial Publishing House'.

Shirley and I walked on past a shed full of newpapers and cardboard — collected for recycling — a small barber's shop, the open doors of a couple of homes, and came to a small garden square almost filled by a giant cedar tree. A security guard stepped out of his hut and stopped us. We explained ourselves and he directed us to the building on the left.

We walked up the tiled staircase. The walls were bare until the last flight, which was plastered with enormous calendars. The covers showed photographs of garish sunsets over pagoda-lined lakes, Dutch windmills under eye-clenching blue skies, and classic Chinese ink paintings, *shanshui:* mountains and water.

We walked along a corridor past open doors marked 'Finance' and 'Photography'. As we looked in, hoping for guidance, the staff looked up from desks piled high with old paperwork. They stared, expressionless, as we passed. No one said a word.

We ran out of rooms to smile into. The door of the last one was half open. Inside, three people were sitting at desks like all the others, stacked with newspapers. Like our own office at the Conservatory, the furniture looked as if it had been borrowed from an old school room. Beside the newspapers, each had a Nescafe jar full of water on a seaweed base of thick brown tealeaves.

A man stood up, looked surprised and mumbled, 'Ah, you've come.'

He introduced himself as Deng Ming, editor-in-chief. Behind his glasses his eyes looked permanently startled, as if he was about to burst into tears. He was self-effacing to the point of shyness.

'This is Mr. Zhang Zhongyu,' he stuttered. Zhang stood up in turn. He did not extend his hand. 'He is the managing editor. Let's go next door. Tea?'

A lady in the corner looked us up and down and went back to her newspaper.

Zhang followed us into the meeting room. He oozed arrogance in that special Shanghainese way. He had barely said a word by way of greeting. His long gray hair was swept back from his forehead. While Deng was dressed like a standard government worker in short-sleeved white shirt and grey trousers, Zhang was wearing a charcoal shirt that tried to be fashionable, and the two top buttons of his shirt were undone. His glasses weren't prescription like Deng's. He'd paid good money for them.

We sat on a long, black, well-worn leather sofa that lined one side of the narrow meeting room. It would not have looked out of place in a student flat. At the far end it curved like the end of a hockey stick, just enough to fit one person who could survey anyone sitting along the shaft. As is standard for a meeting with a Chinese government body, this would be held side on, not face-to-face.

While Deng was handing us flimsy plastic cups of tea a young man burst into the room.

'Sorry I'm late!' he said. 'I did not see you come in. I was waiting for you outside. My name is Gu, Gu Yiming. You must call me by my English name, Alex.'

'Xiao Gu,' Deng used the diminutive form of address: 'Little' or 'Young' Gu, 'will be our liaison, if we work together.' He turned to us. 'Now what is your proposal?'

Thanks to our scramble for a publisher for the September issue and the practice run with Dingxin Antiques, we had a vague idea of what was expected.

We handed out the copies of *Ish* so far. 'Yes, I have seen it,' Deng said when we gave him the latest issue. He passed it immediately to Zhang, who flicked through the pages as if trying to look interested.

We launched into our presentation about foreigners in Shanghai needing a magazine to help them find out where to go and what to do. We emphasized we had no intention to cover news or politics. The magazines were about culture, eating and drinking and entertainment.

Deng nodded. We were careful not to suggest we were aiming to do anything that the *Pictorial* had already so successfully achieved, such as promote Shanghai to foreigners, but we would love to *help*.

We asked about the *Pictorial*. Deng was forthcoming. The magazine barely appeared once every two months. It was distributed to government departments. They never sold a copy on newsstands.

They could not find advertisers. They struggled to survive and print the magazine with grants from the government. Their main income came from the cheesy calendar business, ordered in advance by state-owned companies, once a year.

Deng paused. He pretended to think for a moment. 'Perhaps you could produce the magazine for us.'

This is what we had come to hear. I felt a surge of excitement. I am sure Shirley did too. But we had to be careful.

Shirley spoke. 'Yes, perhaps we could.' She mimicked Deng's hesitation. 'But,' and she kept her words slow and clear, 'we would have to use our name on it.'

Zhang looked up. He was paying close attention. Deng ignored him.

'That might be possible,' said Deng. 'The most important thing for us is that we get to approve everything that is printed. We cannot get into trouble. If we did we might lose our *kanhao*.'

'How do we work that?' we asked.

Zhang spoke. His tone was firm and final. 'We must see the final colour proofs before they go to the printer. And you must make any changes we request. Once we have confirmed the changes have been made, we give you approval to print.'

That was impractical, and colour proofs were expensive. We kept quiet. We could deal with the details later.

'You must also give us 400 hundred copies every month,' Deng said. 'We need to show them to our leaders.' We made a note. Every state run company refers to the bosses as leaders, because that's what they are, government leaders, *lingdao*.

We started to talk about the practicalities of a partnership, how to structure it, what kind of company we could use to sign an agreement. It seemed Shirley's advertising company, even though it was not registered in Shanghai, would satisfy them.

We raised the question of how to arrange the titles. Could we put ours on the top, theirs below? We made up stories of magazines that ran their titles across the bottom of the front cover. We told them it was the latest trend in western magazines. They acquiesced on the spot. We were surprised.

The meeting was going well, but we were steeling ourselves for the big question. What price? The talk of partnership was a charade. We were going to rent their *kanhao* and we would have to pay for it. Only if we made it seem like we were producing the magazine on the *Pictorial's* behalf would the *lingdao* approve such an arrangement. We were going to pay them to produce their magazine for them. We'd keep the revenue from advertising, if there was any left.

We pre-ambled with a hard luck story of how difficult it was to get advertising sales going, our minimal start-up capital, and then couched the question as softly as we could.

Deng looked at Zhang. Gu looked from one to the other. They had prepared their quote. Zhang nodded and Deng spoke, his face deadpan.

'One million a year.'

We gasped. One million yuan? That was 80,000 pounds at the current exchange rate, and 80,000 yuan per issue, way more per month than our biggest cost so far, the printing bill. Two months equalled our entire investment. It would cripple us.

I thought that one day, in a few years maybe, with a legal publishing set-up, we might be able to afford such expensive protection, so long as the protection was rock solid. But we were going to get nowhere if we started at that rate.

Deng twitched. 'Payable in advance. Sorry, I forgot to mention.'

We gave the only possible reply. 'Can we have a think about it and get back to you?'

'Of course.' Deng spoke and Zhang smiled for the first time.

'Let me see you out,' Young Gu said, and leapt to his feet.

Shirley and I were in a state of shocked disappointment. Our hopes had been raised to the heights and dashed to smithereens. We needed peace and quiet to get over it. Alex gave us neither. As we staggered in a daze back along the alley he chatted non-stop, grabbing us by the arm and pulling us to a standstill to emphasize his points. I did not pay much attention. He suggested other government publishers, friends of his who could help. He seemed to be trying to insinuate himself into our good books. It was odd behaviour for an employee of the people we were still trying to work with, though that looked unlikely to happen now.

When Shirley and I returned to the office we asked Kathleen to come out into the corridor. We walked a safe distance along it and told her the basics of the meeting, and the price.

Kathleen exploded in a fury. I was right about her not wanting to come to the meeting. And so was she. I looked over my shoulder to make sure we had shut the door. Once she'd calmed down we debated our options.

There weren't any. The *Pictorial* had been introduced to us by Mr. Wang from the News Bureau. It was clear he meant us to publish with them or not at all. If we did find an alternative we might get away with it for a while, but this was a forced marriage, and upsetting the matchmaker would bring trouble.

Kathleen had an idea: we'd try to get the total price down first, then work out a monthly payment schedule. By pleading poverty — with absolute honesty — we'd see if they agreed to let us pay less than the monthly fee to start with and make up the deficit later, once we'd started making enough money. For us the payment plan had the added benefit that we'd secure their commitment. Long-term security was the key.

Over the next few days I drafted a proposal and had it translated into Chinese by Iris, while Shirley got on the phone and softened up the *Pictorial*. She came up with every sob story in the book. The Shanghainese have a knack for telling sob stories.

When we thought the *Pictorial* were ready I slotted in our numbers and faxed the proposal over. A few days later the reply came back. In principle they agreed. Things started to look up again.

'But,' Mr. Deng told us over the phone. 'We have to get approval from our *lingdao*.' He meant the News Bureau, whose idea it was in the first place that we work together.

'How long will that take?'

'Oh, not long. Maybe a few days.'

There was a week before we had to go to print with the October issue. We had time.

The week passed. Every time we called the *Pictorial* said: 'Any day now.' October itself was approaching. The staff were impatient to get to print and on with the next issue. We waited. Our calls became more frantic.

At last the *Pictorial* called back. 'We need to have a meeting.'

Could this be to sign the contract?

'What about?'

'The Shanghai News Bureau official in charge of magazine distribution needs to see you.'

Our hearts sank. Now what? We realized our proposal was still bouncing from official to official, like one of those shuttlecocks.

The meeting was held at a 'British' pub called Churchill's, down the road from the *Pictorial* offices. It was about as British as fried rice, but the officials lining one side of the room seemed to enjoy the 'international' setting.

It was not even a meeting. It was a lecture. The official in charge of magazine distribution did his best to convince us that no matter what approvals we had or with whom we co-operated, he, and only he, held the key to getting the magazine onto the streets. Since there were no actual rules governing free magazines such as ours, he made them up as he went along. We could only sit and listen, smile, nod and promise to be good. That was it.

Godfatherly Mr. Wang was there, as ever nudging things along. We directed to him our plaintive appeals that approval might be given quickly. October was a few days away. He smiled and reassured us that now we had been approved by Comrade Distribution, we were sure to go to print soon. 'Just a few more meetings in the News Bureau,' he said.

We parted with a round of smiles and warm handshakes, and a sneer from Mr. Zhang from the *Pictorial*. We went back to our office and to waiting.

The first of October came and went, China's National Day, and the start of a weeklong holiday. We were condemned to sit on our hands for another ten days. The whole country shut down, none of it more firmly than government bureaus. Our staff was beginning to waver. They were wondering if they would come back to a job after the break. We resigned ourselves to producing a joint October and November issue. Day by day we cut the events we had dug out for early October, and tried to find some for November.

The phone calls from advertisers started when they got back to work on the seventh of the month. 'Where's the magazine? Where's my ad?'

We ducked and dived, promised and prayed.

At last, on the tenth of October, the call came. It was time to go to the *Pictorial* office to finalise the deal. We were very lucky, they told us, our 'project' had been on the top of the list of things for the News Bureau to decide after the holiday, and they had given the go-ahead. We could go to print. But first we had to sign the agreement, and get the content inspected and approved. Kathleen came with us. We made her promise to keep her cool.

I was surprised yet heartened to see Wang Jianhua. His presence was reassuring.

The senior *Pictorial* staff filed into the room and we squeezed up on the tattered sofa like commuters on the tube. Mr. Wang was given the end bit that allowed him to dominate the room. Deng Ming pulled in a chair from outside and sat facing Shirley, Kathleen and I. Tea was handed out. The three of us sat forward on the edge of the tattered leather.

'You start.' Mr. Deng said in his shy way. He glanced at our faces and studied the low table between us. On it was our proposal. They agreed to our price and the payment plan but they wanted the fee paid in two monthly tranches, in advance. We agreed.

We were keen to get to the details of how we could have the content inspected and approved for print.

Mr. Deng introduced another Mr. Wang who had been stuck at the very end, up at the pommel of the hockey stick sofa. He was the oldest by far in the room. Deng said he was a retired English professor and he would be our content inspector. In plainer words, he was our censor.

Professor Wang had a kindly, academic face and was dressed in a moth-eaten cardigan despite the warm autumn weather. He nodded at me and smiled. His teeth were brown and crooked. There seemed to be only one of his front ones left. It stood out at an angle of forty-five degrees.

Once Deng had explained the complicated procedure of content inspection — which I intended to simplify with the professor as soon as I had chance for a quiet word with him — Wang Jianhua from the News Bureau clapped his hands.

'Mark!' He looked straight past Kathleen and Shirley, directly at me. 'You deserve congratulations. You are the first foreigner to legally publish a magazine in China. How do you feel?'

I tried to look flattered. But I was confused and embarrassed to be singled out. Besides Ismay and Graham Earnshaw in Shanghai, and some Americans who produced a weekly called *Beijing Scene,* what about Kathleen?

To Wang Jianhua, Kathleen was Chinese, despite her American passport.

'I'm honoured, Bureau Chief Wang,' I said. 'But this is only thanks to your support, for which we are all very grateful.' Even Mr. Zhang was smiling, in as patronizing a manner as he could. 'I am sure we will help the *Pictorial* to promote Shanghai to foreigners here and to the outside world. I sincerely hope we can contribute to the city, and help foreign residents appreciate and make good use of their time here,' and more along those lines. Shirley said something similar in proper Chinese. Kathleen looked like she had swallowed a fly. Her face was screwed up tight with anger and helplessness.

Once the niceties had been spoken, Wang Jianhua rose to his feet. He left the room without looking back.

Mr. Deng stared at the table in between us, his face set with his particular awkward determination. He looked up and spoke. 'There is one last small matter to take care of,' he said. 'The name *Ish* has been banned. Our *lingdao* have been very clear on this point. I am afraid there is nothing we can do about it. That means you cannot use the name *Ish* on the cover.' His eyes darted along the three of us and away again.

Out of habit I glanced at Mr. Zhang. He was grinning with genuine delight, from ear to ear.

I felt like I had been hit by a truck. The bitter disappointment on all our faces must have been plain. We were being taken advantage of. And we could not turn back now, not after those congratulations from Wang Jianhua, which we had accepted. No wonder he had just left.

Deng said with finality, 'The magazine will be clearly titled: *Shanghai Pictorial.*'

Chapter Six

The Propaganda Party

We had rented a *kanhao*. We were inside the system, and we were safe. That was great news.

But we had lost our name. That was a disaster.

How could we claim ownership of a magazine whose title didn't belong to us? The *Pictorial* were using us to revive their loss-making magazine. And they were charging us a hefty fee for the privilege.

It was the only way to keep publishing, and we had an overdue issue to get out onto the streets, before it became a Christmas Special. We also had to move office. Too many government bureaus knew where we were, and despite our new legality that was not a comfortable situation. They had seen us get taken down, and pay our way out of trouble. They'd be back for their share.

Through one of our new *guanxi* we went to inspect a new office block, the Golden Magnolia Plaza, with thousands of empty square metres. Shirley persuaded the agents to give us an office in return for advertising, for as long as the building had space available.

Our new home was big. Besides a vast open-plan workspace we had a meeting room, small kitchen, our own bathroom, even a solid, space-wasting pillar in the middle of it all. We felt very grown-up and corporate. We purchased sofas and meeting tables, and a new coffee machine. From our windows we looked south across the city to a bend in the Pu River, and east, across the empty 'plaza' to the other wing, also empty, of the Golden Magnolia. Kathleen and I set our desks up to face each other in the brightest corner.

The first thing we did once we sat at them was discuss how we could sneak a new name onto the cover that would upstage the *Shanghai Pictorial.*

The lead story for our next — double — issue was about the inaugural Shanghai Arts Festival. We had already decided to use the words 'that's entertainment', thinking of the famous Jam song, on the cover. How about we use the word *'that's'* again in December? It would be the end of the year. We could say *'that's All Folks!'*, after Disney. We could use 'that's' for all sorts until, when we felt the moment was right, we morphed it into *'that's Shanghai'*. It was a catchy and appropriate name. One day we could use it for other cities. Renaming *Clueless in Guangzhou* as *that's Guangzhou* was an obvious place to start.

We re-arranged the cover design so that while *Shanghai Pictorial* appeared to be the name of the magazine, above it, in a band of background colour, standing as if on its own, the word *that's* stood out. The only other word near it was the corner tab announcing it was a free magazine. 'Entertainment', while connected by design and font, could be confused for another line.

We had stumbled on the name that would become our brand. For days I couldn't stop humming the song.

Now we had to get the name, and the content, past our new censor.

We sent computer print-outs, not expensive proofs, to Professor Wang. A few days later I was summoned to the *Pictorial* offices. I found the professor dozing on the leather sofa. I stood in the doorway and coughed.

Professor Wang woke with a start. He mumbled, patted the space beside him, and before I had sat down shouted out: 'Bikinis!'

'I beg your pardon?'

'Yes. Bikinis.' He repeated the word in a softer voice. 'You talk about bikinis in here. Girls dancing in bikinis. This is illegal!' The professor shoved his glasses onto the bridge of his nose and leafed through the loose sheets on the low table in front of him.

'Hmm, now where was it? Silly me, I'm sure I marked it.'

'Perhaps I can help Wang *Laoshi*?' I addressed him as 'Teacher', as tradition dictated.

'Ah, hmm, yes, well…' A piece of his lunch flew through the fallen timbers of his teeth and landed on the pages. I shook it off. 'It was in the information bit in the back. Something about a bar where girls dance in bikinis. We cannot publish this.'

I tried to think which bar write-up he could be referring to.

'Oh blast,' Wang muttered. 'I really can't find it.'

'Why is it a problem?' I asked. 'If my editor said there are girls dancing in bikinis then there certainly are girls dancing in bikinis. And if they are dancing in bikinis, why can't we write that?'

'Because it is illegal!'

'But we are not doing anything illegal by writing about it surely,' I countered.

'That's the point!' Professor Wang turning to stare at me over the rim of his spectacles. I leant back, out of range of his lunch. 'If you write about it, and the police see it, then they will go and fine the bar, and the bar will hold us liable because we wrote about it! They could sue us!'

There are many chains of Chinese thought that perplex an outsider. Banning lights on bicycles because they might dazzle car drivers is one. Inverting 'fast forward' to become 'fast back' when skipping through cassette tapes or DVDs is another. It takes time but eventually preconditioned western minds can get used them. Finding out that a lawbreaker, if it really was illegal to dance in a bikini, which I doubted, could sue a magazine for drawing attention to his activities was a new one on me. I struggled with it.

Professor Wang was still trying to find the offending article.

Eventually he gave up. 'Oh well,' he said. 'If you can find it, which I can't, please take it out,' and left it at that.

We moved on to a detailed review of the magazine's content.

I had written an editor's letter so pregnant with hidden meaning it was fit to burst. I had slipped in obvious hints such as 'reading between the lines', and 'names change but the idea stays the same' and used the metaphor of ordering a dish at a Chinese restaurant to be told it is unavailable, then finding the alternative looks and tastes the same. And the piece finished with, 'Get the message? We wish.' It stood for 'We Were ISH'. I wondered if anyone would get it.

Professor Wang skipped it. It became apparent that his English language knowledge while textbook perfect, was based on a textbook published fifty years ago. He was quite out of touch with modern English and idioms. He also appeared to have no particular loyalty to the *Pictorial* or Party propaganda. I began to enjoy the meeting.

'How can a car be 'sexy'?' he asked.

'Of course it can Wang *Laoshi,* especially if it is red.'

We came to the masthead. Here Professor Wang called in Deng Ming and the fun came to an end. It was vital, no matter what the magazine was called, that our readers and potential advertisers knew who was producing it, and how to contact our office.

With his usual embarrassment, Deng told me that his own staff must be clearly named as the editors. That none of them could speak a word of English was immaterial. Our staff, especially the foreigners, could not be called editors or be seen in any way to have produced the content. The *Shanghai Pictorial* would take the top of the masthead, with their address and contact details. To make it absolutely clear who was in charge, the words 'Published by the *Shanghai Pictorial* Publishing House' came first, then in case there was any doubt whatsoever: 'Edited by the Editorial Department'.

I could not help smiling at the tautology, but I was furious we were being bumped to the bottom. I tried to get him to agree that our editors, whilst not allowed to produce content, at least could 'technically edit', make corrections to the text and grammar, and thus be called 'editors', or even 'technical editors' if the *Pictorial* insisted. It was hopeless.

After a long argument I was allowed to give myself the title, 'Planning Manager'. Our new chief editor became 'Planning Assistant'. Kathleen was 'Business Manager' and Shirley 'Operations Manager'. The best I could get for our office was 'Liaison Office'.

I was in a poor position to negotiate. We had to get the magazine out. It was almost mid October. And strictly speaking Deng Ming was correct, only government appointees could edit or produce content.

Deng reminded me that the name *Ish* was proscribed. He had already ordered us to change our email addresses. Now he made Professor Wang and I go through the proofs once again, while he supervised, to remove each and every mention of the old name. He too missed the hidden message in my editor's letter, but he spotted how we had 'accidentally' left *Ish* where it used to appear beside the page numbers. He found every other mention apart from two of them in the text of the magazine.

I made a big show of apologizing for my negligence and carelessness. My aim was to distract him from the game we were playing on the cover. He accepted the position of *'Shanghai Pictorial'*, in a large font across the foot of the page.

The first ever *that's* magazine could go to print.

Meanwhile we discovered that our competitors had been suffering their own regulatory problems. *Shanghai Buzz* had been forced into bed with the Shanghai Tourism Bureau and was due to reappear under the name *Shanghai Today*. Ismay, who I had found were pretending to print in Hong Kong and import their magazine to get around the *kanhao* problem, had also been obliged to call in their local *guanxi*. The November issue of *Shanghai Talk* appeared late in the month at the same time as our long delayed October and November issue hit the streets.

Who and what was behind the September clampdown slowly emerged. The Shanghai City Government was planning to launch its own English language daily newspaper, the *Shanghai Daily*. They had carried out a preparatory manoeuvre that was standard procedure for local government-backed projects: clear the decks of any competition.

This was the first time I heard of the Shanghai Municipal Government Information Office, a name that was to haunt us for years to come. The Information Office was at a similar power level to the News Bureau, but it was directly controlled by the city government, as the name implies, while the Bureau was a Party organ, controlled by Beijing. The Office however, controlled all media in the city and was responsible for the *Shanghai Daily*. It was pouring money into the project. They were recruiting dozens of foreign journalists and editors at vast expense, flying them to Shanghai and putting them up in a hotel on the outskirts of town. The paper was due to launch any day, but the day kept getting pushed back.

Why a daily newspaper considered a monthly arts and entertainment magazine to be direct competition was a question I puzzled over for months, and an enigma I frequently mentioned to people who were close to the *Shanghai Daily*, and then through contacts at the *Daily* itself once I made them. I never got a straight answer.

But we were safe with the *Pictorial*, who in turn were protected by the News Bureau. Our reputation grew, although it was painful to read letters of praise addressed to us as '*Shanghai Pictorial*'. We swallowed our pride and rejoiced when people asked us why we had started calling ourselves '*that's* free'. A sharp-eyed American journalist even commended me for the farewell message hidden the end of my editor's letter.

We got on with building the magazine, for ourselves, not the *Pictorial.*

We had recently recruited our first editor, Arthur Jones, a Cambridge University English Literature graduate who had been teaching English in Shanghai. Appropriately bookish, leftward leaning and with a sharp wit, I was delighted to have a fellow Brit to help me develop the editorial content away from the rather direct American style that Kathleen favoured. One of Arthur's first jobs, which I passed on like a poisoned chalice, was editing Kathleen's 'My Space', and together we delighted in coming up with cheesy titles, such as for a story about the new craze for pets in Shanghai: 'Up *Shi Tzu* Creek without a Poodle.'

Mark Secchia came up with a clever idea to get readers to study the advertisements and thereby reassure clients their advertisements were being read. To be fair to him he pinched it from an American city paper he'd once read. Like all good ideas it was simple and it became one of our trademarks. We called it the Bogus Ad.

We placed a fake advertisement in every issue and gave a prize to the reader who could spot it. They were fun to make up and some of the crazy ideas would have made popular products, judging from the number of people who fell for them and replied to the telephone numbers or email addresses, which we monitored. They also provided a surprise bonus.

Our competitors were calling our advertisers immediately the magazine appeared on the streets, a common tactic in media apparently, and quite flattering if it had not been so annoying. 'Why don't you advertise with us for half the price and we'll give you twice the size?' was the standard approach.

The bogus ad was a popular target for the calls. We usually put one of our less used office telephone numbers on it. The poaching peaked with the daftest of them all, a new Scottish delicatessen we called 'Jock's Trap', which sold imported smoked salmon, oatcakes, and haggis.

I took many of the calls and had a hard time keeping a straight face as I picked up the phone and said in my best Scottish accent, which is terrible, 'Hallo, Jock's Trap, how can I help you?' The office would go quiet and the foreigners struggle not to giggle. One day the call came from my friends *Shanghai Buzz*, now *Shanghai Today*.

In thickest rubbish Scotch brogue I announced I was a piece of sweaty sportsman's underwear. On the line was an American girl, Earnshaw's new advertising sales manager.

'Would you like to hear about advertising in *Shanghai Today*?' she said, starting her sales pitch back to front, not asking a single question about the market for my haggis: bad sales skills. That was reassuring.

'Tell me why I should,' I replied, looking forward to hearing about their circulation, rates and discounts.

She gave me the lot. I had her on the phone for forty minutes, not bad for a complete waste of time for her and some useful information for me.

Once I had learned all I wanted I came out with my counter-proposal, one we heard so often from our own clients. I was having trouble keeping up the Scottish accent and probably sounded like an Irishman who lived in Glasgow pretending to be Welsh.

'How about you give us a wee write up?' I asked, 'You know, I could send y'over a piece o'salmon or the like, maybe a haggis. Have a wee taste and see what it's like. Then you could write a little something, put our phone number at the end, like. If we get some response, for sure I'll consider advertising.'

Her reply was inconclusive and the conversation stopped there.

Two weeks later Mark Secchia walked into the office with a copy of the latest *Shanghai Today*. There were tears in his eyes. He opened it at the listings section and showed me a new category: 'Delicatessens', with one entry: 'Jock's Trap' followed by the text of our bogus ad. We stuck the page up on the wall. The staff loved it. And I had got my own back in a small way on those duplicitous bastards, even if it was childish.

Now we were at the heart of the official publishing system and strictly censored, the jokes and silly games helped keep us sane. While our competitors tried to bribe our new clients away from us and spread malicious rumours, we left them to it and hit back when we could with more originality.

I won the top three places in a *Shanghai Talk* China travel-writing contest with three ridiculous invented stories. In our next issue we placed a prominent recruitment advertisement asking the winners to come and work for us, for a ridiculous salary.

We slipped crude jokes past Professor Wang, such as the St. Valentine's Day poetry competition. The prize was a double bed from IKEA, and the multi-choice question: 'What kept the Princess tossing and turning all night: A tomato, a pea, or a cucumber?' Our prize sponsors spotted the dirty joke. The *Pictorial* didn't. Thank God the Swedes have a sense of humour.

Paul Moclair easily won the prize for slipping smut past the censors, when in the millennium special issue he wondered whether men would be 'snatching a glimpse of the future' in Playboy's millennial centerspread, or 'glimpsing the snatch of the future.'

Like girls in bikinis — who I discovered were dancing at a city district government-owned restaurant and nightclub — problems with content cropped up where we least expected.

There was a new restaurant in a former Russian Orthodox church called Ashanti Dome. It served French food and was owned by a Swiss resident of Hong Kong who owned a vineyard in South Africa, which supplied the wines. To cap the eclectic mix, it had a large portrait of Mao Zedong high on its frontage facing the street. We wanted to publish a photograph of the exterior with our review. Wang *Laoshi* was quick to spot the mole-cheeked Mao.

'You cannot publish a photograph of Chairman Mao,' he told me. 'Use of pictures of the Chairman is strictly controlled.'

'But he's all over the place,' I said, 'and he's the founder of modern China! He's your national hero. And how come the restaurant can put a portrait of him on its exterior, never mind all the pictures in the press of Tian'anmen Square in Beijing, with a massive Mao in the background?'

Immediately I realized it was a mistake to mention Tian'anmen in a debate about content. Wang froze, as if I had just dropped the proverbial pork chop in a synagogue. Since the repression of the Democracy Movement in '89,Tiananmen was a name fraught with hazard and double meaning and the date of the violent clampdown, June 4, or '6/4' in Chinese, had become a code word for all manner of subversive ideas.

I switched my argument to all the Mao-themed restaurants in town, which were plastered in Mao pictures. If we reviewed one of those it would be almost impossible not to get his likeness in a photograph.

Wang was adamant. He quoted some authority or rulebook. The picture had to be replaced. To prove his point he added that the restaurants would no doubt have to remove the portraits soon and all Mao-themed restaurants were sure to be banned anyway. They continue to thrive.

Kathleen found it difficult to deal with the *Pictorial*. She had been wary of them from the start and when we left the final, conclusive meeting with Wang Jianhua, she had said to me with a dramatic raising of her arms, as if she was about to be crucified, 'This is the end.'

She had a point. We were being used. But no amount of insistence on my part that we would have similar if not worse issues to deal with, whichever publisher we worked with, could cheer her up.

Perhaps it was the loss of control that upset her. And her feeling that she was losing control was heightened by her frequent absences on her trips to Guangzhou.

Kathleen's main role in the practical magazine business was overseeing the design and layout. Her *modus operandi* was to brief the production team, leave them to it for a few days and return to see the result. Without regular guidance the team, though they did a good job, never completed it as she expected, or had imagined it in her mind's eye. Her tantrums were spectacular, and demoralizing for the designers. They had no fridges to hide behind. Once Kathleen had stormed out, we picked up the pieces and carried on where we had left off. My own arguments with Kathleen, common after such episodes, were spectacular too. I tried to keep them out of the office.

I had been so obsessed with the magazine and dealing with the *Pictorial* I was ignorant of another problem that had been brewing, until I received an unexpected phone call.

'Hello Mark. My name is Florence.' The woman's voice, which was small and mousey, had a strong Guangzhou accent. She didn't give me a chance to speak. 'I am Kathleen's cousin. I am in a coffee bar just down the road from your office. Could you please come to see me?'

'Er, when?'

'Now. If it's not too much trouble. I have come from Guangzhou specially to speak to you.'

'Florence I'm really busy. Can it wait until later?'

'No. I have to see you now.' It was somewhere between a command and a plea.

I went to find Florence in the coffee bar close to the office.

I had barely sat down when she said. 'Kathleen sent me to see you.'

Now that I was facing her I remembered meeting her in Guangzhou at Kathleen's restaurant. Like Kathleen's cousin Shirley she had helped out in some respect. She was small and mousey like her voice, but as far as I remembered a pleasant, intelligent woman.

'What's happened?' I asked. 'Is there something wrong? Is Kathleen ill? Why have you flown all the way from Guangzhou to speak to me when she could call me?'

'Mark,' Florence's voice became serious. 'Kathleen loves you.'

Oh my God. This is madness. Utter madness. I sat back in horror.

'She has loved you for a long time,' she was saying, 'since Guangzhou. You have to return her love. It is only right that you do. It is not fair to her otherwise.'

'Look Florence,' I was brusque. 'Kathleen is my business partner. That's that. I have no feelings for her other than what is normal for a business partnership. And I have no personal or romantic feelings for her whatsoever.'

I cast my mind back to the doe-eyed look Kathleen had given me on Lamma Island in Hong Kong as we checked into separate rooms, to the time she had turned up at my flat in Guangzhou late one night, claiming she had lost her keys. I had put her in my spare room. I thought of all the conversations and how I had opened up about my personal life. Now it all made sense. I'd had a vague inkling, but I'd ignored it. It had been too much to even think about and I was too busy. Now I wished I'd dealt with this sooner, before it started. Since arriving in Shanghai I hadn't even let Kathleen know where I was living. I had hugged her once, when she was in tearful hysterics outside the office one stressful day. That was the only time we'd had any physical contact.

No wonder the arguments were so violent. I'd put them down to Kathleen's personal feelings about what I saw as simple business decisions. There were countless times we had left the office to talk, or so I expected, about business, and the meeting had become a psychoanalysis session.

I'd listen, argue, and then give up and wait for her to go back to Guangzhou so I could get on with the magazine.

'You have to make her happy,' Florence said. 'It is up to you. Only you can solve this problem.'

Florence was only the go-between. I repeated what I had said.

'So I have come all this way for nothing,' she said, looking defeated.

I was not falling for that old trick. 'Yes, you have.'

I went back to work. That evening I wrote a short and simple email to Kathleen. She replied promptly and quite sweetly, full of praise for my dedication to our business and promising to appreciate that my interest was only in that, the business. I wondered how long the calm would last.

Life was getting complicated. I was building a business on the shakiest of foundations, driving our staff hard and promising them the rewards they were due, whilst my mind was in a constant state of suspended panic at how things were going to turn out with the *Pictorial*. Now I would have to face a woman scorned every time I needed a quick decision on the colour for the cover, or how much to pay a new receptionist.

Angel, my mysterious, sweet, scatterbrained landlady, tried to help. One evening after work she gave me a massage. It was very good. Too good. Why she had to wear a transparent nightdress I have no idea. It showed her perfectly formed girlish figure to full and sensual effect. My excuse might have been the need to push all thoughts of my amorous business partner from my head. It worked, but the last thing I needed was yet another complication. I could not stay with Angel after that night, sweet though it was.

I found a home to call my own. It was the attic of a tall and narrow family house in the heart of the former French Concession. It was more of a garret, perfect for a struggling writer, editor, publisher, designer, sales rep, distribution manager and all else. It was a hideaway and I made sure Kathleen never knew where it was. Angel organized a crew of builders to come and fix it up, and it turned out that she really was an interior designer.

Tucked almost at the dead-end of a *nong tang* off Anfu Road, a short street lined with art galleries, my lodging consisted of a tiny sitting room, a landing cum hallway where I put a desk, and an upstairs kitchen with tiny balcony.

If I craned my neck out of the kitchen window I could enjoy a view of the green treetops in the nearby People's Arts Theatre's garden. From the balcony I could shake hands with my neighbour directly opposite, an electrician. My few visitors had to run the inspection of the Tang family on the floor below, who used their landing as a dining room. The cooking smells came straight up through my sitting room floorboards. Fish nights were bad.

The Tang family comprised two sisters, one husband and a teenage daughter. The daughter's bedroom opened directly below and opposite the small landing that I had to cross to reach my bathroom. I installed a door in the stairwell to protect my privacy, and her innocence.

The Shanghai *nong tangs* — alleys — are tightly packed terraced houses built by the old foreign-run municipal councils to house the constant flow of incoming Chinese who made up their workforce, pre 1949. Where the modern Chinese municipal government hasn't demolished them to make way for glass office towers and apartment blocks, they have survived for many more years than they were designed to. They have an old world charm that is too forgiving of their cramped and unhealthy conditions. A communal rubbish tip is placed at the entrance, whose stench puts of sightseers. Though they are back alleys, removed from the motor traffic, and islands of quiet amongst the construction frenzy of Shanghai — until it is their turn to be demolished — *nong tangs* are not always peaceful. The dawn chorus starts with the handymen and refuse collectors who cycle or walk with their carts down the alley, ringing bells and shouting out what they can fix, what they can sell, what they can take off your hands. Real bells were rare. The regular stand-in was a saucepan lid with a piece of scrap metal for a knocker. The tinny sound was just enough to wake you. In the evenings the alley echoed with the sharp and regular hammering of heavy kitchen choppers on wooden blocks. Then the fierce clack and shuffle of *mahjong* tiles, a sound like prawns crackling in a hot wok, took over and lasted late into the night.

That tiny attic was to be my longest residence after the house where I grew up. I was too busy to find somewhere bigger or more comfortable. Returning home along Anfu Road after working late and a bowl of noodles at a local restaurant, I'd whiff the stench of the garbage tip as I approached. On the right hand side of the alley the *waidi* girls, newly arrived from the provinces like my Miss White, hunched over their sewing machines under pale light bulbs in their tiny sweatshop shack. I'd let myself in as quietly as possible and tiptoe past the door of the Tangs' daughter, up to my tiny attic flat, sit at my desk, pour a whisky, light a final cigarette, unwind and collapse into bed. Every morning I'd wake up to a chopping board, the scrap dealer's saucepan lid or, now and again, the crack and shuffle of an all-night *mahjong* game.

Life began to return to something like normal. I started going out, not to review a restaurant or a bar but to hang out with friends, go to parties that weren't a launch for a product or potential advertiser.

I know we've all been through it, that stage of our lives that's fast and furious, and we think we're living to the max, on the edge, like no one has before or ever will. Every generation has its time, its moment. We all believe they were the best, the craziest, unrepeatable. It's all about the time and moment and being young and living it for all its worth. The 'swinging sixties' must be the most quoted example.

In the late nineties and early noughties, it was Shanghai's moment, and we were young and living it. It was wild, it was new, and the city was like a beautiful virgin who just realized she was a nymphomaniac.

After all, Shanghai had a reputation to live up to.

History does repeat itself. Foreigners were flooding back, with passports this time. Life was one long welcome-back party. Bars, restaurants, nightclubs opened every week. Hotels and fashion brands, whisky-makers and beer companies, car manufacturers, sports promoters, yellow pages... They all came. And then there were the young Shanghainese, rushing to claim the birthright their parents and grandparents had abandoned in 1949, who brought with them everything they had learnt, or copied, from exile, mostly in the States. And the ones who'd stayed, stuck it out. It was their turn too to have some fun.

And the Chinese from the poor provinces up the Yangzi River, who just like they used to in the old days, came to make a better life, the *waidiren* who had built the city for the foreigners in the first place.

While the last of that little lot knuckled down to work their way up as they always did — their turn would come and they knew it — everyone else wanted to celebrate. It was party city, and we were in the thick of it.

Every day we were invited to attend a couple of launch events, a hotel press night, a wine tasting dinner, and a new nightclub hosting a visiting DJ who was going to play until the early hours. They all billed themselves as the 'first ever' in China or Shanghai. Everything had to be brand new, unknown, unseen or unheard in the city. The western press who came along in tow with the 'first China office' of whichever corporation, played up to that, and while they were in town sent back stories of the first this or the first that they had witnessed in China's 'first' city. According to them the Shanghainese had just discovered western music, jazz, theatre, opera, cars, football, fashion, sex, homosexuality...

Of course it had all happened before, pre-1949. But that would have spoilt the story. And they fed into and off of the idea and mood all over the city that we were living a debut, an endless first night at the theatre.

In between the commercial and bar and nightclub parties, the young professional foreign crowd and returnee Shanghainese threw their own parties in villas and apartments and swimming pools. On a 'quiet night', if there was such a thing, everyone packed into YY's Bar on Nanchang Road, owned by Kenny, ex-New York Shanghainese who spoke English like a Chinese Kray Brother, or later at Goya for martinis, run a by a couple of Shanghainese from Milan, or dancing all night in Park 97, set up by the Lan Kwai Fong Group from Hong Kong.

There was a furious, frantic pace to the social frenzy, an impatience. Everyone wanted everything and wanted it now.

And we got it, in every aspect of life, work and play. The speed of the city's resurrection — besides China and its economy as a whole — was unseen, unheard of. We lived fast. We didn't stop.

I don't do drugs, but they would have helped. Every morning was a battle to get out of bed, to beat the hangover, (to show the girl the door), to get to the office.

As soon as I was out on the street it kicked in again, the buzz, the frenzy. And the first thing I saw in the office was a list of invitations to the next night of debauchery, in eight hours time.

One meeting I turned up to, with an international advertising agency and an American executive I'd got to know quite well: he took one look at me and said, 'Mark, you've got to go easy on the coke.'

As I said, I never do drugs. (OK, I've smoked marijuana. But never 'hard' stuff.) But I was living it hard — we all were.

And then there were the actual coke heads.

They really went nuts.

Within six months, Kathleen and I were making money, even with the usurious pay-off to the *Pictorial*. The growth of the *Shanghai Pictorial*, now known as '*that's something*', surprised us.

It was going to be impossible to keep up without more people. Kathleen and I were still involved in every stage of the publishing process. We had no back-up for our hard-pressed staff. I often left an event to return to the office until the early hours, or handed over my glass of champagne so I could rush across town to the output centre to change a font. Then I went back to the party, or on to a new one.

We needed to pause, take stock, build a solid base. We had something. It would work, might make us rich. We started recruiting and training people. The office, for all its vastness, filled up. The massive table wasn't big enough for the weekly sales brief. Kathleen and I had to go out again to talk, because the meeting room was being used by Mark Secchia to interview sales staff, or Arthur was with a candidate for the editorial team.

One day I interrupted Arthur. He was with a young Australian girl. 'Can you read and write?' I asked her, and without waiting for a reply: 'Good. Arthur give her a job and give me back the meeting room.'

I know. That was the most arrogant, chauvinist, un-PC insult you could throw at someone. But I think Kath forgave me. She took over from Arthur a year later and was a brilliant editor-in-chief.

Just as people were falling into place, two days before the February issue was due back from the printers, the *Pictorial* called. It was Alex Gu. He sounded grave and spoke in his usual jumble, leaping from point to point. But the message was clear: Shirley and I were to drop everything and report to the *Pictorial* office immediately.

They weren't butterflies in my stomach. More like a hurricane of albatrosses. I tried to look calm and walked through the office, which was humming with magazine-making, like a Heidelberg printing machine. Shirley was over by production. I motioned to her. Worry flashed across her face. I nodded, and we smiled in unison at the team.

'Got to go with Shirley for a meeting.' I said. 'Won't be long. Call the printers to check they're on schedule won't you?' And we left for Changle Road.

Chapter Seven

Dumped

Gu met us at the entrance of the alley. He stood with his hands folded across his waist like an usher at a funeral. There was no mindless chatter as we walked up to the fifth floor. He showed us into the meeting room where Deng Ming and Zhang Zhongyu were waiting. The silent woman was there as well, and still she did not speak. She seemed to be playing the role of an official witness.

Shirley and I pretended to assume we had been summoned to discuss retail sales, which we were going to try out with the next issue. Maybe we could distract them from the real reason for the meeting, whatever that was, if we blustered. As we talked, Alex Gu scribbled in his notebook.

Deng Ming stopped us short. He spoke slowly and deliberately, yet I had trouble following him. I was in denial I suppose. Then I heard the distinct words: '*Ting fa.*' 'Stop distributing.'

I woke up and caught up. Deng was telling us that he had received instructions from his *lingdao* that our co-operation was to cease immediately. This very minute.

Shirley and I were shocked, caught by surprise. We had expected trouble, but not this. We asked for a reason. Deng Ming would not give one. He said he did not know.

Shirley launched into a passionate speech about the magazine, repeating our pitch of four months ago, how we were helping Shanghai, helping the foreign community. She became aggressive, remarking that the foreign community, investors in Shanghai, would be sure to complain to the city government if our magazine disappeared. We had made our mark. We were popular.

The *Pictorial* people listened. When Shirley was finished they uttered the Chinese phrase that means so much and hides even more. '*Mei banfa*.'

There is no alternative. We can do nothing. We don't give a damn.

They stood up as one and Deng Ming said, straight to our faces, as if determined at last to overcome his shyness. 'It has been a pleasure working with you. But that's it. Goodbye.'

I stared into his eyes. I thought — I believed — for a split second, that he meant it.

Alex Gu escorted us out. Yet again he talked of other publishers, friends who could help, companies he knew that could protect us. He danced and dodged in front and beside us like Gollum in *The Lord of the Rings*. Behind the thick lenses his eyes were a match for Tolkien's creation, and his insinuating, ingratiating pleas that we only had to follow his advice were as sleazy and slimy.

We hailed a taxi and just as Shirley was getting into it Gu pulled me back and said, 'Mark, why don't you work with us? Just you. You could still be in charge of the magazine. We have to continue to produce the *Pictorial*. It is our duty.'

I got into the taxi and turned to Shirley. As we drove off I was fuming with anger. 'Do you know what that little shit just said?'

'Ignore him,' she said. 'Let's get the magazine out before they can stop us.'

I was impressed. I replied that much as I'd love to do just that, it was she who would face the consequences, if there were any.

'They can take us to court!' I said, and corrected myself. 'Sorry Shirley, it would be you who gets taken to court.'

She was still positive, and joked back: 'You might get stuck in China.'

Shirley looked at me out of the corner of her eye and said with a mischievous smile. 'You can marry my daughter, and when I get my American passport,' which she was applying for at the time, 'my daughter will become American and she can get you out! Ha ha!'

Shirley's daughter was pretty. She was also fourteen.

We called our Godfather at the News Bureau, Wang Jianhua. He said he had no idea what was going on. His ignorance comforted us. Maybe the *Pictorial* was playing a game. Maybe they had not been told to stop but were preparing to increase the fees. Or then again, maybe Wang had set the while thing up and was lying through his teeth.

It was a Friday. We decided to get together on Sunday, when Kathleen was back from yet another trip to Guangzhou. I dreaded her reaction. After the recent fights about the business and the emotional sideshow, another intense debate about our future had the potential for cataclysm.

Shirley and I kept our secret from the office. With a dark sense of dramatic irony we watched everyone leaving in high spirits, the issue almost off the press, heading to Friday evening parties.

Shirley's right, I thought, 'Sod the *Pictorial*.'

And I went to a party too.

That evening was the annual foreign correspondents' bash held by a public relations guru and his male partner. Their hospitable camaraderie and good humour cheered me up and the crowd ranged from seasoned and cynical old hacks to the wives of brand new arrivals wondering which kindergarten to send their kids to.

My mobile rang while I was catching up with an old friend from university, now a freelance photographer. I stepped outside into the alley to take the call. It was Alex Gu.

'Are you sure the magazine has not been distributed yet?' he asked.

'Alex, I haven't got a clue. It's the weekend. I'll call you on

Monday.' I went back in to the party. Let them sweat.

As I walked home my anger grew, swelled by the alcohol. How could they do this: dump us with no notice at the very minute we were going to print? We had an agreement. It had been tough to work out and was for a full year. If they were playing games with us then they were a bunch of shits. If this was a News Bureau set up from the start then they were all complete bastards, except for Wang Jianhua, who for some reason I still trusted. I was fuming with rage, at the perfidious Shanghainese and my own helplessness.

I turned down Anfu Road. It was deserted. It was one o'clock in the morning and windy. In my drunkenness I was captivated by the dancing shadows of the plane trees. Under the bright streetlights they looked like fighting cats flailing on the ground.

A young man appeared at the far end of the road. He was running fast and straight towards me. He looked utterly absorbed in his hurry. I had no idea who he was or why he was running, but I hated him. I calculated how to step into the road and punch him in the face. The combination of his speed and my fist would smash his nose. I stepped down off the pavement. We would pass right by each other. I swayed to my left to allow for the swing.

He ran on past. I was very drunk and very angry. The fantasy had made me feel better for a fraction of a second.

Over the weekend I slept late, my mobile switched off, and dragged myself to the office to inspect the February issue. The in-house copies, about a thousand of them, were stacked in the usual place along a wall inside the door. I was alone. I slouched at my desk and stared at the piles of brown packages. The cover was taped on top of each one. Would we ever get it out onto the streets? The other twenty thousand were waiting at the printer for our word to release them. Thank God the *Pictorial* did not know where the factory was.

Once again Kathleen, Shirley and I debated our options. First we had to decide what to do with the February magazines. Shirley's determination hadn't faltered. Stick to our tested formula: act first and say sorry later. But what about the next issues? We needed a partner and we needed one fast. Chinese New Year was coming up in a fortnight. As it had during the October holiday the whole country was about to shut down, this time for at least ten days. If we couldn't get a publisher before then we were going to be stuck, like the millions of China's migrant labourers unable to buy a train ticket home because they were owed a year's unpaid wages. The *Pictorial's* timing was perfect.

'You must understand,' Shirley said to us both, 'there are no rules in this business, no laws governing it. It is run by individuals. If there is no benefit for them then they will stop you. Why shouldn't they? And there is no set line defining legal from illegal. Whoever has the power can decide where to put the line and dictate who has crossed it.'

She warmed to her theme. 'The *Pictorial* has wasted our money instead of doing what they should have done with it: spent it on our behalf for whoever they needed to keep in favour with. No trips abroad, school fees for someone's son or "business" trips to Beijing; that is what they should have been arranging with our money, for the person who is trying to stop us now.

'We have to find the right person. Or we have to go above them and get them instructed to let us carry on.'

For the first time I heard Kathleen say, 'Is it worth it?'

She had read my mind. I had decided that if we did not come out in March, I would pack up and go home. Taking a note from Kathleen's own book and drawing on a personal metaphor, I remarked that most soldiers have a rest between battles. Not that I had even been in a battle, but she knew I had been in the army.

Ever since we had come to Shanghai, I reminded her, we had been fighting without a break to set up the magazine, to deal with the everyday problems of business in China, like disgruntled employees we had fired, Jenny in sales for example, who sneaked on us to the tax authorities. We had been shut down, hassled by the news bureau, the tax bureau again, the foreign affairs bureau and attacked by competitors, by malicious rumours, imitators, potential competitors who weren't even competitors, slandered by jealous expats and jealous locals and now dropped like a hot brick by our partners at the *Pictorial*. I thought it best to not remind her of our own fights.

I spoke in English, which Shirley did not understand. That was a good thing, because she carried on where she had left off and she carried us with her too.

She had talked to Wang Jianhua again. His suggestion was either use a book publishing licence, a *shuhao*, which was easier to find than a *kanhao*, so long as we made some subtle changes to the format, or find someone in Beijing. A powerful publisher in the capital would outrank and have better connections than whoever it was in Shanghai who was on our case. Wang was being remarkably helpful.

We had one lead in Beijing. Shirley was to look into it. I was to deal with the *Pictorial*. We instructed the distribution company to go to the printers and get the magazine out. We were still in business even if we were acting like a band of guerillas.

One last effort for March I promised myself. Then that's it.

As I expected, Gu called first thing on Monday.

'Mark, why is the magazine being distributed? What happened? You know we've been told to stop!' I heard him sniff, as if he was crying.

'I'm so sorry Alex,' I lied. 'Truly. I had no idea the printers had finished ahead of schedule. I tried to call them over the weekend and could not get through and when I did it was too late. This is very embarrassing I must say. And I didn't have the number of the distribution company. And our office was shut for the weekend so I could not get in to find it. It's really *mei banfa.*'

The more lies I made up, the more of his own medicine I threw at him, the more I enjoyed myself. I savoured the helpless silence at the other end of the line.

'Oh, and Alex,' I carried on, just to get another squirm out of him. 'We need to see an official document stating why we must stop. After all, we do have a signed contract valid for one year. And,' knowing it was useless, but hoping to put him onto the defensive, 'of course you must return the money we have paid in advance.'

Alex was surprisingly submissive. 'You'd better come round to our office.'

'Sure, as soon as I have time.' I rang off.

I could not wait to go and give them a piece of my mind. My impatience was goaded by Mark Secchia, who walked into the office as I put the phone down. He had been out on a sales call. He looked furious. We went into the meeting room.

'I can't believe it!' he said. 'Over the weekend I discovered that bastard Gu has been telling our advertisers the magazine is fully booked for the next three months.' He reeled off a list of clients. 'And those guys I just met? He called them, the little creep, and told them not to advertise anymore because we have been banned. What the hell is going on?'

I had some explaining to do.

As I spoke to Mark, I realized what I had been too frightened to suspect until now. If the *Pictorial* were telling clients we were fully booked and to call them back in three months, they must have been planning all along to take over as soon as we had got 'their' magazine back on its feet. No wonder the insistence on the title, the masthead. 'Edited by the editorial department.' I began to doubt if the name *'Ish'* really had been banned. Come to think of it, how could it have been?

We had been scammed, conned by the *Pictorial* and their leaders, the News Bureau. It was one thing to be used and know we were being used, but to have been set up like this was worse.

How stupid, how naïve we had been. Myself especially. I had stuck up for the *Pictorial* in arguments with Kathleen, partly because I had been more involved in the negotiations and partly because I truly felt we had no alternative. Her fears had been justified. But we had got four issues out and we had a new name that the goons had not cottoned onto yet. I stopped feeling helpless. I felt wronged, personally insulted.

I thought back a few weeks to a call from a young girl, a Korean student, who had asked me if we were the 'real' *Shanghai Pictorial.* An odd question, and I had answered as best I could. Why did she want to know, I asked back.

'Because I am working as an intern in their offices and they do not seem to be producing a magazine,' she explained. 'Are you the guys who are really doing it?'

I had innocently assumed the *Pictorial* had other business they wanted her help with. If she wanted to work on the 'real' *Pictorial* magazine I said, she was welcome to come over and work with us. She turned up the next day and could not help telling us how happy she was to get away from the non-job she had been tricked into.

Mark Secchia, no fool, knew something of the deal with the *Pictorial* and had guessed a fair bit more. He took the let-down calmly. Then he went further and gave support and encouragement I did not deserve. His faith in the trio of us who were trying to build the magazine boosted my morale.

I set off for the *Pictorial* offices.

Deng Ming was out. No sign of Gu. Zhang Zhongyu was talking to someone in the meeting room. That left me in the office with the woman. I took a seat at one of the empty desks.

'Mark, you do not look happy. Why do you not smile? It is almost Chinese New Year! Relax. Have some tea.' Those were her first ever words to me. I wondered for a brief a minute if they were genuine. It would have been nice to give her the benefit of the doubt. But there was none, I was sitting in a den of thieves.

I glanced over the desk in front of me. There were a couple of sheets of fax paper. When she turned back to her newspaper, I gently nudged them apart with my elbow and uncovered another underneath.

The fax was in English and addressed to Deng Ming, from someone looking for a job at the new look *Pictorial*. The sheet below was his reply. It was positive and asked the girl to give him a call and arrange an interview.

As I daydreamt of how I would deal with him, Deng's face flashed past in the corridor. He glanced in, saw me, and hurried back the way he had come. I leapt to my feet and chased after him.

'Mr. Deng! We need to talk!'

He turned back like a truant schoolboy. For once his sheepishness was straightforward.

'Have you got the document that can officially terminate our agreement?' I demanded, trying to sound formal and businesslike.

Deng confessed he did not.

'Then we are still partners. And there'll be no problem with the February issue appearing, will there?' I could not help behaving like a bully. It seemed to be working too.

'Err, I guess not,' Deng mumbled.

'And Wang Jianhua says we can use a book publishing licence in March. Did he tell you? Isn't that good news?'

Deng made a pathetic attempt to look pleased. I had scored my point. They would leave the February issue alone. There was no use in forcing him to own up to his trickery.

First thing the next day, Shirley and I barged into the Shanghai News Bureau, the lion's den. We didn't have an appointment. The Bureau was housed in a large concession era villa on Shaoxing Road, which had a long association with the Shanghai literati. It was once home to six publishing houses, and we knew it well because of the 'Old China Hand Reading Room,' a coffee shop and bookshop where we'd had some of our first meetings in Shanghai. I had never noticed the plain strip of official characters a few metres along from it, at the gates of the Bureau.

We stuck our heads into an office and announced that we had come to see the Bureau Chief. A young man was so surprised to see us, a local and a foreigner, that he assumed we must have an appointment. He ushered us into the main meeting room, and asked us to wait. The big room was darkened by heavy floor length curtains. I noticed the floor was bouncy. It was an old ballroom.

We only had a to wait a couple of minutes for the Bureau Chief. He invited us to sit down but did not offer us tea. He was polite but said he had a busy morning ahead of him. He agreed to give us ten minutes.

We started to speak, but the Bureau Chief cut us short. He listed our problems, betraying an intimate knowledge of our case.

First, he said, we were foreign. Therefore we could not work for a magazine in China, let alone publish one. I glanced at Shirley who, as a Chinese person, was responsible for everything we did. Now I understood why we had been granted the meeting. I proved we were 'foreign'.

Second, the *Pictorial* was obliged to produce its own magazine. They had no authority to delegate the responsibility to another party. To do so was illegal. And that was that. No argument.

He went further. We might be interested to know that the *Pictorial* was planning to come out with a new bilingual version of their magazine after the Chinese New Year. Perhaps, he suggested, we might consider helping with the English language portion. Maybe we could even sell the advertising in that part? He smiled.

Hang on a second. A minute ago he'd said foreigners could not be involved in magazines.

The blatant contradiction, the double standards, the pure hypocrisy amazed me. More was to come.

When we stood up to leave the bureau chief asked me for my name card. He ignored Shirley. It was as if she did not exist. 'Maybe we can do something together in the future,' he said, and started interviewing me.

He asked about my experience in publishing. He was under the impression I was a professional. I was careful with my replies, and to hide my anger. It was obvious what he wanted. While we spoke he looked me up and down, as a slave-trader would, or a punter sizing up a prostitute. I felt repulsed by the man, and humiliated. He was arrogant, sleazy, and he had power, over me. On top of that, his hypocrisy, and the fact that I had to stand and listen to it and could do nothing to show how sick it made me, made me feel physically sick.

I steeled myself, looked him in the eye and took it all as best I could. I shook his hand, smiled, and left.

A fax from the *Pictorial* was waiting for us back at the office. It was a copy of the official document from the News Bureau instructing Deng Ming to cease all co-operation with us. I smiled as I read it.

'You are unable to produce the magazine *Shanghai Pictorial* in co-operation with another party,' read the key line, 'therefore you will stop.' The four issues we had produced 'in co-operation' meant nothing. Mr. Deng had well and truly set us up. I imagined him dictating the content to the Bureau, who had typed it out and put their chop on it. The double meaning of the word 'unable' was a nice touch. In Chinese, when coming from authority, it can mean 'not allowed to', or 'incapable'.

We started work on the March issue. Over on the production side of the office Kathleen was briefing two freelance designers. One of them, a pleasant looking young student, was keen to help but clearly lacked any skills. As her frustration peaked, Kathleen threw a tantrum and stormed out. Shirley went after her to fix a date to fly to Beijing. We were going to follow Wang Jianhua's advice. I had asked Shirley, on our way back from the News Bureau, why we hadn't seen him there. She told me that he was about to retire, and that might have been one reason he had helped us. He would not have to face the consequences.

So he might have been a good guy, after all.

We needed to get to Beijing as soon as possible. Chinese New Year was a week away.

A few days later the three of us were in the offices of the magazine publishing division of the China Light Industry Bureau. The room was cluttered with the familiar bashed-up school desks, piles of newspapers and Nescafe jars of stewed cold tea. Light poured in through high swing windows. The Beijing winter sun cut beams through the fine dust that was stirred by the slightest movement.

'So you want a publishing licence, a *kanhao*?' Mr. Hao Gang said.

Mr. Hao was short, rotund and happy. His bean-shaped face could not help smiling as he spoke. Every other sentence he broke off to laugh at himself. We had no idea of his position or his power. His name had been given us by a *guanxi* of a *guanxi*. This was a long shot and a long way to go for it, but we knew he had a licence somewhere in this shambles of an office.

'Well I do have a licence. And I am not using it right now. It is for our Bureau magazine, *China Light Industry* it's called. You want that one?' Mr. Hao giggled.

It couldn't be this simple. We had spoken to dozens of publishers in the past few months and got nowhere, more often than not before we even started. Some had stated up front that we must change our name again or switch to Chinese language, or at best become bilingual. Others explained patiently yet adamantly that we must package our magazine with their faltering publication and could only sell it via newsstands. Weeklies who published once a month had offered us one of their three 'spare' *kanhao,* so long as we changed our page size to match theirs, and understood there were two other parties they were talking to for the other two weekly licences. Once they had finalized an arrangement with them, they might change the format again, depending who paid the highest price.

We had been led up more alleys than there were *nong tangs* in Shanghai, and just like the *nong tangs,* they were all dead ends.

We mumbled our reservations to Mr. Hao, hinting at the problems we were sure he'd raise. We might as well get them on the table.

'Oh I am not concerned about any of that stuff!' he said with a grin. 'I think the magazine's supposed to be in Chinese but what the hell, it's a licence isn't it? That's all you want! It's monthly and so long as you put our name on the cover — put it in a light grey font at the bottom of the page, I don't care, so long as it is there — and let me run through the content before you publish, that's all there is to it.'

'And the price?' we asked, with bated breath.

'How about twenty thousand a month?' It was a fraction of

what the *Pictorial* had demanded, and he hadn't even pretended to think about it.

'Um, sounds possible...' Shirley and I looked at each other.

'Good. Now that's all settled,' said Mr. Hao, 'let's go for lunch.'

We could not believe our luck. Here was a publisher who dished out *kanhao* like he was lending you his car for the weekend. Look after it and do what you want, go where you want, as long as you stay on the roads.

Over lunch we drew up a basic agreement and Mr. Hao polished off a mug of *Er Guo Tou,* a vicious Beijing brand of *baijiu.* He made me join him. Kathleen and Shirley refused. My incredulous relief that we'd found a way to stay in business became a drunken contentment with the world and all in it, including Chinese bureaucracy. I liked Mr. Hao very much. His good humour was infectious. I liked Beijing. Things could get done here. The people were far more confident and straightforward than the Shanghainese.

Mr. Hao promised to draw up a simple contract and have it ready for us the next day.

He kept his word. Within 24 hours in Beijing we had a signed and chopped agreement with a new publisher and another *kanhao.*

We were back in business. I couldn't wait to get back to Shanghai, tell the team, and get on with the simple work of magazine production, and then enjoy the Chinese New Year break. Nor could I wait to see the faces of the *Pictorial* and the News Bureau when we came out with Beijing backing.

The following few months passed in a happy, hardworking blur. Compared to 'co-operating' with the *Pictorial,* which had been like dancing with the devil, Mr. Hao was an angel. Shirley and I took turns to fly to see him, present the documents we needed him to chop, deliver the payment and pick up a barcode for the next issue.

'Put them on the desk,' he would say to me, pointing at the

sheaf under my arm. 'Let's go for lunch. They'll be chopped by the time we get back.' And off we went for drinking session.

We had established ourselves as *that's Shanghai* by now, and our reputation was growing. So were advertising sales. The numbers went up by half as much again every month. The sales team was raking in clients, cash, and their own commissions. They were happy, confident we had a winning product.

Late one afternoon a local businessman called and declared over the phone that he wanted to advertise his new bar and restaurant. It was on my way home so I volunteered.

'What sort of bar are you going to make this?' was my first question.

'I don't know.'

'Are you going to serve food? Perhaps a restaurant?'

'I don't know yet.'

'Please forgive me, but why do you want to advertise with us when you don't even know what sort of business you are going to set up?'

'Because I know it works. I've seen all the other bars in your magazine and I know it helps. And,' he looked embarrassed, 'I was hoping you could tell me what to do with this one.' He waved his arm at the empty space.

The steady flow of foreign corporations moving into the China market via Shanghai went from a flood to a deluge. One of the first things they saw in the city, that they could understand, was *that's Shanghai*. Their international headquarters were dishing it out with the airline tickets. We picked up almost the entire Virgin Atlantic marketing budget for the year, paid in advance. Like us they were starting with the international community and spreading to the local market.

The petty tricks played by our competitors didn't bother us

anymore. So they tried even pettier ones. Some months into the deal with Virgin I asked the marketing manager how come I was seeing his ads in all our competitors. He had become a good friend. (His contract with us had nothing to do with me mentioning him as a candidate for the job to Richard Branson.)

He laughed at my concern. 'Mark, it's brilliant. Whenever my ads appear with you, all your competitors try to lure me away with free ones. It works a treat. I spend my money with you and the rest is free. You're doing me a massive favour mate [he's Australian]. And you're still getting all my print budget.'

Wine importers, insurance agencies, airlines, the dozens of international bars and restaurants that were opening every month, the foreign DJ parties, the dot coms, they all used us to get their name out to their new market. Pickings were rich. We started making serious money. Kathleen and I took a small dividend and passed on a bonus to Shirley. We promised flights home to foreign staff. We increased editorial salaries and paid ourselves our own first real ones. I gave up KFC, switched from sushi to teppanyaki, and flew to Vietnam for the Chinese New Year holiday.

We planned our first anniversary and dreamt up an idea for a street party, an international food festival to draw in even more advertising, and make money. Virgin took title sponsorship and gave us yet more hard cash. We secured the rights to be the official English language media for Shanghai's 'Swedish Week'. I was granted a one-to-one interview with Benny Andersson and discovered Abba thirty years late. I even got Sandvik, a Swedish metals company I used to trade with years before, to take a half page at full price to congratulate themselves on being Swedish and in China. We were on a roll.

It did not last.

Of course it didn't.

In May we got the call from Mr. Hao. He apologized. He had no idea why, but he had been instructed by his superiors to stop working with us. It was *mei banfa* again. He did sound sorry. I could picture him in his dusty office, laughing sadly. I was disappointed that our run had come to such a sudden end so soon after it had begun.

We knew what was behind the end of our honeymoon with Mr. Hao. After long delays and political infighting with the *China Daily*, who had an office in town, the *Shanghai Daily* was up and running. We were hearing regular reports from friends who worked there that the senior management hated us with a recalcitrant, debilitating fury that would have been better suited to a school playground. Apparently one of the trio who ran the paper could not mention our name, and when she heard it went red with anger. They were out to get us.

There was no semblance of professional rivalry, let alone commercial competition. They envied our success and blamed it for their own failure to make even half the impact on the foreign community. Their source of funds and power, the Shanghai Municipal Government Information Office, had contacts in Beijing. The word had been passed.

Just to put us back into the Shanghai 'picture', the News Bureau had at last launched the new, bilingual version of the *Shanghai Pictorial*.

Its name was *SH*, in precisely the same font we had used for *Ish*, and in the exact same spot on the cover.

Chapter Eight

Sent Down to the Country

I once fancied myself a half-decent fencer. I captained the school team, represented my university and the army, and trained with Olympians, both British and Chinese.

I had been put off team sports because they all involved balls or bats, or both, and I could never connect them, and I loved fencing all the more because it was all down to you, one against one, and you don't only want to be fitter and faster than your opponent, you have to be smarter than him too. The best description for fencing is 'physical chess'. You try to predict what your opponent will do, or coerce him into doing it, then take ruthless advantage and hit him when he is on the wrong foot, or his blade is in the wrong place.

Our battle with the Shanghai and national publishing authorities and whoever was encouraging them was beginning to remind me of a fencing match. We had to think ahead, anticipate their next move and prepare a counter. We deliberately led them astray, made feints, like we did with the building a separate name under the noses of the *Shanghai Pictorial*. That had been a perfect one. And then we had let them think we were retreating defeated along the piste, when actually we were running up to Beijing and finding Mr. Hao.

We knew all along there would be a counter-attack coming, once they saw what we had done with the China Light Industry Bureau. And sure enough it arrived. But we hadn't let our guard down. Even while working with Mr. Hao we had been preparing our next move, the next safe haven, and while we were doing so we always enjoyed one small advantage: until our enemies got to know us better, they always assumed we'd accept defeat.

Our counter attacks had to be so fast that they did not see them coming, so smooth and swift that the next issue of *that's Shanghai* came out on time and none of the spectators, our readers and clients, saw the flash of the blade.

There are many bouts in a championship.

It was tiresome, all the more so because it seemed so unnecessary. After a day's work in the office, or interrupting one, Kathleen, Shirley and I would drag ourselves to a meal or meeting with yet another potential publishing partner, government bureau, or new-found *guanxi*. The conversation, as far as we were concerned, could only be hypothetical. We were hedging our bets. But if you start a discussion about co-operation with a government-related Chinese businessman or official, he will assume a deal is imminent. Sometimes we set in motion a chain of events that were hard to stop. We upset many potential partners because we had to leave them hanging in limbo. But business is business and *guanxi* are *guanxi*, and in China they are inseparable. We had to be mercenary about it. Many of the people we talked to would never be able to deliver on their promises of support, their boasts about how they could protect us. Some were genuine however. We made it up to them with free advertisements.

The stakes were higher now. We had a reputation, a name, and a solid readership. The business year was beginning to pick up. We had a list of clients ready to book advertisements. We had also taken some major upfront payments. The date of the Food Festival was approaching. Virgin Atlantic was depending on us to stage a massive public event that would help launch their name in Shanghai.

I remembered the look of confusion on Richard Branson's face over dinner a few months ago, when I explained the intricacy and upside-down logic of publishing in China. He either missed my point, or didn't bother himself with it, and I couldn't blame him. But he'd for sure be blaming us if we screwed up the event his company had paid a small fortune for the title rights to.

We needed a new, powerful publishing partner, fast.

Through a distant cousin of Shirley we had made contact with the News Bureau in Shaoxing, a city a couple of hours from Shanghai, famous for its plum wine and being the birthplace of Lu Xun, an influential writer in the Republican era. The official made supportive noises but that was it. He did, however, drop a hint that a distant colleague of his, an old classmate, who was an official in the News Office in Yangzhou, a mid-sized city a couple of hours the other side of Shanghai, might be able to help, he knew not how. Yangzhou was the hometown of Jiang Zemin, then president of China, so its star was on the rise. We made a note and left it at that.

The day we heard the bad news from Mr. Hao we called up Shaoxing again and asked for an introduction to Yangzhou. The next day, a Saturday, 22 May 1999, the three of us, Kathleen, Shirley and I, boarded the first train out of the city.

The flat Jiangsu plain rolled past the windows. The view wasn't inspiring. Grey clusters of farmers' cinder block houses gave way to green fields of mulberry bushes, blankets of broad leafed squashes and the ponds of fish farms, the water's surface cluttered with ranks of white polystyrene floats. Rows of larches sprang up and then away beside long stretches of the track, breaking their step and our boredom as we bridged the canals that cut through the repetitive landscape. Long strings of barges chugged slowly along the waterways, loaded so heavily that their gunwales barely surfaced above the tiny waves that splashed against them.

Shirley helped pass the time by telling us stories of life during the Cultural Revolution, when she had been 'sent down to the country' to learn from the peasants. An entire generation missed out on their education thanks to the organized anarchy led by the Gang of Four. The view from the windows held a special significance for her. I had always assumed that when you were 'sent down' you were sent miles away, to far distant provinces, or the borders with Russia and the Central Asian 'stans. It seems the Shanghainese, or many of them, were only sent down the road.

A car, driver, and a junior official were waiting for us at Zhenjiang, a railway town beside the Yangzi River, the dividing line between North and South China. No trains go to Yangzhou. There are no railway bridges.

We squeezed into the back of the black sedan and were driven to a car ferry. We waited in a queue while a long procession of rattling blue trucks and buses that heaved and lurched, came up the riverbank past us. The smell of low-grade diesel exhaust brought to mind memories of journeys I had made as a student into the poor hinterland of China.

We drove onto the ferry and Yi Ming, our escort from the Yangzhou News Office, took us up onto the top deck. He pointed out the supports for a new bridge that were setting off from opposite banks of the broad river. In the grey haze the vast lumps looked like the rows of mythical beasts that line the avenues leading to the imperial Ming Tombs near Beijing. The bridge that would bestride them was a personal project of the president, Jiang Zemin. One day he would drive over it from Shanghai, where he was expected to retire, on his way to his hometown to sweep his ancestors' graves and choose the site of his own one, perhaps.

On the opposite bank a brand new road led to Yangzhou, about ten kilometres away. Our driver barreled down the middle of it as if we were VIP guests on our way to visit President Jiang's grandmother. He swerved past trucks, blasted the horn, and forced the oncoming traffic into the far verge.

The outskirts of Yangzhou were similar to any one of the tens of thousands of Chinese cities and towns that in the late nineties were undergoing not 'urban renewal' so much as rebirth by violent C-section. Roads straight as chopsticks, lacquered black, cut through weed-covered patches of dust and rubble where next year a factory or housing complex was to spring up. Brick and plaster walls, riddled with holes like they'd been blasted by tank shells, enclosed the barren building plots. Sections of podgy concrete piping were laid along the roadside, roughly end-to-end, like a toy wooden snake, waiting to be buried underground.

Downtown Yangzhou was tidy. It was a city blessed with high favour. From Yi Ming's brief introduction we learnt that Yangzhou today was the same size, by population, as it had been in the fourteenth century. It had been a key post on the salt trading route from the south to Beijing, thanks to the Grand Canal, which joined the Yangzi a few miles up the river. Marco Polo was the city's governor for seven years, by appointment of the Mongol Emperor Kublai Khan, founder of the Yuan dynasty. The place really did have connections, ancient and modern. The significance was not lost on us.

Our car turned in through the gates of the Ying Hotel, 'Welcome Guests Palace'. It was an enormous building, perhaps a few years old, and it looked like the exterior was polished daily. A vast lawn stretched across its front, big enough for a football pitch, maybe two. The grass was perfect, as if it had been brushed and combed. Yi Ming pointed to another block diagonally across from us, set among cherry trees and magnolias, its rear overlooking a private park with a small river running through it.

'That's where Jiang Zemin stays when he comes home,' he said with pride.

The director of the Yangzhou People's Government News Office, Mr. Sun Xiaofeng, was waiting in the lobby. We introduced ourselves.

'Have you eaten?' he asked, the standard polite greeting.

'Yes thank you,' we replied politely, and untruthfully. It was after midday and Mr. Sun would have had lunch. We were impatient to get to the business at hand. We did not have time for food and small talk.

'Let's sit over here.' Sun guided us to a coffee bar set back from the lobby. We ordered drinks and pulled out packets of cigarettes.

'This is a five star hotel,' Sun said, as the waitress placed cups of cheap instant coffee on the table.

We told him it was beautiful.

Sun Xiaofeng was about five foot eight and comfortably chubby, not fat. His face was full fleshed, his high cheekbones buried under puppy fat. I imagined he might have a dash of Mongol blood. He looked faintly noble, and northern. That inspired confidence. Those people were straight talkers. He was more relaxed than many of the officials we had met, and while he had a sense of humour, it was sophisticated. He was an intellectual; very different to the equally charming, yet almost childish Mr. Hao. Sun spoke with a reassuring confidence.

His sidekick Yi Ming, on the other hand didn't say much but when he did speak it was with an arrogance that was almost insulting. He was a *'gao gan zi di'*, son of a high official, with a sense of entitlement. Those youngsters could be dangerous.

We came to the purpose of our visit.

I did not expect Sun Xiaofeng to help us. We were half a day's journey from Shanghai. What interest could he have in a magazine designed to promote that city? He wasn't even a publisher. He didn't possess any *kanhao*, let alone book numbers. He had no magazine he needed resurrecting. Surely there was no personal interest, let alone an official or commercial one.

We made our rambling presentation, skipping from point to point, from Shirley to me to Kathleen. When we had finished we looked at Sun, our faces transparent with nervousness, our eyes pleading.

'Yes, I think we can support you,' Sun said. 'You can help us promote Yangzhou. That is my department's job. But you can basically carry on doing what you are doing, use your title, and run your business.'

We were amazed. I made an effort not to gasp, or shout for joy. This was too easy, like the China Light Industry Bureau again. It could only be a flash in the pan. Without a *kanhao*, how could this turn into a long-term arrangement? Perhaps his support could last for a few months until we found another publisher, a proper one. All the signs said this would be another temporary refuge. But we could hardly turn him down. We asked the price.

Sun seemed confused. He glanced over at Yi Ming, who looked nonplussed.

'Er, I don't know,' he said. 'I suppose there are some costs for us, administrative, or something like that.' He paused for a long minute, thinking hard, and looked up.

'How about fifteen thousand a month? Does that sound reasonable?'

That was cheaper than the China Light Industry Bureau. And a fraction of what the *Shanghai Pictorial* had extorted from us. This man had no idea what he was getting into, or its worth. And he had made the decision there and then, on the spot. There had been no request to let him talk to his *lingdao*, his leaders, no quiet conference with Yi Ming on one side, in their local dialect. Sun seemed to have the power to make decisions. He hadn't finished.

'Ten thousand will be the fee for content inspection and other administration. The other five can be our expenses, travel to Shanghai for example. It's what I estimate we will need. Don't worry, we'll give you receipts.'

So we were getting published for a mere ten thousand. That really was incredible. And he was promising to give us receipts for expenses. We accepted without a moment's hesitation.

We moved onto the practical details. How to get the content to Yangzhou for inspection, how long he needed to go through it, how to credit his office on the masthead. What about the publishing permission? Could his office get hold of an actual *kanhao*?

Again Sun was relaxed. 'I cannot get a *kanhao*, at least certainly not for your next issue. We'll get one sooner or later. In the meantime we can give you a printing permit.' He looked at Yi Ming, who grunted.

Sun explained. 'We produced a brochure for Yangzhou not long ago. A printing permit, as opposed to a publishing one, was all we needed. I don't see why it cannot do for your magazine. Your publication is free after all.' We kept our concerns to ourselves. He sounded so confident.

The only condition of Sun's that made us nervous was the inclusion of promotional articles about Yangzhou in the magazine. We might look just a little stupid if we published regular articles about a small city three hours away from Shanghai. On our way into town I hadn't noticed any obvious tourist attractions.

Then again, if this partnership only going to last a few months then it and the price were worth a little editorial embarrassment.

To keep Sun on side, I asked for his suggestions for the next issue. What could we write about?

'We are trying to attract investment to Yangzhou. That is my key responsibility.' My heart sank. Horrifying images of double-page spreads about factories and tax breaks flashed through my mind. I thought of the industrial wasteland we had driven through on our way into Yangzhou. Not pretty.

'Bureau Chief Sun,' I replied. 'One of the best ways to do that is to write about the attractions of the city. What, for example, is Yangzhou's appeal for tourists or for people thinking of living here?'

'Yangzhou is famous for its water culture,' he offered.

I had not seen any canals. 'Water culture?'

'Yes,' Yi Ming said, brightening up. 'We have lots of public baths, saunas. We spend a lot of time in them.' He seemed to be remembering his last visit.

I knew perfectly well what he meant. The word 'sauna' in China is nearly always a convenient synonym for a brothel. Sun and Yi Ming were smiling.

'Um, any historical sights?' I asked.

'Well, there's the Slender West Lake. It's even more beautiful than the real one.' The original West Lake is the key attraction to Hangzhou, a tourist city a few hours south of Shanghai. Why do Chinese cities have to copy each other so blatantly, I wondered, not for the first time? Why can't they give their own names to their attractions and be proud of them? I feigned interest.

Sun was silent for a long while, and then said. 'Oh, and we have the last working woodblock printing press in China. It still produces books. They are handmade, as they were centuries ago.'

At last something I could relate to and so could our readers. My interest was genuine. I showed it, hoping to make a good impression. The pictures could be good.

'How about Yangzhou fried rice?' Kathleen asked. 'You're famous for that.' She had an excellent point. Yangzhou fried rice, staple of fast food restaurants and backpacker hostels, was the fish and chips of China. It was the ubiquitous standby when menus got confusing. And to slap together a story about it would be as easy as throwing the simple ingredients in a wok.

Sun Xiaofeng told us with evident delight how the Mongols, when they swept south through China in the thirteenth century, by the time they reached Yangzhou, had run out of the flour-based mush they kept in their saddlebags to eat on the move. It was in Yangzhou that they started using rice, which they fried up with whatever was to hand; bits of meat and vegetable, and put that in their saddlebags instead. I pictured Sun Xiaofeng on a horse, riding south at the head of the propaganda bureau of the Mongol hordes, filling his chipmunk cheeks with handfuls of fried rice.

We had the first of our Yangzhou stories. Kathleen agreed to write it. She must have served thousands of plates of the stuff in her restaurant.

We were set. Sun was happy we had a story about Yangzhou that he liked and we had a publisher, or at least a government supporter. We had to get back to Shanghai and to work. We declined the invitation to a celebratory banquet and a night in the five star guesthouse.

A fortnight later we came out with the June issue of *that's Shanghai*. Manchester United were on the cover. They were making their first ever off-season appearance in Shanghai. The production process, output and printing went without a hitch. No raids, no visits, no telephone calls. Our enemies were confident they had put a stop to us. When the magazine appeared at the distribution venues, we stood by for the reaction.

There was none. Nothing. Silence. Not a whisper, not even from the Entry and Exit Police.

The lack of a reaction was almost worse than having the door kicked down. I was a nervous wreck.

I set off to Yangzhou again, with Adrian, photographer and university friend who was coming along to take shots of a traditional woodblock printing press. I would be writing the article.

As soon as I could, while Adrian wandered around the old building I pulled Sun Xiaofeng to one side.

'Bureau Chief Sun,' I said. 'I can't help wondering, I mean, I'm just curious, nothing more: but did anyone call you about us, say from the Shanghai News Bureau, just for an example? I'm not trying to, you know…'

He cut me short. 'Oh, yes, they did call. The Shanghai News Bureau in fact. How did you guess? I know them quite well. They asked me a few questions and I explained you are promoting Yangzhou for us. I'll go and see them soon. Don't worry. They won't give us any trouble. Now, let me show you a reprint of a volume of *sutras*, and then the works of Deng Xiaoping.'

And that was that.

Slowly it dawned on us that the words: 'Yangzhou People's Government News Office' punched way above their weight. They clearly confused the officials in Shanghai because they knew what they meant: we had found a powerful guardian angel. And no one, not even the Shanghai bureaus, could guess how powerful, which made them even warier. For all they knew a relative of the President of China might be behind us now, or the President himself. Whatever or whoever it was: you don't mess with government officials from the President's hometown.

Meanwhile the Yangzhou News Office was happy. We had run a full-page story about fried rice.

I got to know Mr. Sun on the trip to the printing press. He gave us a personal tour and was a knowledgeable guide. He had been a student of Chinese literature, a subject close to my heart. I told him I had been awarded a first in Chinese poetry in my university finals and that my Chinese name, Ji Yiduo, was inspired by a famous poet of the early twentieth century, Wen Yiduo, who had lived in Nanjing, Yangzhou's provincial capital. Sun liked that. He was a charming host and good conversation.

On our way to the State Guesthouse for lunch Adrian remarked how green and clean the city was. He mentioned he would love to bring his family for a weekend.

If that's what Adrian thought, maybe our readers would forgive us for constantly pushing the place on them. Perhaps there was a way to turn propaganda into readable content after all.

Over lunch we discussed other Yangzhou topics that we could cover in the magazine. Expanding on the morning's literary theme, Sun told me what I should have remembered but had quite forgotten: that the fictional family in the Qing novel, *Dream of the Red Chamber*, the Jias, were originally 'from' Yangzhou. Hence much of the food in the novel — and I certainly remembered that, the descriptions of banquets went on for pages — was from Yangzhou. Maybe we could do a story about that?

Once Adrian and I had swapped stories of lectures at the School of Oriental and African Studies spent thinking up different English words for rice, Sun Xiaofeng rested his chopsticks beside his plate.

'There is something else that will make a good story for your readers.' I leant forward. This was enjoyable, and so much easier than I had feared.

'We have a major event later this year. I would like you to come,' Sun said. 'The city is launching a special investment zone. We will have some ground-breaking ceremonies at factories. They are Korean invested. The mayor will host the event personally.'

'Oh bloody hell,' I thought. 'I should have known better.'

'I would like you to bring the press with you — the international press,' Sun said. 'You do know them all don't you? We'll take care of the accommodation of course.'

Adrian grinned at me. He was finding it funny, damn him.

'Err, yes Bureau Chief Sun, I am sure it can be arranged.' Now I was in trouble.

I had a good idea of what was in the offing, and the foreign correspondents would have one too. No way were they going to drop their hot stories about political corruption and property market bubbles to spend three days in a backwater like Yangzhou, listening to propaganda dressed up as investment incentives. And even if they did, they were not going to write what Mr. Sun expected.

But *that's Shanghai* would have to.

I drew comfort from one potential benefit. We could count on Sun's support until the press trip had taken place.

'What date have you set Bureau Chief Sun?' I asked with that in mind.

'October.'

Brilliant. That gave us five months.

On the downside, October was a busy time for foreign journalists. Getting even a single one of them out on a pointless press junket to Yangzhou would be impossible.

In the Shanghai office life carried on as normal, our own version of normal. The staff soon learnt of the switch from the China Light Industry Bureau in Beijing to the Yangzhou News Office. There were bemused looks from the foreigners and knowing ones from local staff. Yet again we had got away with it at the last minute. And they knew it. There were some nervous moments as we made the changeover. But the staff either bounded back with renewed confidence in our ability to ensure the survival of the magazine, the business and their careers, or quietly rewrote their CVs ready for the next crisis.

The main problem with our new partner was Mr. Sun's paranoia about the personal classifieds in the back of the magazine. These were free and very popular. I heard it was common after-dinner entertainment at expatriate parties to pull out a copy of the magazine and see who could find the most subtle reference to threesomes, homosexuality, or which was the most blatantly false search for a 'language partner', a common euphemism for a one-night stand. I also heard from gossip about town and chat rooms on the web that the advertisements were very effective. 'Found a tennis partner through *that's* classifieds,' was one chat room entry. 'She wasn't that interested in tennis.'

We tried to self censor the most obvious cases of 'escorts' announcing their services but it was impossible, and would have affected the popularity of the magazine, to cut every single possibly dodgy advertisement. And how could we tell if a 'semi pro', a cross between a party girl and a prostitute, prevalent in Shanghai, was genuinely looking for her true love at last or if that was just her regular sales pitch?

Sun Xiaofeng recruited a young woman, whose English name was Annie, to be a his moral arbiter. We became quite skilled at what Shelley in the office called the 'lonely heart bypass' operation, splicing the original submissions with innuendos that would have confused a champion crossword fanatic, unless he himself happened to be a 'fan of Oscar Wilde', one of our code words for the gay community. One evening Mr. Sun called me in person.

'The personal advertisements have to stop,' he said. 'I've had a call from the Shanghai Municipal Government Information Office and they say we are selling sexual services.'

So the *Daily's* de facto pimps were accusing us of being real ones. It had to start again somewhere.

'That's ridiculous Bureau Chief Sun,' I replied. 'You know we have done our best to cut any illegal advertising, and we have met all your requests to cut the ones we think are innocent too. You should see the ads that we do not even send you!'

'That's as may be, but the safest thing we can do is to stop them altogether.' He proceeded to give me a lecture about Chinese morality, starting with Confucius and finishing with the Communist Party.

You have to understand — and I hope admire — the irony. There was a gaping moral vacuum in China. Thanks to its rampant corruption, the Communist Party had little moral authority. Newspapers frequently exposed cases of cadres blowing their ill-gotten bribes on gambling and mistresses. As for sexual prudery, despite the western press's bold and boring proclamations that China was undergoing a 'sexual revolution', the Chinese have been going at it like bunnies for centuries. Prostitution was rampant. Saunas and hairdressers were barely disguised brothels. Streetwalkers openly solicited for business outside the smartest Shanghai hotels and whole districts were known as *er nai cun*, 'second wife suburbs', where rich businessmen kept their mistresses.

I couldn't say that to Sun. I took his tirade patiently, waiting for the escape clause that was sure to come.

'Now,' he was saying, 'genuine advertisements seeking marriage partners are OK.'

'But Mr. Sun, you just said that people looking for partners of the opposite sex were not acceptable.' I could not resist joking: 'Are you saying that you condone same sex marriage? Homosexuality even?'

'Don't try to be clever with me.'

I chipped away and eventually rescued the classifieds. I also learnt a lesson that would be useful for the future: let Sun lecture himself into knots while making notes of the holes in his mangled web of an argument. Once he finished, appear to agree to everything unreservedly, but slip the key article through one of those gaps as if it was an afterthought.

The summer months passed with minimal interference from the Shanghai bureaus. They still seemed flummoxed by our move to Yangzhou. I guessed they were gathering evidence or support for an attack that had to come sooner or later, but our confidence in Yangzhou was growing. We had put out five issues with them. The date of the press trip, our propaganda payback, was approaching.

I sent an email to all the foreign correspondents I knew in Shanghai explaining the real reason behind the invitation, humbly admitting they would be doing me a favour. I got the answers I expected. They were all polite and sympathetic, but far too busy. I wracked my brains. I needed journalists, or people who looked and acted like them. I knew the prime qualification was that they were Caucasian. I had been to many press conferences and remembered how the television cameras spent as much time on the round-eyed, big-nose faces in the audience as they did on the presenter. A news item or press launch doubled in value if it could be shown that the foreign press was showing an interest.

I called up an American friend, Brent Beisher, whom I'd helped get a job at the *Shanghai Star*, the *China Daily's* local paper. He was working as a copy editor, known as a 'dechinglifier' because the main work was polishing English copy written by local journalists in 'Chinglish'. He knew the form and agreed. Anything to get out of his office. He put me onto another candidate, Anna Scott, a young Scottish girl at a new travel website called C-trip. She had something to do with content, so she could be a reporter.

Then I scored a major coup: a foreign television journalist and a real one, or so he would have us believe. John Johnston was a retired Canadian, who claimed to have been a television producer.

We joked that he had probably been a porn director. He had the name for it. He worked as a consultant at Oriental TV in Pudong.

I commandeered one of our own editors, puffed up everyone's experience and position and sent the name list to Yangzhou. Sun Xiaofeng was happy. He told us where the bus would be waiting in Shanghai. Shirley came along for the ride.

As soon as we arrived in Yangzhou we were shepherded into a welcome lunch banquet. Apart from a few Yangzhou journalists, the rest of the party seemed to be friends or business contacts of the city government. The only other outsiders were the Korean investors in the industrial park.

The press conference came straight afterwards and was true to form. We had barely sat down, foreigners in a convenient lump together, when the bright lights of Yangzhou TV cameras blinded us. They put the big lenses right under our noses and panned along the row. We fiddled with the pencils and paper in front of us, and tried to look professional.

A vice mayor stood up to make a speech. He extolled the virtues of investing in Yangzhou, at length. The city's main attractions, he claimed, were its safety and convenience. The safety he spoke of was for daily life. A few months ago a German family had been murdered in nearby Nanjing, supposedly during a robbery that went wrong. The vice mayor took brutal advantage of the tragedy. As for convenience, the brand new highway to Shanghai, which we had sat on for hours that morning as we squeezed past road works, had made travel to Shanghai far quicker.

The city mayor, who was sitting in the centre of the row of officials behind the speaker, leant forward to his microphone and quipped. 'The trip can be done in three hours in my official BMW. And if I let my chauffeur off and drive myself ... two!' At least he had a sense of humour.

The cameras swung on us as we laughed.

After the press conference the TV crew pulled me to one side.

'So, what do you think of investing in Yangzhou? Is it a safe, convenient place for your business?'

'I think Yangzhou is a very safe and convenient place to invest,' I declared straight to the camera. 'I am seriously considering setting up my business here.' That I was supposed to be a journalist and my business was already closely connected with Yangzhou was best ignored. They wanted their sound bite from a foreign face and they got it.

I imagined the evening news preluding my comment: 'A foreign businessman who is about to invest millions of US dollars in Yangzhou said today...' At least it would only be broadcast in Yangzhou. Sun Xiaofeng would be delighted. I wondered if I might get another five issues out of that.

In the late afternoon we were taken on a tour of showpiece factories. The toothbrush one was full of toothbrushes, the textile factory full of shirts. The directors of both pulled us into their boardrooms and entreated us to invest in their operation that had so much potential, if only they could secure the funds. In their presentations the balance sheet played second place to their government connections. We walked away with enough toothbrushes to stock a small village store.

In the evening the mayor hosted another banquet, making more off-the-cuff jokes in his speech. Yangzhou officials really were a breed apart. I was happy to rent out my soul to them for a couple of days, especially if it meant more protection in our battles to keep *that's Shanghai* safe. The bottles of *bai jiu* scattered across the tables went further to relieve my conscience and animated the warm praise I dished out to local reporters over plates of Yangzhou fried rice. 'Did you know this was invented by the Mongols?' I asked them back.

Once the mayor had left, Sun Xiaofeng and Yi Ming took our impostors up to the hotel's bar. Everyone was happy thanks to the fried rice and copious drink. The trip was turning into a painless and mildly amusing diversion.

A large stage filled a third of the bar, which was also a disco. A karaoke TV stood on a pedestal to one side, lit by a spotlight. We sat at a couple of low tables pushed together in the semi-darkness on the dance floor. We were the only customers.

Without asking which media they worked for, now that he had them all to himself, Sun asked my friends' opinion of Yangzhou. They said the right things and Sun smiled. We sat back.

'I haven't seen many pretty girls though.' John Johnston flicked the words into the conversation like a cigarette butt.

'What did he say?' Sun Xiaofeng said.

I translated.

'Off you go Yi Ming!' Sun shouted. Yi Ming leapt to his feet and disappeared into the gloom. Five minutes later he reappeared with a shy and almost pretty girl. He sat her on the other side of me to Johnston.

'You translate,' he commanded me.

I stuttered some small talk. The girl replied, her face a picture of confusion. Why was this foreigner chatting her up as if he wanted to date her? Anna was watching with frank surprise. Brent was smiling.

'No not like that!' bellowed Yi Ming. 'Stop beating about the bush! See if your friend likes her. Find out if he is OK with the price.'

'Um, OK then. John, what do you think of her?' No point putting it delicately. John approved.

I turned to the girl. 'Miss, sorry I did not catch your name, but what, err, do you charge?'

'Whole night?' she asked, glad to be getting down to business. I referred to John.

'Yes.'

'Four hundred.'

'That OK with you John?'

'Fine thanks. See you later.'

And a couple of weeks ago Sun had given me a lecture on morality and accused us of selling sexual services in *that's Shanghai's* classifieds.

John was smiling the next morning. We did not ask.

The Special Investment Zone was set on the edge of one the barren wastelands I had grown familiar with on the outskirts of the city. Multi-coloured flags surrounded a vast area of farmland beyond it like a bridgehead. A large stage with red backdrop had been set up. An arch of balloons stretched over it. Our bus had to stop short where the tarmac road finished and a wooden footbridge crossed a canal. We walked the last two hundred metres along a dusty track. A red carpet had been laid down the middle.

On our right a school band was lined up in blue and red uniforms. Each child wore the red scarf of the Young Pioneers. Boys were on trumpets, girls on drums. The music was raucous.

Held back by a line of police, local villagers and farmers looked on as our brigade of suits marched through the fields they had farmed for generations. An old man stood alone in the middle of a field of wheat, visible only from the chest up. His face signaled nothing but idle curiosity.

'Many of these people will be given jobs in the factories,' I was told.

Behind the gaggle of farmers, a column of earthmoving trucks and JCBs were backed up. Peasants struggled to heave tricycles laden with vegetables over the elevated dirt road and its red carpet and then down the other side back onto a path that led to their homes. Their farming lives had already been cut in half. Soon they would be obliterated.

During the speeches an impish boy with a pair of cymbals made a two-fingered pistol and shot the mayor. I got him to repeat his gesture for a photograph. Then the band struck up again, fireworks exploded, and bright balloons were sent up into the breeze. Pigeons were released from baskets and flew into the fireworks, chasing the balloons. Some of the peasants looked up and prayed that a pigeon would be hit by a firework and land on their dinner table. Our calvacade marched back to our buses and the next banquet.

A Korean businessman paused by a placard marking the site of his future factory. As he smiled for his translator's camera, a local farmer on a small motorbike sped past, churning the dust into the Korean's face and his smile into a grimace.

We re-crossed the footbridge. In the thick vegetation covering the canal an old man paddled a wooden bathtub collecting *lin jiao,* water chestnuts. I snapped him with my camera. His family on the bank laughed and tried to attract his attention to the fact that he was being photographed. He took not a blind bit of notice and continued collecting the water's harvest as he probably had done all his life.

There would be no canal soon. I wondered if the old man's family looked forward to sticking bristles in toothbrushes.

I felt saddened by the whole show, the whole two days. I felt sorry for the farmers, and I felt sorry for Yangzhou, which I had begun to like, as a city and a people.

Chapter Nine

Double Life

The well-dressed Shanghai society crowd filed into the sparkling atrium of the brand new Times Square Shopping Mall on Huaihai Road. It was the Shanghai launch of the Hong Kong mall chain that takes its name from the New York original. The members of the press were easy to identify in their scruffy clothes. Pretty girls in *qipaos* served champagne. Yet another media party. There was one every day. At weekends I might attend four or five.

Glass in hand I set off to schmooze. I bumped into one of the government-appointed directors of the Shanghai Grand Theatre. We'd met several times and he'd impressed me with his passion for his work, even though his hands were tied by his *lingdao*. He couldn't be more different from the man I'd shocked with a copy of *Time Out* at the Concert Hall

'Ah Mark,' he said, 'Good to see you. Do you have a copy of your magazine? There's someone I'd love you to meet. Here they are.' A small party of overseas Chinese was trailing behind him.

'This is my cousin from New York and his family. They are back for a short visit. Left Shanghai ten years ago.'

The man shook my hand and introduced his wife and son in perfect English.

'Now come on,' my friend from the theatre was saying. 'Show them your magazine. I want them to see how things have changed in Shanghai, how sophisticated the city is.'

I dug into my briefcase and pulled out our latest issue. He

snatched it from my hand and flicked it open.

'Look at that!' He had turned to his cousin. 'See? We have a proper city entertainment magazine in Shanghai. It tells all the foreigners and locals who can read English what's on, including of course what's on at the Grand Theatre. We have even been reviewed in it a few times, haven't we Mark?' He turned back to me with a grin.

The cousin looked impressed. 'My God,' he said to me. 'This is just the kind of thing we have in New York. I am amazed to see it in Shanghai. Boy, things have changed! May I keep this? I'd love to show it to my friends back home. Show them how my old hometown is getting ahead! They'll be amazed.'

I was happy to let him take it. I caught up with the news from the Grand Theatre and we passed on.

I spotted a young journalist I knew and moved towards him. He was from the *Shanghai Times*, a Chinese language weekly that did a good job of covering party — with a small p — gossip and events. I had interviewed the publisher for a story in the current *that's Shanghai*. I had another copy on me.

'Hi Xiao Peng,' I touched him on the elbow. 'How's things?'

Xiao Peng and his friend I didn't recognize looked slightly perplexed.

I blustered on. 'Have you seen the story I wrote about your boss? Here's a copy for him. Be grateful if you could pass it on.' I pulled the magazine out of my briefcase and opened it at the story.

Xiao Peng opened his mouth to speak when a middle-aged man who had been lingering behind him reached round and snatched *that's Shanghai* out of his hands. He spoke in Shanghainese, the anger plain on his face. I couldn't understand him but it was obvious he had a strong opinion. I watched in silence as he rifled through the pages, jabbing his finger at the advertisements. He was turning puce with fury. I strained to pick up the gist of his diatribe in the harsh Shanghai dialect.

'Illegal... should not be allowed...unfair...too much advertising... too much money...stop...' He drew a finger across his throat and then stabbed the same finger on the cover. Xiao Peng and his friend looked as embarrassed as I was confused.

'Excuse me,' I said in Mandarin, struggling to be polite, 'But we have not met.' I offered him my card, the substitute for a handshake. He waved it away.

'You don't need to know who I am,' he spat back with venom. I had never seen such spite. He sneered at me.

'Yet you seem to know who I am and what I do,' I persisted.

'Huh,' he grunted. 'Since you are so ignorant, you may as well know I am one of your *lingdao*. I am in charge of you.'

'So you are from Yangzhou then.' I couldn't help being sarcastic.

'Who is Yangzhou? We know what you are up to. Your magazine is going to be banned soon. I'll make sure of that.' He thrust it into my hands and strode away without a backward glance.

'Who was that?' I asked Xiao Peng.

'He's from the Shanghai Tourism Bureau.'

Five minutes ago a Shanghainese cultural official had been praising *that's Shanghai* to the skies. Now a tourist one was wishing us dead.

There was a side to Shanghai that I was only beginning to understand. The Shanghainese, the ones in charge, had a major hang-up. They knew that much of the city as it stood — and almost all of its reputation — was built by foreigners, and they themselves, the 'natives', were immigrants, refugees even. That's what their grandparents had been, when they fled from the chaos of early twentieth century China: the warlords and bandits, the famines and disease that ravaged the countryside around the city, and found a safe haven in the foreign city on Chinese soil.

Now, fifty years after the foreigners had been run out of town by the Party, the Shanghainese leaders had been instructed by the Party to restore that reputation, but this time, the city was to be entirely Chinese, from top to bottom, and the Party also wanted them to create the perfect example of a 'market economy with Chinese socialist characteristics', to attract the foreigners back again.

It was a classic top-down Party command: 'You will recreate the old Shanghai, which was foreign and free market, but you will make it Chinese and we, by the way, control the market.'

Hence the Shanghai leadership's awkward relationship with foreigners, especially ones who were recreating something in their city and doing it better than they could, as we were with the magazines.

And we were making money. That was really galling.

You could even say we were a perfect example of their dilemma. We were foreign, we behaved like we were operating in a free market — a free country even — by employing English speaking natives to write and create content, which the *Shanghai Daily* was absolutely forbidden from doing — foreigners on their staff were only allowed to 'dechinglify' — and we were cocking a snook at the Chinese controlled economy. Meanwhile they had to listen to their leaders' crass non-commercial instructions and were forbidden from employing foreigners in any meaningful capacity. Worst of all, we were making Shanghai look better than they made it look. No wonder they hated us.

I'm talking mainly about our bitterest enemy: the *Shanghai Daily*.

I got to know the people behind it quite well. The semi-retired foreign journalists the paper employed as 'experts', and the foreign students who 'dechinglified', popped up at the same events we went to, like life buoys, looking for someone to rescue them, something useful to do, some news to write about. Their constant complaint was that they had come to China expecting to make a difference, to build a modern Chinese media industry, and all they were doing was correcting bad grammar. I discovered they were given one-way plane tickets. If they resigned they had to pay their own way home.

Some of the paper's local journalists were bright young things. I became good friends with one of them, Eddy Mu. He was entertaining and enterprising, and quick to criticize. He also saw through the charade he was part of, and admitted to his self-interest in playing it. He told me the *Daily's* management studied *that's Shanghai* every issue, to see how an English publication should be produced and to pick up story ideas. And to find something to complain to the authorities about.

The paper was run by a triumvirate, not one of whom was clearly in charge. It was a common Party trick of spreading responsibility and indecision. The man most often mentioned as the boss was Peter Zhang. He was the Information Office appointee, and maintained his position in the government hierarchy. When we first heard rumours that the *Daily* was out to get us, I phoned him to arrange a meeting and see if we could work things out. He refused to take my calls and when I found his direct line he hung up on me. Equal, but not quite, in the hierarchy was Ms. Jiang Jun, who was famous for her temper. I imagined Kathleen with political power and the idea terrified me.

The only person in the trio who had any real experience in newspapers, and no political position as such, was Max Wang. Max was a class apart. He was charming, friendly and competent, for a state-run newsman. He became a close ally over the years, and admitted with unabashed respect that he admired *that's Shanghai*. He loved to tease me by introducing me in public as a 'publisher', as opposed to 'planning manager'.

But one out of three was not enough. When the *Daily* realized our move to Yangzhou had secured powerful government support that could suppress the local attacks they set up via the Shanghai Information Office and the Shanghai News Bureau, they resorted to small scale yet persistent trouble making with the one national bureau that was obliged to act, no matter how petty-minded the accusation or hypothetical the evidence. Within days of an issue of *that's Shanghai* appearing, Sun Xiaofeng would tell me that he had received a complaint about our content from the General Administration of Press and Publications in Beijing, GAPP again. The *Daily* really did study every issue, with a Communist Party ideologue's magnifying glass. That we were selling sexual services was the first of many complaints.

Next up we were accused of being pornographers. We had published a photograph of an oil painting of a nude woman, on public display. The following month they said we were supporting Falun Gong, the outlawed religious sect that had recently put the wind up the Party in Beijing by staging a surprise demonstration outside the government's secretive compound, Zhongnanhai, on the fringe of Tiananmen Square. We had run a story about the ageing population of Shanghai that included a picture of a pensioner doing Tai Qi, the ubiquitous and gentle Chinese keep-a-little-bit-fit regime. Falun Gong practiced similar breathing and physical exercises.

They caught us out when we ran a review of a music CD by Taiwan's favourite pop star, Zhang Hui Mei, better known as 'Ah Mei'. We had only just distributed the magazine when Ah Mei sang what passed for the unofficial Taiwanese national anthem at the inauguration of the 'renegade province's' first ever elected president. Her music and concert appearances were banned on the mainland. So was any reference in the media to the charismatic star. The *Daily* dumped us in the Taiwan Straits with that one. Then they complained that we published the words Mainland China with a capital 'M'. This was secessionist. The mainland, small 'm', was only part of Greater China. Or is that greater China? I asked Mr. Sun to complain that the *Daily* had referred to the first ever post handover rugby match between Hong Kong and the Chinese national team as an 'international'. It did not wash.

My favourite was the accusation that we were promoting illegal societies. In a panic I looked through the magazine for any reference to triads or organized crime. I found the offence in the community pages where we listed various expat wives' groups and the dates of their coffee mornings, Alcoholics Anonymous, and the Macintosh Users' Society, amongst many other gatherings, none of which were officially registered, as required by the strict letter of the law.

Each month, one by one, we dealt with the complaints. That entailed listening to a long-winded ticking off from Sun and me coming up with a reply to pass back up to Beijing. We played Ah Mei albums back to back in the office.

For the lesson on Chinese national unity Sun Xiaofeng came to Shanghai in person. I invited him to dinner at a Hunanese restaurant. The walls were plastered with pictures of Mao like the one we had been ordered to remove from the magazine by the *Pictorial* the year before. A large bust of the Great Helmsman greeted clients at the entrance.

We started with Tibet, where I had recently been for a story. To be precise, I had not been to Tibet but to its borders, where Tibetan culture had survived remarkably intact, as I was describing to Mr. Sun.

'You see,' I said, 'when China *liberated* Tibet in 1951,' I watched my words, 'the first thing China did was cut off swathes of Tibet's eastern regions and give them to the neighbouring provinces of Gansu, Sichuan and Yunnan. That meant they were no longer Tibetan. So when the *revolt'* — careful use of words again — 'occurred in 1959, those slices of what was once Tibet were left alone because they were already Chinese. This had the unexpected benefit of allowing Tibetan culture to survive and all but flourish, whilst in Tibet proper their heritage was suppressed.'

'I must correct you Mark,' Sun said. 'You have one thing quite wrong. It was not China that took those eastern regions of Tibet.' He paused. 'It was Gansu, and Sichuan and Yunnan.'

'Ah, I see.' He'd got me there.

A waitress thrust a plate of ham and peppers between us. She leant over and adjusted by a few millimetres every dish on the table. We waited.

'Now, since we are talking about provinces,' Sun said. 'Let me ask you: how many of China's provinces have you been to?'

'I'm not sure. I imagine I've visited about half of them.'

'Aha, there you are you see. I have been to every single province in China! So, when it comes to Chinese provinces, you have to defer to me. Case closed.'

'Really, Bureau Chief Sun?' I laid on the respect. 'If that's the case, can you tell me what Taiwan province is like?' I grinned like an obnoxious schoolboy who has caught out his teacher, which I had.

He laughed. 'You cheeky bastard!'

I enjoyed our debates. I think Mr. Sun did too.

Eventually the *Daily* ran out of patience and protests. Amongst their final whining complaints passed up the chain via the Shanghai Information Office was: we were foreigners, and then, to cap it all, a simple childish plea, 'It's not fair.' They finished off by accusing me of being a spy.

That last one was quite effective. Such accusations are never put on paper, which would make the accuser answerable and give the target a chance to kick up a fuss by going to his embassy, as I was dying to. All that is needed is a quiet rumour. It spread like wildfire. I remembered Kathleen's concerns in Hong Kong, when we went into partnership, and my days in the army and Military Intelligence's doubts about me being a Chinese spy. It was so ironic it was almost funny.

With Sun Xiaofeng's help I invited the State Security Bureau to come and check me out, which they did over a cordial dinner. I showed them my passport and visa, now legitimate thanks to Yangzhou, and went through my background. They smiled and left to make their report. As usual the *Daily* had wasted my time. But they had also paid me an unintended compliment. Accusing someone of being a spy is the last resort. They had run out of ammunition. I could relax.

I had a call from Eddy Mu one morning soon afterwards. 'My boss is out to get you. Big time. Watch it.'

'Eddy, can't you tell me anymore? Which bureau is it going to be this time?'

'My friend, I do not have any more info. Sorry. I guess it will be today. Good luck.' He put the phone down quickly, and quietly, I guess.

That afternoon, immediately after lunch, three uniformed officials burst into the office.

'We are the Cultural Investigation Bureau,' one said. From the looks of them I doubted they would know a piece of culture if it punched them in the face. But they for sure knew about throwing punches — they looked like thugs.

I ushered them into the meeting room. I had long ago learnt it was vital to keep these people away from the staff, especially the junior or new members. The bureaus' favourite trick was to corner one, preferably in the finance department, and bully him or her into telling them what little they knew about our business operation. When the staff member ran out of their minimal knowledge the officials encouraged conjecture. At the end of the terrifying experience a statement would be written out by the official and the staff member told to sign it. Then they confronted me, or Shirley, with the 'evidence' and a closed case that we couldn't argue with. I had got into the habit, when the bureaus arrived, of throwing myself in front of the staff, physically, like I was trying to stop a bullet. One day I performed the feat in front of a potential client who was dressed a little too much like an official, in plain clothes. The sales staff had a hard time explaining my behaviour.

Shirley was out of the office. It was me and them across a table.

'We'd like to interview your accountant.' They went straight for our weak point.

'Of course, I'll go and get her. But I must tell you she is only authorized to talk in front of me. Please wait here. Can I get you some tea?'

'No, and be quick about it.' They frowned at my pre-emptive defence.

I crossed the corridor to the new office space where we had put the sales team and the finance department.

Only two cashiers were in. Just who the Bureau would love to interrogate.

'Get out now, both of you. No questions. Come back tomorrow morning.' The pair grabbed their handbags and disappeared in a flash. They knew the drill.

I walked back into the meeting room. That had been easier than expected. 'I'm so sorry.' I faced down the senior of the three. 'The finance department is out on a training course.' They looked upset. 'But don't worry, I'm sure I can help with your enquiries.'

'Yes, I am sure you can,' he sneered up at me. 'We want to talk to you anyway. Sit down.'

I sat and sized them up across the table. They were the nastiest looking bunch of officials I had ever met, and they knew it.

'We're here because you have been investigated by the News Bureau, and they could not complete their case.'

I went straight on the counter attack. 'Then why can't the News Bureau come here themselves? Surely if it's their case, then it's their responsibility to finish it. It has nothing to do with you.'

The man looked at me as I had told him to go jump off the Great Wall, which in a way I had. No one talked back like that.

'We have been ordered to come and investigate,' he said, his tone cold and ruthless. 'So we will investigate.'

I knew damn well who had given him his orders, probably over a slap-up lunch half an hour ago.

This was not a 'say sorry and ask for forgiveness' scenario. These men were not acting with any official mandate. This was straight up bullshit. And the only way to beat bullshit was with bullshit.

'How much profit are you making every month?' he asked.

The answer would go straight to the *Shanghai Daily* and help the bureau set the figure for the fine. They would find us guilty of something. All it took was a little imagination. Not that this chap seemed to have much of that.

'I am sorry,' I said. 'I do not have the authority to give such information, even if I knew it. You will have to ask my *lingdao*.' I relished giving him some of his own poison.

'We know you are in charge.'

'No I'm not. I just work here. I'm the Planning Manager.'

'What is that supposed to mean?'

'What it says. I make plans.' I settled in.

'What sort of plans?'

'Plans.' I smiled.

'Look, we know a lot about you. We have seen the reports from the News Bureau.' I am sure he wished he could tell me to stop talking in dog farts, the Chinese equivalent to bullshit. 'I am going to ask you again, how much income do you make with each issue?'

'And I tell you again,' I said. 'I don't know.'

The question and answer session was frustrating him. He leapt to the verdict, like the King of Hearts in *Alice in Wonderland*. 'This magazine is illegal. It will be shut down.'

'Then you had better tell my *lingdao*. The Yangzhou People's Government News Office.' I reeled off the full title. 'Would you like me to give you their phone number?'

'We have already spoken to them.'

'Well, there you are then. No need to ask me any more questions.'

He glared at me.

The interrogation went on for another half an hour. When it finished, the main man ordered one of the junior goons to write out a record. I watched while he scribbled. The three of them conferred in Shanghainese while he was at it. There were three sheets. It took some time.

The leader pushed the handwritten sheets of thin letter paper across the table. 'Sign here, and here, and here,' he said. To him this was a standard procedure.

'I want you to make a copy for me and you to sign it as well.' I was not finished with them, even if they thought they were with me.

He lost it. He screamed, 'Against procedure!'

'I'm sorry, but I cannot sign anything without authorization from my *lingdao*.' I paused, as if thinking hard on their behalf, while I watched the man's face twist itself into a knot of pent-up anger. 'I know what,' I said, trying to look helpful. 'Why don't you fax a copy to Yangzhou right now. If they approve, I will happily sign. You could use our fax machine.'

The man was on the point of having a fit. He seethed and stared at me, speechless. I had got him. They had never been in touch with Yangzhou. I was right. This was intimidation set up by the *Daily*. It was unlikely he even had a warrant, or whatever official authorization he needed. I had not asked for that. I had been too easy on him.

He turned to his colleagues. 'Let's go.' He didn't look at me as he walked out.

I called Eddy once they had left. 'Thanks mate, it was the Cultural Investigation Bureau. We dealt with it.'

'Cool.' Eddy stretched out the word. It suited him. 'But Mark, I think this is serious. Watch out, they might be back.'

Two days later, when I was eating a bowl of noodles down the street from the office, Iris Zheng called my mobile. She sounded panicked. 'Mark, they're here again and they're taking our computers.'

I sprinted back to the office and found a pitched battle in progress. The same officials were screaming at Shirley, who was shouting back. One of them was tussling over a computer with Douglas Gong, our distribution manager. Douglas was a retired factory worker, aged about 50, but fit and strong, with a pugilist's face and bearing. Iris was shouting at the officials too. All three on our side were Shanghainese. They're good at screaming matches, which is what this was, so far.

Douglas blocked the door and refused to let anyone out. I was impressed. Neither he nor Iris knew the background, but sixth sense told them it was a set up. Shanghai natives also have an uncanny sense for weakness in an opponent.

The situation calmed but the Culture Investigation Bureau officials continued to demand our computers. The entire staff was standing in a circle around them. Shirley started to reason with them. She pointed around the room.

'Those four over there do not belong to us,' she lied. 'And these here are the official property of Yangzhou People's Government News Office. The Macintoshes have no commercial information on them, they are for design, so you have no right to take those.'

She selected four computers that we could spare, insisted that only the hard drives were any use to the officials, they could leave the screens and keyboards, and demanded an official receipt. The goons filled out a form and walked out with the computers under their arms, scowling.

We were stunned by the suddenness and ferocity of the attack. The staff had been brilliant. And we had been lucky that the goons had not noticed we had a whole new office across the corridor, with all our sales and financial records on countless computers. They had walked past it four times by now, including the raid the other day. They really were dumb thugs.

Marcus, our lanky Swedish webmaster came over to me and whispered in my ear. 'In the confusion I got one of the drives out of those computers.' He grinned. In one hand he held a screwdriver, in the other a paperback sized black box. I slapped him on the back.

We resigned ourselves to never seeing the computers again. We knew they were going straight to the *Shanghai Daily*. No doubt whatsoever.

The fight was getting dirty. We might have high-level support from Yangzhou, but even they could not prevent such ambushes at the local level.

That Yangzhou was three hours from Shanghai had its advantages. Genuine enquiries from local bureaus had to either travel in person to Yangzhou, which it was highly unlikely they would bother to, or wait for Sun Xiaofeng to come into Shanghai. The delay gave us time to prepare. But against surprise attacks like the one we had just experienced we were almost defenceless. Our only weapons were quick wits and pig-headed stubbornness.

Shirley and I phoned Sun and told him about the skirmish. It was like a contact report from my army days in Northern Ireland. What, where, when and what we were doing about it. And then an extra section for a Chinese media fight: who was behind it. Sun promised to get onto the big guns in Beijing and see what they could do for us.

We got back to work. Sales were still breaking records every issue. Every week we added someone to the payroll, bought them a desk and a computer and in no time had overloaded them with work and needed yet another member for the team.

Some new staff were not so necessary, or even effective. Zhang Hailong, who had chosen for himself the English name John Halo, was the son of a senior official in our local tax bureau. He was due to go to university in the UK in a year's time. He needed to practice his English. We needed to keep the tax bureau happy, not that we had much choice. That included paying John a salary for a non-job we had to create for him. He pottered about the web department, handicapped by a level of English that would barely have got him into nursery school.

The Entry and Exit Bureau, not my old friends but our neighbourhood branch, called Shirley in for a casual chat about our foreign staff's visas. The subject moved onto a niece, who like Halo was on her way to study abroad and wanted to work in an English-speaking environment for a few months.

This time we had a fortuitous communications breakdown. Shirley arranged for me to interview the girl but forgot to remind me. I was interviewing potential staff every day.

A shy teenager who couldn't speak a word of English and had no qualifications, skills, or experience, sat mutely in the meeting room with me for fifteen minutes. I had a formula for each department. For sales, I asked candidates to tell me their ambition. If it was an expensive one, they got the job. Editors I asked if they could read and write. If they laughed, they got the job. For any job, I asked them why they wanted it. If a local told me, 'to practice my English,' or 'improve myself' they were shown the door. The days when we had time and no alternative but to train people were in the past. And we could afford to be choosy. We had money to pay decent salaries and there was a bottomless pool of young people, local and foreign, looking for work in boomtown Shanghai.

This girl was wasting my time. I gently explained we could not fit her in, thanked her for coming to see us and showed her to the door.

When Shirley returned to the office she asked me where the niece of the Entry and Exit bureau official was and what work she was doing.

'Who?' I asked.

'I arranged for her to start work today. She should have turned up at ten this morning.'

'Oh shit. I thought it was just another interview. And the girl didn't say anything that indicated she was here to start work, I promise!'

'Well, where is she?'

'Err, I think you could say I fired her before she started.'

Shirley swore. We never heard any complaint from the Entry and Exit twins.

The bureau visits continued. I developed a paranoia about Chinese in uniform. If I saw them leaving our building's lobby as I entered I'd rush upstairs and ask if we had been raided again. If I happened to go up in the lift with them I would pray they stopped at another floor. Policemen on the street gave me the jitters.

One day I looked up from my desk to see Shirley escorting some severe looking people into the meeting room. They were in plain clothes but had that look of authority about them that gave away they were officials.

Shirley showed them into the meeting room and came over to my desk.

'City Propaganda Department,' she whispered. 'I can handle it.'

My day's work was ruined. I sat at my desk and worried. Were they ever going to leave us alone? Was there no way of satisfying them? Was it possible for us to live in this suspense forever?

An hour later Shirley reappeared, smiling. She saw the guests to the door and came over again.

'No problem?' My voice was trembling.

'Good news!' she said. 'They want us to help them with the Shanghai bid for the World Expo in 2010. We have to edit their text and design the first bidding materials. And guess what. They're going to pay!'

'I don't believe it.' I said. 'Did you ask them to get our computers back? They must be senior to the Cultural Investigation Bureau.'

'Different departments, though they're under the same authority,' Shirley said. 'I don't think it will work.'

'So you're telling me that while one city bureau is investigating us for whatever they can find to screw us with, most likely "illegal income"; another, probably more senior one, is asking us to help them and is going to pay us what will amount to "illegal income".'

'Precisely.'

We called Sun again, this time with some good news. He was pleased.

'One small thing, actually something similar,' he added. 'I have just been called by the Propaganda Bureau in Beijing too, the national one. We are going to be visited in Yangzhou. They want to see how *that's Shanghai* is produced. It will partly be an inspection, but I think the real reason is to find out how we do it.'

'Tell them to come to Shanghai,' we said.

'Err, that's the problem,' Sun went on. 'As you know, you officially work in Yangzhou and *that's Shanghai* is officially produced by my department. You need to move your office to Yangzhou. Now.'

Chapter Ten

Break Up

We called Kathleen and she rushed to the office. We were waiting for her in the meeting room. We looked at each other in horror. No way could we run the magazine from Yangzhou.

'Shirley, can you call him back and see what Mr. Sun really means,' Kathleen said. Shirley went to her desk. Kathleen and I waited.

'It's OK,' Shirley said when she returned. 'We do not actually have to operate from Yangzhou but,' she carried on, 'we do need to set up an office there.' She saw our expressions change again. 'Calm down. It is only for a few days. Just for the duration of the visit from Beijing.'

'How the hell do we pull this one off?' I asked.

Kathleen loved this kind of challenge. 'Simple. We get a van, fill it up with a few computers, some back issues and a load of scrap paper. We take along a couple of staff and drive to Yangzhou. They must have a room available in their building that we can pretend is our office. Remember when we went up there?'

I did remember making a rare visit to the Yangzhou Municipal People's Government News Office. Usually we met Sun and Yi Ming in the coffee shop of the Ying Hotel. On one occasion, we'd been invited up to their floor in the ugly white-tiled block of the government offices. It was soulless: new, shiny and cheap.

The next morning we scrambled together our props, stuffed them in a van and drove for three hours to Yangzhou. We took

Iris Zheng with us. Her mother was an opera singer. She knew how to put on a performance.

We drove straight to government building. Yi Ming greeted us. 'Hurry,' he said. 'They are on their way. Bureau Chief Sun has gone to meet them in Nanjing. He could be back any minute.'

'Where's our office?' we asked.

'Follow me.'

'And take this with you.' We gave him a computer screen.

We shuttled our bits and pieces up to the News Office floor. Yi Ming had opened up a tiny box of a spare room.

'Hey Kathleen,' I said. 'This is like being back in the Music Conservatory, or old 63 back in Guangzhou.'

There was barely room to move and certainly not enough to produce a city magazine like *that's Shanghai*. The Beijing people were sure to rumble us. They can't be that stupid. Then I remembered the tiny office of the *Shanghai Pictorial*. Maybe this is what the top people of the Propaganda Bureau would expect, what they were used to. They had probably never seen a commercial magazine in operation.

We borrowed a fax machine, stuck its cable out of sight behind a desk and threw some scrap paper into a filing tray beside it. Iris squeezed in behind a desk with a phone on it. We plastered the walls with old faxes, restaurant menus, and a cheeky cartoon from the Guangzhou office, drawn by the editor, of himself holding a phone away from his ear and the earpiece shouting, 'Fuck! Here come the listings!' He had an on-off relationship with our Shanghai production team, which was laying out Guangzhou's magazine as well as *that's Shanghai*. It was a nice touch of realism.

Finally we spread a selection of back issues like a deck of cards across a side table. We were ready. Everyone tried to look busy but there was nothing to do. So we and sat and waited.

Yi Ming's mobile rang. He listened and turned to us, 'They're coming.' We prepared for the reckoning.

Ten minutes later a matronly woman marched into the room, ushered by a smiling Sun Xiaofeng. Behind her were a couple of young men. They were well dressed. The lady looked impressive, with a natural air of authority. Her name was Madam Wu Wei and she was the chief of the National External Propaganda Bureau, the *Duiwai Xuanchuan Ju*. Her responsibility was spreading the good news of China to foreigners, inside China and out. Of medium height, she was plump but only so much as a distinguished and powerful woman should be. She had a kindly face and smiled graciously as she was introduced. She was clearly no fool. Sun Xiaofeng introduced us in turn.

'So this is where you produce your interesting publication,' she said. 'I am very impressed.' Whether she was referring to the magazine or the fact that we were publishing it from a shoebox in a small provincial town, who could tell.

She glanced about her. We held our breath.

'Very good,' said Madam Wu. 'I look forward to talking to you all over dinner.' And that was it. She turned to leave and caught sight of the back issues on the table.

'May I have a look at those?' she asked, just as a benevolent aunt would ask to be shown a favourite toy. She ran her fingers over them.

'But of course,' Sun Xiaofeng said.

Madam Wu turned to one of her young men. 'Bring them!' She sounded like an empress, her voice was sharp and clear. The young man swept them up and shuffled them under his arm.

She turned once again. 'Goodbye for now, and thank you,' she said and swept out.

You could have poked the atmosphere of relief with an empress's jade hairpin. 'Well, that was simple. So far.'

Shirley, Kathleen and I retired to the Ying Hotel to await our summons to dinner. Iris went for a wander.

The banquet that evening was special. To capitalize on the city's association with the fictional Jia family in *The Dream of the Red Chamber*, Yangzhou's top restaurants served up 'Dream of Red Chamber' dinners, replicating the complicated meals in the novel. This was to be my first experience of one. It was like eating your way through all 120 chapters of the novel itself. Amongst the vast array of dishes were Yangzhou *shizitou*, lions' heads — meatballs to the man on the street, abalone, chicken boiled in egg white, fine strips of bean curd disguised as noodles and to fill the gaps, Yangzhou's eponymous fried rice.

We sat around a large table in a private room of the State Guesthouse. Waitresses in Qing Dynasty-style embroidered silk *qipaos*, tottering on shoes made of one wooden stiletto, designed to make them walk as if their feet were bound, served us portions of each dish on small plates, one after the other, as is the form only with the smartest banquets.

The conversation was about the food. We were not expected to do anything so forward as to ask Madam Wu for her support for the magazine. Sun Xiaofeng would have covered that in his own way during the afternoon. Our task was to make polite conversation and demonstrate our appreciation of Chinese culture. My basic knowledge of Tang poetry and Qing fiction came in useful once again. The lecturers at SOAS would have been impressed, and no doubt amused, that I was putting their lessons to practical use.

Now and again Madam Wu slipped in a sly question about *that's Shanghai*. Sun's ears pricked up like pointer's. He need not have worried. We knew a game was being played. Just as obliquely, we threw in offhand references to business trips to Shanghai, how

Yangzhou was a wonderful place to live, so clean and healthy compared to a big city, convenient for transport and so on.

Nothing significant was said, let alone achieved that evening. It didn't have to be. The dinner was a resounding success. Sun was delighted. We had secured his and Madam Wu's support for a few more months. Our record-breaking run without being dumped or forced out of a partnership was almost up to a year.

The next day we packed up our 'head office'. I felt a momentary tinge of regret that we really couldn't run the magazine from Yangzhou. It was a pleasant city.

Back in Shanghai things were not running so smoothly, although advertising sales were still going off like a chain reaction.

The problem was me and Kathleen.

The arguments had grown fiercer, and her solution was to disappear from the office for days, sometimes weeks. She had decided to open a restaurant in Shanghai and had already found a location. She was going through another of her creative frenzies.

The food festival, the big event sponsored by Virgin that had been so important to us in the early days, had been a resounding success. Kathleen had thrown herself into it — although it was Kirk and his deputy who had sold it to the sponsors and made it work. We had even reprinted all 10,000 copies of the brochure because Virgin had objected to the red for their advertisements, and still we made a profit. Kirk had been given his share, as agreed, and left us to set up his own business.

The festival had exacerbated the fiery nature of my relationship with Kathleen. In one meeting I had insisted we broke down the plan and analysed it. I was beginning to get the hang of being a businessman. Kathleen had flipped out. She saw the festival as a personal labour of love. The practical questions, which as a business partner I felt I had to ask, had infuriated her. She stormed out of the café where we were meeting, on the point of tears. Kirk went after her. I stepped outside to explain myself, if I was given the opportunity.

Kathleen was kicking one of the trees that line the streets of the old concession areas. Passers by looked on.

'He treats me like a child!' she screamed at Kirk.

'Well,' said Kirk in a soothing voice, 'look at what you are doing Kathleen. Doesn't it look like it too?'

Kathleen did not reply. She bawled.

We worked that one out, but there were many more. It was becoming distracting and upsetting for the staff. I started to receive private messages complaining that their jobs were becoming impossible because of the conflict.

Then one of the final straws landed on my desk. The managing editor in Guangzhou, our amateur cartoonist and an enthusiastic young American, had recently done a masterful job of rebranding *Clueless* to become *that's Guangzhou.* I liked Neil very much and loved what he was doing with the magazine.

One day, out of the blue, he sent in his resignation. In his letter Neil stated that the reason was management conflicts. I was upset and embarrassed. Although I thought I was the good guy, I felt responsible. Not for the first time I cursed Kathleen's restaurant in Guangzhou that gave her an excuse to visit the city and muck about on her own with our magazine there.

In Shanghai Kathleen's mood swings became so violent I had to engineer excuses so our meetings took place outside the office. I had no way of predicting whether I was going to face a sheepish Bo Peep or a screaming banshee. One day she told me with breast-beating emotion that the magazine was really my baby, that she appreciated all I done for it, all I had taught her about herself, that her role in it was finished and she wished me and the magazine all the best for the future. She would remain a partner but step back and concentrate on her restaurants. A few days later she declared that it was her right, as the original founder of *Clueless*, to destroy all she had built. She was good at destroying things she said. She destroyed her personal relationships, why couldn't she destroy her creation too?

We made one last ditch effort to keep the partnership together. The success of the food festival had given Kathleen the idea for another event branded by *that's Shanghai*. It was to be a lifestyle exhibition, interactive, for the new generation of Shanghainese. We had run a story about them in the magazine. We called them the *'kuaku'* generation. *Kua* means crossing boundaries, synonymous with progress. *Ku* is the phonetic Chinese character that has been hijacked to mean 'cool'. I agreed there was something in it, though it sounded ambitious. When Kathleen suggested she set up an office across the street from the magazine, I went through the rough budget with her and agreed that too. She took a couple of staff from the magazine and recruited her own designer.

The exhibition never happened. Having started with the kernel of a good idea, Kathleen then asked for the input of all and sundry and lost all sense of direction. In December of that year, 2000, she called the whole thing off. The exercise had cost us 100,000 yuan. I was happy to have been left in peace to get on with the magazines, but that was an expensive price to pay. I told her so, omitting the bit about being left in peace.

Kathleen pulled out her personal cheque book. 'I'll write you a cheque for 100,000, right here and now.'

'Don't be silly,' I replied. 'We're business partners. I agreed to the idea. OK, so you screwed up. That's business. We took a risk and lost.'

She stared, not sure what to make of me.

Kathleen was dynamic and creative. She had energy and drive. But she needed a solid and practical partner to take care of the details, the brick by brick process that every creation needs, no matter how inspired.

She had a new partner for her restaurants, an American called Bob, who filled a similar role to mine at the magazines. We got to know each other and often exchanged notes, and empathy. The path of his partnership with Kathleen was to mirror mine, beginning well and ending in acrimony. At least Bob did not have to fight off her personal affections. He was gay.

It was over a cup of coffee at her new restaurant that the end finally came. It was a cold and damp January day. Shirley joined us. She was helping with the restaurant too.

As was our custom, I briefed Kathleen on the latest news from the magazines.

She went all the way back to our brainstorming session on Lamma Island, almost three years ago.

'Mark,' she started. 'Remember how I always wanted long and in depth features to be the main attraction of the Shanghai magazine?'

'Of course.'

'Well I think now is the time to totally re-launch it and make it into a serious read. The listings have served their purpose. You have got people to read it, you have built your market. But look at all the imitators out there now.' She was referring to half a dozen English magazines that had launched in our wake. None of them was a patch on us. We were the market leader. 'They are all doing listings too. So we should move away from them. Give our readers a proper magazine, like I wanted in the first place.'

I kept calm. 'Kathleen, the listings are our lifeblood. They are the whole reason for the magazine's success. We have made it indispensable. They are the very reason people pick up the magazine and read the features. You can't just take them out like that, and to do so just because someone else is copying us? It makes no sense. It would be commercial suicide.'

'That's your problem Mark. You can never see things my way.' Kathleen was winding up. I braced for the explosion. She turned red, the colour filling her face like mercury in a thermometer. 'That's the whole problem with our partnership.' Suddenly she was spitting with fury. 'I want out. I cannot work with you anymore. You are impossible!'

There was no point countering that we had hardly worked together for a year. She was mad enough.

'You can buy my shares in Klau and Benedict. My price is half a million yuan.' Kathleen shouted. 'I have some other conditions. I'll send you the details.'

'Let me think about it,' I replied.

I had already decided.

It was a lot of money, almost everything I had saved. I had been living frugally — I had got stuck in the habit during our first days in Shanghai. And the risks were considerable. We were still operating in a legal and corporate vacuum. The bureaus' attacks never let up.

Then again, we had got this far and the business was profitable. Why could it not stay that way and one day, somehow, I could lock in my interests. There had to be an exit plan out there somewhere. There was no point spending half a million yuan, about 60,000 US dollars, for day to day control, peace and quiet, and a chance to keep the profits to myself for as long as they lasted. Besides, we were building all the time and that's what I wanted to do: build. I was not motivated by the short term. I was on a mission to create a successful business and a chain of magazines.

I wanted the big prize and I was prepared to gamble for it. I reasoned with myself this could be the best bargain ever, or a lot of money for a whole lot of nothing. But I would be in control of that destiny, whichever way it turned out.

Kathleen could change her mind in an instant, but she would be as good as her word if we did the deal over the table and a handshake. I had to decide on the spot. There and then.

I looked at her face. She had calmed down but it was set in stone. She meant what she said. Now was my chance.

'OK Kathleen, I agree, subject to seeing your conditions.' The price had been fixed. We shook hands over the table.

'What about Shirley?' Kathleen asked. Shirley had stayed silent.

I turned to her and spoke in Chinese. 'I hope she will stay with the magazine. Perhaps she can have some of your shares.' While she had not invested anything, nor even paid for the setting up of her company as far as I knew, Shirley had taken a significant risk and played a frontline role in the battles with the bureaus.

We had set aside the limited liability of Shirley's company, another half million yuan, in a deposit account under her name as a guarantee. I hated to see that money not being used — although I discovered it had been once, to set up Kathleen's restaurant and buy Shirley a house. They paid it back when I took my turn to throw a tantrum. Maybe if Shirley had some shares we could free up that money.

Shirley said she was keen to stay involved. I was pleased. I felt we could work well together, better than I had with Kathleen.

Thus my only real business partnership came to a close. Despite the ups and downs, we had achieved something together. I was grateful to Kathleen for that and wished things could have been different, skipping the personal relationship bit. I was happy to pay her what seemed a fair price.

Her conditions turned out to be unusual, including the right to make decisions about any future *that's* magazines, which I denied her, and we worked out an agreement. The key was that I acquired her shares in our Hong Kong company, Klau and Benedict.

I was on my own. I planned to make Shirley a minor shareholder, but I was effectively the owner and controller of the business. Unfortunately that business did not exist. My priority and preoccupation for the years to come, whilst always growing it, was to make it real, make it safe.

Shirley helped me take the first step. We set up a foreign co-operative joint venture between Klau and Benedict and her Chinese advertising company. We made the joint venture a consultancy, the most flexible model we could afford. Consultants, while they are limited to doing just that: consulting, can consult in any field they like, which opens up possibilities. No way could a consultancy be a publisher. Nor could anyone else, apart from the Chinese government.

We called the company Gao Bang Ltd, a rough transliteration of Klau and Benedict. *Gao* means 'high' and *bang* is a slang word for 'good', rather like Americans use the word 'shit'. High shit. The name raised eyebrows.

The immediate problem was to raise the funds, not that we needed any. We were making plenty of yuan. But to register a foreign joint venture in China in the year 2000 you had to invest a minimum of 140,000 US dollars, in US dollars. I was lucky to have some money set aside for a rainy day in the UK. I had meant to keep it safe and dry, but other than going through a usurious mainland based fixer, who could take our yuan off shore and then bring them back into China for a large fee, we had little alternative.

I wired the money to China. We satisfied the rules, and Gao Bang was approved. For three nervous months every penny I had in the world was stuck in the Chinese commercial regulatory system being counted and certified. Once we were a company I slipped it out again. I had made my small contribution to China's annual foreign investment figures that the government so loved to shout about.

I became the legal representative, the Chinese way of saying chairman, of my own company. In the meantime I gave twenty per cent of Klau and Benedict to Shirley as a reward for all she had done and to motivate her to help me put the value of our business into the company, somehow. Under the joint venture contract Klau and Benedict paid Shirley's company an annual fee of 30,000 yuan. Otherwise all profits were due to Klau and Benedict and Shirley's company had no liabilities. I was solely responsible. I thought it slightly odd at the time that a flat fee was all she wanted, but I was too excited that we had a legal international entity to pay much attention.

My ultimate aim, as planned with Kathleen in the beginning, was to bring the Hong Kong company as close as possible to the magazines in Shanghai and Guangzhou, and one day — if possible — to own them. As things stood, the magazines did not belong to anyone. They did not even exist except on their own paper, once a month. We had not registered the name because we never knew when we might have to change it again. We did not even know if we could, as a foreign company, own the rights to a name for a publication in China. And I didn't want to ask because I would need Yangzhou's help and I didn't see Sun Xiaofeng letting me have the trademark rights to what he insisted was 'our' publication.

Shirley's company, unregistered in Shanghai, was only directly used in Guangzhou to collect local advertising income. In Shanghai she had made an arrangement with a local company, Goldlion Advertising Ltd. In return for one per cent of our turnover Goldlion issued our advertising contracts, paid taxes on our behalf and channeled the payments to our printers, and then passed whatever was left to us. Our business was all going through their books. If they decided to drop us we would be in big trouble. Aside from that, we were running a business bringing in over one hundred thousand US a month and we had no company to put it into, let alone through. I was building a load of nothing, which I had just agreed to pay half a million yuan for. Things had to change.

The plan was simple: make consulting contracts with everyone we dealt with, take the hit from the extra tax because money would be transferred one more time than was necessary to Gao Bang, and start bringing income into Gao Bang and profit to Klau and Benedict.

Shirley heard me out as I explained the bigger picture, smiled, and said, 'We'll get round to it one day Mark. But things are fine for the moment.'

She had one point on her side. We were putting all the profits back into developing the magazines. There was no profit for Klau and Benedict yet. I let it pass.

It was raining the day I made the payment to Kathleen. I was wearing a three-piece suit, overcoat and a trilby hat. I was due to attend yet another hotel launch party in the late afternoon, a smart one.

Personal cheque accounts are rare in China, so I kept my money at the Post Office. I had called ahead to ask them to prepare half a million.

'I'm going to buy a house,' I said. It was less likely to raise any questions.

Without a word to anyone in the office I slipped out and walked the couple of blocks to the Post Office, sunk in thought. Was I being a fool? Did I know what I was getting into? I was going to be broke, in Shanghai at least, once I had done this. My UK reserves were still rattling around in a bank somewhere nearby. Would I be able to get them out again as planned? I was about to stake everything I had on a very brave, or foolhardy, gamble. Was it really worth so much to be shot of Kathleen and all those fights?

I pulled my coat up around my chin and my hat down over my forehead. Damn this Shanghai rain. It was so fine it seemed to soak you right through your clothes.

I glanced back over my shoulder, up at our office windows. There were thirty people in there, working like mad to produce the best English language magazine in China. Ideas were flying around like confetti in the editorial department. They were making up titles and 'standfirsts', selecting 'pull quotes', writing captions, laughing as the puns and alliteration got cornier. A sales rep was on the phone asking a client why they should be given a discount, what were they going to do for us in return? One of our freelance photographers might be going through his shots with the production department. Our new marketing manager was planning another party.

It was worth it. They were worth it. They believed in the magazine. They believed in me too. Someone had to stand up and take the responsibility, devote himself to the magazines and the team and nothing else. I knew it could not be Kathleen. And I was damned if I was going to step away from it. It was a part of me, and was the best thing I'd done in my life. I loved it and I was good at it.

I picked up pace. The cashier at the Post Office was ready. I wrote out a chit and he started passing bundles of ten thousand yuan over the counter, fifty of them. Only half of it fitted in my briefcase.

The man pulled out some plastic carrier bags. 'Will these help?'

More money than I had ever handled in my life and I was going to wrap it in carrier bags like an East End gangster. Images of *Lock, Stock and Two Smoking Barrels* flashed through my head. The film had just appeared at the pirate video stalls. I was dressed for the part, from trilby down to my shiny shoes.

Back out on the street the traffic was heavy. The rain increased from a light, all-pervading drizzle to a steady downpour. I searched for a taxi. They were always difficult to find on days like this.

I began to feel uncomfortable, standing alone in the wet holding the GDP of a Chinese village to my chest. Migrant workers from just such a village trudged past, hunched against the rain in their worn out Mao jackets, and gave me the usual stare. 'A stinking rich foreigner,' they were thinking.

I smiled back. 'Too right, for once.'

A *motuolao*, a freelance motorbike taxi, pulled up beside me. I stepped back instinctively but the man was grinning. He pointed to the pillion seat.

It was the only thing for it. I gave directions, climbed on and we moved off into the lane jumping traffic. Now I was not only worried about being robbed but even more about skidding on the slippery road or being taken out by a taxi. Today seemed to be the day I was destined to take risks. I might as well get them over with all at once.

The rider drove carefully. I gripped the plastic bundles and briefcase tightly to my chest with one arm and held my hat on with the other. Halfway down Fuxing Road the *motuolao* started gesticulating wildly at his jacket pocket. He turned round to explain, almost giving me a heart attack.

'Please watch the road!' I shouted.

'It's my mobile!' he yelled. 'My wife I guess! Can you pull it out and tell her I'll be home soon? Please.'

I couldn't believe it. I am either going to break my neck or lose a large bundle of cash so this guy does not get screamed at by his wife. Shanghainese men are notorious for being henpecked.

I couldn't very well explain: 'Sorry but I'm holding onto half a million yuan and an expensive hat. Do you mind getting it yourself?'

Maybe it was in my best interests to act normal.

I transferred my hat to my money arm and reached into his pocket. Raindrops hit the mobile the second I pulled it out. I prayed it would not slip out of my hand. I clicked 'accept' put it to my ear and spoke, fast. 'Hi. You don't know me but I am on the back of your husband's bike. He says he'll be home soon.' I hung up and stuffed the phone back in his jacket. It did not ring again, so it must have been his wife. That was a relief.

We stopped outside Kathleen's restaurant and I felt a cheapskate as I handed over a tattered five yuan bill. The man will never know what he did for me, or how grateful I was to get there.

Kathleen was waiting at a table upstairs. The restaurant was quiet but this was hardly private.

'I have the money,' I said, sitting down opposite her. She wasn't in the mood to hear about my journey. I pushed over the bags. 'Want me to pull this out here?' I asked, indicating my briefcase.

'Here's fine,' she said.

'Want to count it?'

'No. I trust you. I'll check it later anyway.'

'Can I have a receipt please?'

'No problem.' Kathleen ripped a page out of a notebook and scribbled on it. She signed off with her clear and legible signature, which I had seen on the bottom of so many intensely personal business memos over the years. 'There you are.'

She didn't want to talk. I wished her luck with the restaurants. She was already looking for a second venue. We shook hands and I stood to leave.

'Just one thing Mark,' she caught me by the arm, softly. 'You really think it will be easier working with Shirley, with me not around?'

'Yes, I do,' I replied evenly.

'Be careful Mark. Shirley is not what she seems.'

Those were the last genuine, friendly words Kathleen ever said to me.

Chapter Eleven
Breakdown

Anyone who has ever owned a business, or been responsible for one, knows what a wonderful sense of freedom comes with it. You're living to the max as you, a human being, were meant to. It's you and no one else. You are the hunter, the gatherer, the provider, the Everyman. You are alive. It is fulfilling. It is real. Real life.

It is also bloody stressful. There's no one you can turn to. You are alone. You have to face everything that comes at you, and protect and look after your staff too.

For my first couple of years in Shanghai, despite our differences, I'd had Kathleen, even when I had to wait for her to come back from Guangzhou. When she wasn't beside me I had Shirley, who had been brave and confident. And there were the staff, who had been with me for so long, or left and become friends, like Mark Secchia and Kirk Jobsz.

But the friends were getting on with their own lives and businesses, and Shirley was my partner, no longer a buffer between me and Kathleen. And Kathleen hated me.

I had brought it — bought it — on myself.

The bureau attacks didn't become less vicious. I suppose it was never likely that the officials would say to each other: 'Poor boy's all on his own, now, we can ease off a bit.' If anything they became worse. They like to go for you when you're weak.

'Reacts well under pressure,' those army reports had said. I was about to find out.

It didn't help that the most popular, and just about the only, escape from the pressure was to party.

I had no problem finding invitations. My evenings were a repetitive whirl of launches, press events, free tickets to one-night shows, model contests, fashion parades, champagne receptions, DJ parties, concerts. The same people: the models, the party crowd, with the same hangers-on: PR managers and press like me, were herded like sheep from one to the next, swapping comparisons with yesterday's event or anticipating tomorrow's. There was nothing to it. You attended, drank the free booze, and now and again I picked up a useful tidbit of news or gossip, or a girl to take out for dinner afterwards, perhaps a whole gang of us, to drink late into the night, often at Goya, which I'd stumble out of in the early hours, groggy with three too many martinis.

I got to know the regular taxis drivers who queued outside. Once I found one who lived in my own *nong tang*. He'd heard about the late night business outside the bar.

'Take me home Mr. Zhang,' I slurred, laughing at the fantasy of employing a chauffeur.

As might be expected at an endless party, in a transient society fueled by alcohol; casual relationships were all too easy. Ask for a girl's phone number and more often than not you ended up in bed together. All it took was a snack at an all-night restaurant, a banal conversation you'd repeated countless times: 'How long have you been in China?', 'Why did you end up here?', 'What are you going to do here?'

One evening at an art gallery launch party I admired a beautiful Japanese girl from behind. She was wearing the classic black party dress. The sheen of wafer-thin silk clung like shrink-wrap to the upper slopes of her perfectly formed backside and flared ever so slightly, especially when she moved, as it fell towards her knees.

I only glanced, I swear, and thought how sexy, nothing more.

The next morning I woke up beside her. I have no clue how.

There were many girls, for a night or two. Long-term relationships were difficult, long-term friendships hard enough. The city moved too fast and so did the people. It was a selfish city. We were too preoccupied with our own dreams to allow anyone to share them. It was easy to find a partner for a night, a dinner companion for a few more, until you each went back to your small world.

As quick and easy sex does, it left me feeling hollow.

They said Shanghai has no soul, and I was coming to agree. It was beginning to suck mine out of me like a leech.

It seemed impossible to find a kindred spirit on the circuit of press launches and events. Everyone had an agenda. Friendships, if you could call them that, were based on benefit going one way or the other. PR people are hardly the most deep and meaningful conversationalists. It was like 'Ab Fab', but without the wit or the characters and everyone speaking three different languages.

There were two young women writers who were the talk of the town, or doing their best to be. One of them had published a novel called *Candy*. That was Kika, who wrote under the name Mian Mian. The other was Wei Hui, who would go on to exploit the western literary appetite for all things Chinese, modern and sexual, with her own novel *Shanghai Baby*, a plot-less litany of soft porn that has been translated into several languages.

The pair of them, Kika and Wei Hui, were their own answer to the West's new 'chicklit', and they wanted us to know it. Their rivalry was vicious and couldn't have been better staged if someone had scripted it. Instead of writing novels they were trying to live them. The contest was who could be the most outrageous, the most talked about.

Kika was robustly attractive, not unfeminine but certainly not a flower-like beauty. She was accompanied by her sidekick, Caspar, a short, spiky haired, gap-toothed, cigarette-chewing androgen, who did make Kika look like an English rose. Kika loved to shock with talk of bisexuality, hard drugs and dirty sex. I have never heard a Chinese woman say the English word 'fuck' with such perfect intonation. There was a rumour she'd been a gangster's girlfriend in Shenzhen, the wild southern city on the border with Hong Kong. Another said she was a drug dealer. She had a sharp and ruthless intelligence.

Wei Hui was the opposite, in a physical way at least. Small, petite and soft-spoken, she appeared to be feminine inside and out. Her long black hair fell down the sides of her delicate features. She spoke as if she was singing to herself, and looked out at you with doe-like eyes, tenderly... until Kika was mentioned, when she transformed from fairy to witch. Her eyes burnt with hatred and she spat her words like daggers.

Somehow I fell in with both of them. I also fell into bed with them, one after the other. They wanted scandal, and something to fight over. I was happy to give them some ammunition and I thought I was getting somewhere near the heart of the elusive cultural scene of Shanghai. For all their posturing, Kika and Wei Hui had spirit, a desire to do something different. Each was jealous of my friendship with the other. The coincidence that a German character in Wei Hui's *Shanghai Baby* was called Mark had Kika shouting across a crowded bar soon after the book appeared, 'Hey Mark I hear you fuck like Hitler!'

Kika swore blind, and every other way, that the name *Shanghai Baby* was her idea and had been stolen by Wei Hui.

Another Shanghainese who stood out was Coco, a gay jazz singer, who sang at the Cotton Club and almost every launch event, even for car manufacturers. Coco was in the Kika camp. She did fag hag well. He had genuine talent and like Kika and Wei Hui's books, he drew the ire of the cultural authorities.

That was it. Those were the only three Shanghainese who made life interesting, who stirred up the repetitive parties, particularly if all three were at the same one. There was also a circle of artists, painters such as Ding Yi, Shen Fan, Pu Jie and iconoclastic Zhou Tiehai, whose main oeuvre was a satire on Camel cigarette packaging. But unlike the Bohemian cliques of artists that any city with respectable artistic aspirations has, and even less like the artists' villages and communes in Beijing, to find more than a couple of them at the same table in a bar or café was as likely as catching Damien Hirst in Tracy Emin's infamous bed. As for the subjects of our first ever feature, Mi Qiu had disappeared to Europe and Chen Yifei was managing a model agency, a chain of home knick-knack stores, and producing saccharine semi-documentaries about Jewish refugees in Shanghai during the Second World War, a shameless rip-off of Spielberg's *Schindler's List.*

If you thought about it — and I thought about it a lot — Shanghai's indigenous cultural life was as shallow as Suzhou Creek and as the empty office blocks springing up in Pudong. For entertainment we relied on international acts and exhibitions that were beginning to divert up to Shanghai from Hong Kong, where they stopped off on their way to Australia on world tours. The idea of 'breaking into the China market' was just occurring to them and they were happy to accept the subsidies the municipal government dished out to make the city look like a 'centre of international culture'. There were plenty of free tickets, or cheap black market ones sold on by the *huang niu,* the Yellow Cows, Chinese for tout. They picked them up for nothing from government officials who had been given them. But such shows and events were as censored as magazines were, and few and far between.

So, in the absence of any meaningful distraction, we partied some more or reverted to the simple, ago-old method foreigners in China used to employ to cheer themselves up: we drank and ate to excess.

I'd begun to build a circle of friends, almost all foreign — unlike the cosmopolitan cross-cultural lot in Beijing or Guangzhou — starting with Kirk and Mark. As with all close friends, we'd been through stressful times together. And now they were starting their own businesses and going through the same fights I had, wondering if they'd have an office and jobs for their staff the day after next, we had even more in common. None of us were the type who joined chambers of commerce, or the Young Entrepreneurs Organisation. We got together now and again, and swapped stories, and advice, and drank ourselves stupid.

A favourite venue was *Bao Luo,* a popular twenty-four-hour Shanghainese restaurant. The food was sweet and oily, and cheap, but delicious. Thanks to an honest and glowing review in an early issue, Mr. Chen the manager always had a table or private room for us. We drank *bai jiu* and behaved badly, more like rowdy students than businessmen. If I was Mr. Chen I'd have thrown us out, especially after the incident with the fire extinguisher. But the review had given him a boost, and we always apologized and paid in full.

One evening just Kirk rang me. 'Kitto, I need to go somewhere where I can say 'cunt' a lot and not upset anyone.'

'Know how you feel. What time you going to be out of the office?'

'Probably make it by about ten.'

'Me too.'

We chose an out-of-the-way bar, Garçon Chinois, run by a Japanese, Takashi San, who also suffered regular visits from the bureaus. His bar was next door to an apartment block for retired army officers who resented a successful Japanese under their noses.

Garçon was in a beautifully restored villa. Takashi had set up a very simple and well-run restaurant and squeezed in a tiny bar, again simple yet perfect. The service was the best in town. Takashi did not have the right business licences. His neighbours had seen to that. Hence his regular visits and our sympathetic support and large bar bills.

Kirk and I pulled stools up to the bar and ordered double whiskies. Kirk had set up a free postcard advertising business, the first in China — since 1949.

'So what's up?' I said.

'They're just such cunts,' Kirk said. 'How do you build a business in this city when people you have worked hard to build a relationship with rip you off the first minute they see a chance? There's no trust. There's no long-term view. It's just grab all you can the minute you can and everyone else get fucked. So they fuck everything up and ultimately fuck themselves.'

'Bit like the cunts at the *Shanghai Pictorial?*' I asked. Their re-launched 'SH' magazine was now filling seat backs on airport buses.

'Yes, just like them.'

'Who was it this time?'

'Our printers. We've been using them for months now. It was hard work, getting them to produce to our requirements, but we stuck with it, gave them the chance, and it was beginning to look fantastic, worth all the effort. Now they've gone and screwed me on a massive deal I had for the States. I set the whole thing up and they screwed it up just to save a few cents. So that's the end of that. I can't understand why they had to go and ruin everything, just for one deal.'

We slugged our whiskies. Takashi came up to the bar and joined our conversation. He knew us both well, and our situations. We caught up with his latest dramas.

'Takash'san,' I asked. 'How do you think you will end up?'

'It is not how I think I will end up,' Takashi said in his soft-spoken English with only a hint of an accent. 'It is how they will *let* me end up!' He laughed.

Garçon Chinois was gutted by fire in an arson attack during one of the regular, government-approved, anti-Japanese riots a few years later. Takash'san rebuilt it.

I had no idea how I would end up either.

My answer was to work harder, sell more ads, print more pages. It helped, took my mind off the big problems. But as I began to lose myself in the little world I had created. I withdrew from old friends in the UK, and family too. My excuse was my fear that if I communicated with them I'd only be passing on misery. No one likes a constant complainer. And who would understand the madness I had brought upon myself? Better keep it to myself. I forgot what friends and family are for.

One of the few pre-Shanghai friends I kept in touch with was Joanna, in Guangzhou and a long-term relationship. On my trips south to check on *that's Guangzhou* we used to meet for dinner. Our feelings simmered beneath the surface. I hadn't met anyone like her in Shanghai. Joanna listened with patience as I poured out my anxieties and frustrations and then we'd go drinking with a gang of her friends. Guangzhou was a good place to unwind. The Cantonese know how to enjoy life and don't mind making fools of themselves, very different to the Shanghainese. In the early hours Joanna drove me in her BMW roadster back to my hotel and I went to sleep alone, wondering what might have been.

As for keeping in touch with the UK, every time I planned a trip home another government attack was launched and I had to cancel at the last minute. My father complained about my disappearing to China to make a career. He was approaching eighty, lived alone and thanks to polio, which he'd had all his adult life, was dependent on carers and home help. I am an only child and I wasn't there for him. He had expected me to look after him in his old age. That was not a life I wanted to lead and probably explains why I was in China in the first place. My mother, long-divorced, had warned me about the emotional blackmail that would come my way. She made it her mission as a mother to make me independent, to push me away. In so doing she had turned to alcohol to compensate. So that was another reason for my being in Shanghai, perhaps.

There was a man I called my surrogate father too, though never to his face. His name was Laurie. He had been my mother's long-suffering partner for many years. Not only did he have the patience of an angel, he had blue eyes and bore a resemblance to Paul Newman, the actor. Whenever I went to the UK, if at all possible I went to see him in North Wales. He put me back together.

'Now next time you fly back, I expect a private jet.' That was his favourite joke.

There came a day when at last I thought I had enough good news to write some letters. We hadn't been busted by the bureaus for weeks. I sat down to write, first of all to Laurie. It was a long, cheerful letter, and ended with a joke about a private jet. I had written it in my apartment. I sealed it in an envelope and took it to the office.

There was a fax from my father on my desk, with one simple message. 'That friend of your mother's, Laurie, has died. I thought you ought to know. I am sorry.'

I walked down the corridor, let myself into an empty office and blubbed like a baby. I was weeping for Laurie, but also for my neglect of the people who were close to me, who cared.

I was losing touch, and losing myself. Was I going to lose 'it' too?

I remembered stories of foreign businessmen driven mad by China. There was a Frenchman who had run naked around Tiananmen Square in the eighties when I was student. He had worked for years on a major deal only to have it written off at the last minute.

Suicides were common, in history and the modern day. On a flight home I sat next to a young British guy, about my age, on his way to see his mother for the last time. She had a terminal illness. A month later he was dead too. He'd jumped from his apartment in a Shanghai tower block.

Or look at my gang when we went out drinking and partying. To the Chinese we must have lost touch with reality — though there's more to their view of us than that. But we would never behave so badly back in our home countries. We'd be locked up. Maybe we wanted to be locked up. One of our group was, on a regular basis. He was famous for doing a runner from police stations. Some years later they succeeded in keeping him in detention for two weeks. His clients and family were told he'd gone on a long business trip.

I know I wanted to be locked up, or kicked out, on many occasions. It would have made the end so much neater, and explicable. Honourable even. I remember leaving the office in the Conservatory after a bureau raid, walking round a corner and sliding with my back to the wall, down to the floor. I hunched up and pressed my head to the heels of my hand and prayed that next time they come and finish the job. I'd had enough. I couldn't cope, no more fights.

The next time they came however, I fought like fury.

My tiny flat became my refuge. I shut myself away, stumbled home drunk from another party, pulled out a bottle of whisky, and wondered if it was all worth it. And then I poured another. I watched, night after night, a video of '*Cool Hand Luke*', the story of a man who never gives in, who fights for the hell of it. The famous line: 'What we have here is a fundamental lack of communication,' looped through my head while I sat through another session of double talk with Sun Xiaofeng, or a bureau raid.

Thanks to the drink and the stress I started dreaming. Big bad dreams. When things got really bad I dreamt I was back in the nice safe army, where everyone knows their place, what to do, who's going to tell them to do it and who they can tell to do their bit. I missed the order, and having someone to turn to, the training and procedures for the situations you were likely to encounter. In business life in Shanghai there were no rules and nothing could prepare you for the impossible situations.

I jerked awake around five every morning when the sugar in my blood readjusted. Getting back to real sleep was impossible. I was drinking enough to qualify as an alcoholic. I'd been to AA with my mother. I knew.

Instead of drinking I started visiting the sauna a couple of blocks away from my flat. It was a brothel, like most Shanghai saunas, but tasteful. Full sex was not on offer, just a 'happy ending'. I know it's a cliché, but that's because it's true: I went for the company, the comforting touch of a pretty girl massaging my neck and shoulders, chatting about her life and asking about mine. It was pointless trying to explain what a state I was in but it helped to talk about the general difficulties of life for a foreigner in China. Some of the girls gave surprisingly sound advice. Some just gave good massages and chat. Both were effective.

I remember one girl, a graduate working to save the money for a university place in Australia, sitting at the end of the bench, cross-legged and topless, lecturing me as if I was the student not her. She offered to meet up for a drink after her shift. She was attractive and had a big heart as well as beautiful breasts. It was tempting and I should have done. I held back. I didn't want to become a *'dage'* a big brother with a kept woman on call, however golden-hearted. I asked after her a month later and she had gone.

I was losing touch with my old friends and couldn't even bring myself to buy new ones.

That Christmas, the year 2000, was miserable. I joined some waifs and strays for lunch on Christmas Day at the club, bar and restaurant, Park 97 in Fuxing Park. The Australian manager and her brother the chef prepared a spread for some Shanghai stragglers without families or tickets home. We were united by our homesickness, distanced by vague acquaintance.

We tried to make merry, with copious amounts of alcohol. I'd just heard that my father had gone into hospital with a serious lung infection. He'd been knocked flat but would recover. His housekeeper had told me that when he got out he'd better go into a nursing home, for the rest of his life. I had called him and promised I'd come and get him out of hospital, and back home. Despite running away to China, and my mixed up feelings, I didn't want to let my father fade away in an old people's home. The loss of the independence he treasured would destroy him. I kept it to myself.

A week later, on the eve of the year 2000, I joined another leftovers party at M on the Bund, Shanghai's newest western restaurant on the top floor of one of those picture postcard buildings. My companion was a young, pretty, American-born Chinese girl I'd met on the party circuit. I can't remember her name.

The party was lively, drunken, and from a distance and the photographs it looked like a wild night in the good old days of Shanghai. The pretty girl made a pass at me. I was too drunk to take her up. I returned alone to my flat and got out another bottle of whisky.

On New Year's Day, 2001, I set out to wander the back streets of the concession area and walk off my hangover. It was one o'clock in the afternoon, a bright sunny day. The knock-off market at

Huating Road was packed with bargain hunters. People crushed round stalls lined with fake Lacoste shirts, Gucci and Louis Vuitton bags and ranks of sunglasses with 'Real Leather' stickers on the lenses. Farmers from the suburbs were selling fresh vegetables at the illegal market on the corner of Anfu Road.

Walking the concession area's tree-lined streets was one of my few ways of unwinding that didn't involve alcohol. I could do it for hours, mind blank, staring at people and buildings. If I was spotted by friends outside a bar or café I'd pretend I was on my way somewhere and walk past with a cursory greeting. Sometimes I stopped for a bowl of dumplings or noodles in a street-side hole-in-the-wall. An old lady would serve me with a smile and one or two words of kindness and that was all it took to cheer me up for half an hour. Perhaps it was simple humanity I was looking for in this surging sea of people.

That day, the dawn of a new century, a day of hope and optimism, I had barely walked a hundred yards from the entrance to my *nong tang* when I burst into tears. I was taken by complete surprise. I had no inkling, felt no warning.

Through my tears I saw two friends on the other side of the street. It was Paul Moclair, my favourite freelancer, and his girlfriend. I couldn't let them see me like this. They were bent over a pirate VCD stall, absorbed with the difficult choice of a trashy movie for a lazy bank holiday type afternoon. If there was anyone in Shanghai who understood, and had the kindness and patience to let me get whatever was screwing me up out of my system, it was Paul. I could picture him walking me to a bar, buying me a stiff drink and giving me as long as it took. His girlfriend Melissa had put me up for my first week in Shanghai. She was an old friend. But I was too ashamed.

I slapped on a pair of sunglasses I had brought for the hangover and walked past with my head down, praying they would not see me. I passed within feet of them. They did not look up from the rack of VCDs.

I walked further down the street, turned into a deserted *nong tang* and cried until I wondered if I'd ever stop.

What the hell was going on?

This was ridiculous. Was I having a nervous breakdown?

Jesus Christ. Not me, please.

I used to think the standard foreign businessman in China, with his family and villa, car and driver, and month-long holidays, was a wimp. Why live in China if all you thought about was escape and that's what you did every evening when you drove through the guarded gates of your compound, ordered a pizza delivery and watched the BBC on satellite television while you ate it. You could be anywhere in the world. The hassle was taken out of your working day by armies of local assistants who spoke perfect English and never told you when there was a problem. They just waited till it went away of its own accord, or you were replaced by the next foreign manager and they blamed it on you. Where was the China experience in that? What did you contribute? Why did you even come in the first place?

China wasn't brand new office blocks and villa complexes. It was a teaming, noisy, cut-throat market like Huating Road, which to most expats was a quaint source of fake designer goods for cheap Christmas presents and an amusing place to take visiting friends and family. Those markets represented real China, desperate to make a buck any which way and damn the next man in line. If you wanted to get into real China you had to get in there and fight on your own, one to one. You guys can't take it.

It was people like me who lived and worked in the thick of it, who spoke the language, who uncovered and tackled the problems head on: we were the people getting the most out of China and putting something into it too. We were living it and we did not need to escape. We could hack it.

That sunny day, hiding in an alley with tears pouring down my face, I realized I could not hack it, not alone. China was too big, too tough. Those big corporations and their expat managers might be right. You need to keep some distance. You need shelter.

I wiped my cheeks and headed back the way I had come. I turned south across Huaihai Road and ducked down the alley that led to Garçon Chinois, my secret hideaway and home of a kindred spirit. The patio was deserted, Takashi was out. I ordered a cappuccino and pulled out the book I had stuffed in my pocket. It was Turgenev's *Fathers and Sons*. I had started it a few months ago, put it aside, and forgotten about it until today. I stared at the cover, the title. The irony made me smile, cheered me up even. I needed a break from China. I needed to go home for a while.

A week later I climbed into a taxi at Norwich train station, in Norfolk, UK. It was late in the evening and I had missed the last connection to Sheringham, the station closest to home, up on the coast. I faced an expensive drive. I was so happy to be back it didn't matter.

It was a London black cab. I relished the chug of the diesel engine I hadn't heard for so long, the space in the back. I put my feet up on my bag.

The driver slid back the partition. 'Come a long way?' he asked over his shoulder in thick Cockney. He must have semi-retired from London. His accent was music to my ears.

'Shanghai,' I said.

'That's in China innit?'

'Quite right.'

'I had some Chinese in my cab once.' He started off. I sat forward to better hear what promised to be a proper cabbie conversation. 'Goin' to Lowestoft they was, gambling. They like that don't they?' He paused for my agreement. 'Well I tell you, there was four of them in the back, and the 'hole way there they was chattering in that language of theirs. You speak it?'

I told him I did.

''Kin hell, get on wiv yer! That ain't no language. I mean, not really. It can't be. It's just an 'hole loada noise, innit?' He was throwing in more tones and changes in pitch than a Peking Opera. 'They was just making all these sounds they was. I couldn't hear no words for the life of me. How they understood each other I have no blinking idea.' He paused, as if coming to terms with the disappointment of having his theory proved wrong. Then he spoke again, as much to himself as me. ''An' you can speak it. Blimey.'

I smiled. He was making me feel better already.

The next day I got my father out of hospital and took him home. I didn't mention the nursing home.

I checked he was going to be looked after, could cope. When the time was right, I told him about China and the magazines. I was reminded there is nothing quite a like a fatherly chat to sort out a son who has got into a mess. When I explained the massive risk I had taken, buying out Kathleen, how I had no idea how things were going to turn out, he didn't question my decision.

He heard me out, slipped in some words of advice and told me he was proud of me. Living with disability had given my father that rare determination people in his situation develop. He was stubborn, often obstinate. I suppose he saw some of that in me. If he worried I was going to disappear again for who knew how long, he kept it to himself.

He took away the shame, the pressure, and the worry.

My determination to make or break myself in China with the

magazines, my magazines now, came back stronger than ever. And I swore that I would stop shutting myself away, that I would never again try to be so brave or stupid, and selfish. I had to get a life, make time for friends. I would not let China consume me. I would do everything I could to win.

On the plane back to Shanghai I started drawing up the plan for a new magazine, in Beijing.

Chapter Twelve

The Bigger City

The longer I lived in Shanghai, the more I missed Beijing. This was perfectly normal for a foreigner living in one of the two places. The Beijing ones envied the sophistication, the party times, the old concession era housing we enjoyed in Shanghai. Long-termers in Shanghai who knew something of the capital did not take long to become jaded by the shallowness of Shanghai life, despite its comforts, and dreamt of heading back north where life was rich yet down to earth and the locals open and friendly.

Whenever I flew to Beijing, the happiness hit me the minute I walked out of the airport. The simple act of getting a taxi exemplified the difference between the two cities.

Beijing taxi drivers are polite, know how to get to your destination, drive like chauffeurs, and talk about interesting stuff, like Chinese embassies getting bombed, Blair sucking up to Bush, or football.

Shanghai taxi drivers assume you are in a rush and drive like racing drivers in a dodgem car, jerking from lane to lane. They honk their horns, communicate in grunts and gesticulations because they assume you can't speak Chinese and often have no clue where they are. Beijing-based foreigners of course prefer Shanghai taxis. Maybe just for a change.

It is a classic case of the grass being greener. At least grass is green in Shanghai. In Beijing they really did paint it for the 2008 Olympic bid. An acquaintance witnessed it.

For the Chinese of each city it is straightforward. They hate each other. The Shanghainese think of Beijingers as uncouth louts whose breath stinks of garlic while the Beijingers view the Shanghainese as a bunch of arrogant upstarts who cannot do anything for themselves. In fact all Chinese outside Shanghai hate Shanghainese, until they move to the city themselves. Such is the curse of an immigrant population anywhere in the world. And Shanghai was and forever will be an immigrant city.

The foreign communities are almost as different as the natives. Beijing is home to the China hands, young and old, overseas students, China career diplomats, foreigners who come to China to discover the country, to do something useful, creative even. The Shanghai expats come for jobs and money. They come to see if Shanghai can do something for them, make their dreams come true, make their fortune. Everyone in Shanghai is on the make, local and foreign.

I had foreign friends in Beijing who got by, switching jobs once or twice a year, earning enough money to rent a cheap flat or rooms in a *hutong*, the low rise courtyard housing of old Beijing. They were not there to make their fortunes, though they would not have turned down the chance. They were in Beijing because for all the financial and indulgent attractions of Shanghai, Beijing was the centre of the country. It was where things happened. It was real China. One of those friends was Steven Schwankert, an occasional contributor to *that's Shanghai* I had known since '96.

When I sent him a copy of our first issue of *Ish*, Steven emailed me. 'Mark, we know Shanghai sucks, but you sure as hell make it look good.' He signed off with a question that had rattled round my head ever since. 'When are you going to come to a real city where there's real stuff going on and a real need for a magazine like yours?'

It was time to think about our next step. We were minting money in Shanghai. Every issue made a profit of approximately 25 per cent, sometimes more. If a fortune was all I wanted, and I did want one, it would have been easy to sit back and watch the cash flood in. And nearly all of it could be mine now I had bought out Kathleen.

But I wanted more. As well as profit, we had made a difference in Shanghai, as we had in Guangzhou. The subtle message, which sometimes we slipped in between the lines, sometimes shouted about: that life in China could be international, could be enjoyed not suffered, had got through to our audience. *that's Shanghai* had become a bible for the foreign community and a bridge for the locals into the international life we preached about.

In 2000, two things happened that convinced me the time was right to expand. One was tiny, the other affected half of China.

During a visit to Guangzhou I dropped into a bar we had featured in *that's Guangzhou*. I wanted to check the editorial. Joanna was coming by later.

I leant on the bar and ordered a drink. There was a young Chinese already in place beside me. The conversation opener was predictable.

'You speak good Chinese,' he said. 'Where you from?'

'England, and you?'

'Shanghai,' he replied. 'You like this kind of bar?'

I looked around. The review seemed to have been accurate. 'Yes. You a regular?'

'No,' he replied. 'I just found it.'

'How?'

'I read about it in *that's Guangzhou*.'

We had been talking in Chinese. 'But it doesn't seem like, er, forgive me for being rude... but can you speak English?'

'No, not really. I can read a bit though.'

'Then how come you are reading *that's Guangzhou*? Why not a Chinese magazine? How did you even hear of it in the first place?'

'Ah,' he said. 'In Shanghai we have a *that's* magazine. Bigger than the Guangzhou one of course. You should see the pile of them I have at home there. I used it all the time. It has everything I need. You being a foreigner, you must have heard of them. When I was sent by my company to work in Guangzhou and found they had a *that's Guangzhou,* well, I was so happy.'

He had made me extremely happy. I owned up to what I did and thanked him for giving me an enormous boost to my confidence. We parted like old friends. As soon as possible I repeated that conversation to the sales team. It was worth a lot of money to them.

I was given another confidence boost from the most unlikely of sources: the Government of the People's Republic of China.

The third anniversary of *that's Shanghai* was approaching. We were planning a major party. We went out in search of a venue and found a seedy, badly run bar in a vast expatriate villa and apartment complex in the suburbs, Mandarine City. I think they meant to call it Mandarin. It reminded me of an Eastern Bloc city in the eighties, apart from the pagodas scattered in the dinky communal gardens and our target, the enormous swimming pool in the centre. The bar, which was right beside the swimming pool, was called Swing. It was patronized by the Taiwanese and Hong Kong businessmen and their mistresses.

The management had asked us about advertising so we suggested a barter: we take over for a night and throw a party, you get advertising space. Their eyes lit up at the thought of hundreds of thirsty expatriates ordering drinks at their inflated prices. We kept quiet about our plan to have the alcohol sponsored.

'One more thing,' we said. 'We need the pool.'

This was a problem. The pool was managed by the property management company, not Swing. And the lifeguards knocked off at 6 p.m.

'Well, how about we give you the overtime pay for the lifeguards? And you arrange for them to be on duty, and the pool open of course?' we suggested.

'That might work,' the manager replied, his eyes flashing again. 'But why do you need the pool anyway?'

'It is for a water ballet,' explained J.R., our new events manager, in his sing-song Filipino accent. He really was planning a water ballet. That much was true. We were also planning a pool party on a scale that would have terrified the bar management.

Two weeks before the party, when the band was booked, as were the lifeguards, and the water ballet all set, every bar in Shanghai was shut down.

Bust. Every single bar. No exceptions.

Restaurants were allowed to open. Restaurants with bars attached had to pull out their best *guanxi* to stay open. Anywhere that served drinks and played music was slammed shut. The district *gongshangs,* supported by police, swept through the city late on a Friday night, throwing clients out onto the street and explaining to bar managers that the order had come down from Beijing. A convoy of Armed Police trucks pulled up on Julu Road, known for 'girly' bars, and ordered all women up onto the back of the vehicles. Innocent female bystanders and legitimate girlfriends had to scramble for their ID and proof that they were not 'working', or they went too. An urban myth was born that night that a Scottish man on a stag party, in a kilt, was taken to the police station with the hookers, because he was wearing a dress.

One bar cum restaurant owner on the wild side of Mao Ming Road reported how the gongshang barged in, pointed to the speakers on the wall, and screamed, 'This is a disco! You are banned. No dancing in Shanghai from now on!' It was a puritan party-killing pogrom carried out with a fanaticism reminiscent of the Cultural Revolution.

All bars south of the Yangzi River, in other words southern China, were closed until further notice. This was incredible. A blanket ban on drinking and dancing across half of a very large country.

Rumours started flying. The one repeated the most was that the son of a high official in the central government, some said a vice president, had been thrown out of a nightclub and beaten up in Shenzhen, down on the border with Hong Kong.

It was easy to imagine an obnoxious playboy princeling making himself unwelcome in a club where the management thought they had the *guanxi* to put him in his place. Perhaps he had made a pass at the wrong girl, or maybe been a bad loser in a high stakes game of *ma jiang* or poker.

This particular little prince obviously had high connections. Getting his revenge by shutting down the bar industry from Shenzhen to Shanghai was spectacular. I dread to think what happened to the place that offended him, not that they would have been angels themselves.

Nightlife in Shanghai stopped. Our party looked as if it was going to be cancelled. J.R. was devastated. His debut was going to be postponed until God knew when. We called Swing, ready for the bad news.

'Oh, no,' they told us. 'The ban does not affect us. We are not a public bar. We are for residents of Mandarine City... officially speaking, and their guests. We also have some good *guanxi*. Your party is fine. It can go ahead.'

A fortnight later, 1,200 people turned up for what became the party of the year. The vast majority were foreigners desperately needing a night out. Clubbing, drinking and partying were their only diversions and they had been deprived for two long weeks.

In an attempt to put an innocent innuendo on Swing we had proclaimed a jungle theme, as in Tarzan 'swinging' through the trees. There were quite a few Tarzans and Janes. Once the water ballet had surprised everyone and the management made clear there was to be no swimming, a couple of hundred half-naked drunken expats jumped into the pool. It was mayhem. I struggled to escape sodden embraces as people thanked me for saving them from another dull night watching a pirated movie. I was thrown in half a dozen times. The drinks stands set up by our sponsors could not pour fast enough. There was an atmosphere like a graduation party coinciding with New Year's Eve on the same day that the US Pacific Fleet came ashore. It was a fantastic birthday for *that's Shanghai*, and we knew we had finally put our stamp on the city's foreign community.

Sun Xiaofeng came to town for the celebration, with Yi Ming in tow. He was impressed, in a government official kind of way. Standing around drinking as a horde of foreigners behaved like the barbarians he had been brought up to believe we were was not his favourite idea of a night out. Officials prefer to have their fun in private.

I had a perfect opportunity to show him how popular the magazine was becoming. I carefully selected the more senior and sober of our guests and introduced them. They said the right thing, and then I took Sun to a quiet table and started work.

'Bureau Chief Sun,' I said. 'You see how we have captured the foreign market in Shanghai?'

From behind him a pretty young Chinese girl ran past in a bikini, water dripping off her wet body and flicking from her hair as she turned her head towards her pursuer. A burly westerner in soaking Bermuda shorts trotted after her, flat footed on the slippery floor. Not exactly the image I wanted Mr Sun to go away with. I wished I hadn't used the word 'capture'. But he nodded, and brushed the droplets of water off his arm. He stared with a shadow of a smile at the girl's retreating back. From the angle of his head I could see he was focusing on her pert backside.

'Yes, not bad,' he said, still looking over my shoulder.

'Sun Xiaofeng,' I slipped into informality. We were at a party. 'I think it's time we thought of setting up in Beijing.'

'What?' he switched attention back to me. 'Beijing did you say?'

'Yes. It's time we considered *that's Beijing*. Can you support us?'

'Mark, we still do not have a *kanhao*. I keep telling you. It's on its way. Madame Wu is giving us her full support. The application is in. It's being processed. But we cannot start a new magazine until we get a *kanhao*.'

'Sun Xiaofeng, even if we get one it will only apply to the magazines we already have won't it? We can't use a *that's Shanghai* magazine *kanhao* on another one in Beijing can we?'

'Yes we can. There are ways.'

'But that's against the rules. You know perfectly well. And I know if we apply for a *kanhao* for *that's Beijing* before we launch it we might have to wait years. We would never get started. Why can't we do what we're already doing, which is publish with your and Madame Wu's support and get the *kanhaos* all together, for all our magazines, how ever many we have by then? Besides, you keep telling me the *kanhao* will be issued any minute. If that is really the case, then...'

The band started up below the roof terrace where we were sitting. The persistent bass line seemed to match the way I was plugging away at Sun's resistance.

'I tell you,' he interrupted me, 'the *kanhao* are almost ready. I am not lying to you. If you hadn't made so much trouble with those people you've upset in Shanghai we'd have them already...'

I had touched a nerve, and so had he. It was my turn to interject. 'Sun Xiaofeng, you know damn well why those people are doing all they can to stop us. You cannot blame me for the attacks, for the trouble they made for us with GAPP in Beijing. That's unfair.' I spoke with a tone that made clear I was tired of repeating myself. What the hell I thought, if we have a tiff we can get drunk and make it up later.

'But still you insisted on the personal classifieds!' he shouted.

I moaned. Not this again. It had become a regular and tiresome subject.

'Sun Xiaofeng, please,' I said. 'Besides, I've made friends with the *Shanghai Daily*. You know we're selling classifieds in their paper once a week — we even put personals in there! And they're making money from us.'

I was proud of the way I had wangled that arrangement. It had been painfully difficult to make the deal, which was loaded in favour of the *Daily*, and it was damn hard to make any money from it, but there was hope we might one day. At least we had got the *Daily* off our backs for a while. Peace has its price.

'Yes, exactly! There you are see! You are losing money on that project!' Sun was pleased to have caught me out.

'Sun Xiaofeng,' I made no effort to hide my exasperation, 'It's a price we have to pay, and when I say 'we' I am talking about my business, not you. You're not paying. We can afford it. You should be thanking me, not criticizing me.'

As usual, we were getting off the subject. These conversations could go on for hours.

A couple of attractive Shanghainese girls, fully dressed in their party best, passed by. 'Sun *Laoban*!' one of them exclaimed as she grabbed her companion's arm, using the word for 'boss' that signifies a familiar respect. The boss pays for dinner. 'We did not know you were in town!' Both girls were standing over him and smiling at Sun.

'Er, well, yes I am.'

'Call me later,' the first girl said. 'We won't disturb you now.' They moved on. It was my turn to watch them walk away, and throw in a double entendre.

'*that's Shanghai* classifieds?'

'What was that?' Sun missed my dig. His mind was elsewhere.

'We were talking about the classifieds.'

'Oh yes, anyway, well, you know my opinion of the classifieds.' He dismissed the subject.

'I certainly do now.' I couldn't resist.

'And about Beijing,' he got back to the point. 'You must wait for me to say it's OK to start preparing for that. Understand?' Then he gave me the let out clause that always came at the end of our chats. 'But if you want to think about it, you can go ahead and think about it.'

I had declared my intention. I fully intended to carry on, not just with thinking. We had proved *that's* magazines were city magazines widely read by English speaking locals and expatriates. The formula worked. It was time to move onto the real first city of China, the capital.

Kathleen, Shirley and I had made several trips to Beijing when we were all together, to meet more publishers our Shanghai *guanxi* had lined up for us. Those meetings really did drag us away from the task in hand, compared to a quick dinner or two in Shanghai, but we could not turn them down. Whilst Yangzhou and Sun Xiaofeng were our best ever partnership and we got on remarkably well, we could never rest from the tiresome job of making sure we had a back-up should they suddenly drop out, nor could we deny ourselves the remote possibility of finding someone even better.

We had danced our way through sham negotiations like someone practicing *tai qi* at sunrise, ever conscious that word might get back to Yangzhou. We never knew who knew whom. We told white lies dirtier than day-old Beijing snow.

One of those white lies, and a convenient way to give credit to the Yangzhou News Office where credit was due yet allow for a discussion about a new publishing partnership, was to pretend we were considering launching a magazine in Beijing.

Now I began picking the brains of old friends, such as Steven Schwankert, who knew the publishing scene in Beijing. I had left the city as a metal trader. I was coming back as a publisher. The circle had a few kinks in it. But this time, unlike our brash, naïve and impetuous jump from Guangzhou to Shanghai, I knew what I was talking about.

There was only one patronizing old time foreigner, reminiscent of that conniving trio in Shanghai, who told me my only chance to achieve anything in Beijing was to partner with him. I told him to get stuffed. When he called back having done a little research, and asked for a job, I told him he could stay stuffed.

That was a one-off. Maybe it was luck. Maybe I had developed a nose for sourcing decent magazine people, or maybe the people who moved in media circles in Beijing were different than those in Shanghai.

I think it was more a case of the people. And I suppose we had created something of a reputation, which attracted them.

I was introduced to Jeremy Goldkorn, a South African of English heritage, who had been an editor at *Beijing Scene*, a publication which could rightly claim to be the first — post 1949 — independent

English language magazine in China. The founder had cracked under the pressure, attacked a policeman and been kicked out of China.

Jeremy had gone on to work for other media start-ups in Beijing, often Chinese language publications, and knew the city's media industry as well as he knew his way round Ghost Street, the late night restaurant district where we spent many evenings and early mornings getting to know each other. He gave me the benefit of his knowledge and experience and we became close friends.

Beijing had changed for the better since I left. Sanlitun, the bar area, was packed with locals and foreigners every evening of the week. Houhai, the 'Back Lake' north of the Forbidden City, where I remembered eating steamed fish washed down with a beaker of Er Guo Tou at a solitary family restaurant, under a single street-light, was now a mass of sparkling neon that circled the lake like a halo. The shores were crammed with bars. Shopping malls and Starbucks coffee shops were scattered across the city like pinpricks of progress. Jeremy took me to meet some potential freelancers at a punk concert in an upstairs backroom dive. The all-girl band, Hanging on the Box, belted out a song called 'My Cunt'. The foul language was a breath of fresh air after the saccharine cover bands of Shanghai.

One development in Beijing was cause for concern. An English language magazine called *City Edition* had filled the void left by *Beijing Scene*. An American, Anne Stevenson Yang, was behind it with her Chinese partner, Max Yang, no relation. There was a story that Max had played a key role in the end of the *Beijing Scene* by setting up the bust that tipped the founder over the edge. He had government *guanxi* and was not shy to use them. He was one to watch out for.

I liked Anne. She seemed a decent woman, if a little pre-occupied with the social issues she wanted her magazine to cover. We had met in Shanghai when she was thinking of her own expansion and had got on well. We agreed that the more people there were like us, and if we could present a united front to the authorities, the better chance we had of building our businesses and decent magazines. She had been true to her word and given some helpful advice when we had been in trouble.

Anne and I had a mutual understanding that we would compete fairly. *City Edition* had moved into Shanghai soon before I set off for Beijing and it had trouble making ground against us. I was confident we could do much better in Beijing than they had in Shanghai.

In the spirit of that mutual understanding, the first solid step I took in Beijing was to poach her general manager.

To be fair, he approached me. His name was Mike Wester and it was Jeremy who dropped the hint.

Mike and I hit it off. He was from Boston and had completed an MBA before moving back to China where had studied Chinese, to take up the job at *City Edition*. I frowned when he mentioned the MBA. 'It's OK Mark,' he said. 'All they taught me was a few good words and how to use Excel.' That was reassuring, and might come in handy. I still used a computer as a typewriter.

The job at *City Edition* had turned out to be a non-job, but Mike had picked up valuable knowledge of how a magazine works. Best of all, he had a passion for Beijing and we shared an ambition to create a magazine that conveyed that passion to the English speaking residents. He knew the city, he knew the magazine business, and he knew how to manage people. All he needed was a magazine. And I liked him very much. Mike had a genuine honest-to-God decency about him. I signed him up and left him to find an office and a team. The launch date for *that's Beijing* was set for October first 2001, National Day.

Now all I had to do was get past Sun Xiaofeng.

Over the late summer I made frequent trips to Yangzhou. There was no shortage of excuses, most provided by Sun. We had stirred his curiosity in what we actually did by publishing our first ever bar and restaurant guide to Shanghai, in English and Chinese. For the first time he could read what 'we' were publishing. The English version had its content approved with little comment. The Chinese one had been a nightmare.

'The washroom attendants are a rather glum lot,' we had written in a review of an exclusive bar, 'but then wouldn't you be, stuck in the lavatory all night while everyone outside the door was drinking champagne and eating caviar.'

'This is classist!' Sun screamed down the phone to me late on the evening we were due at the printers.

I was alone in the office, standing beside the fax machine which was spewing out pages of the Chinese guide, covered in a mess of hand scrawled characters as if a spider had stepped in ink and run across it.

'Look at my fax!' he shouted. 'You are suggesting that there is a low class of worker in China, that workers' employment can reflect their status in society. This is impossible in China. We are a classless society!'

I thought of all the street sweepers, garbage sorters, and the beggars. And that very day I had almost been run down by a black Buick with government number plates driving the wrong way down the one way street outside our office. Classless society my foot.

'And you cannot say that people are unhappy, even if they are doing a low class job, either. This is promoting dissent, discontent!'

'So you admit there are people who do low class jobs Mr. Sun?' His argument was so unreasonable I could not resist answering back. 'But they should be happy to do them?'

'Mark, I have told you many times, you do not understand China. You are a foreigner. And you are obstinate. Sometimes you really make me angry.' He sounded it.

'Mr. Sun,' I replied, 'I think I understand China in a way that you do not quite understand. Besides, what we are saying in this item that you are upset by is that we sympathize with the lower class workers.'

'There you are you see! Promoting dissent... and inequality!'

This was pointless. Much as I wanted to give Mr. Sun a refresher course in his own dearly held Communist ideology, this was not the time. It could wait for my next trip to Yangzhou. It always helped if Mr. Sun could see me smiling when we argued. I had a book to print.

'OK Mr. Sun, we'll cut it,' I sighed.

'All right. I am glad you have learnt your lesson. You can go ahead.'

He did not say the same thing about Beijing.

By September Mike Wester had the office set up and a staff working like mad to get the first issue ready. By an amazing piece of luck Shelley Yip, who had moved to Beijing a year or so ago to work for a PR company, agreed to come back and repeat her role from *that's Shanghai,* setting up the listings. Jamie Wilson, another of the original Shanghai team, had returned to China after university in the UK — his thesis had been on drinking songs — and asked for a sales job. It was great to have him back. But he wanted to work in Shanghai again, which is where he landed. I told him not to unpack and sent him straight up to Beijing. I could not help joking with him at the irony of me doing to him what his father's chief China representative had wanted to do to me five years before.

To cap it all, Jeremy Goldkorn was in between leaving his last job and setting up his own business. He needed something to do and some quick cash. He agreed to be the launch editor of the magazine.

I could not have planned it better if I had tried. A magazine was in the making.

I invited myself to Yangzhou before the national day holiday. I enjoyed the trip by train and ferry. The journey gave me time to think, to plan my strategy for the next confrontation, like a schoolboy on his way to the headmaster's office, or an officer travelling back to headquarters to see if he could persuade them to give him more support, call up the heavy artillery. That is exactly what Sun Xiaofeng had become for me, a headmaster with heavy artillery, and I had taken the role of the rogue unit that did the job, the maverick pupil, who exasperated those who thought they were in control.

There was always a room waiting for me. This time I was put into the West Garden Hotel. Early the next morning I waited for Sun in the glass fronted lobby that looked onto another vast Yangzhou lawn. He kept me waiting.

'I am sorry I'm late Mark,' he said when he arrived. 'I'm looking after a delegation from Nanjing, the News Office there, my provincial superiors. They're here to inspect our work.' He looked puffed with pride. Our magazines were reflecting well on Sun Xiaofeng. Senior officials like Madame Wu Wei were praising the Yangzhou News Office for *that's* magazines and Sun was happy to take the credit. It suited us both, and it might lead to a *kanhao*.

Sun had told me every month for almost half a year that the *kanhao* was imminent. Every question I raised, every problem we faced, he repeated like a mantra, 'Next month we will have the *kanhao*, then I can answer your question, then there will be no more problems.'

I reminded him of this every time we met. I must have

exasperated him. But there was always another excuse: the people in Beijing were away on a trip, there was one more bureau that had to give its approval, and so on.

One time the problem had been the name of the magazine. Someone in the General Administration of Press and Publications had raised the question that the word *'that's'* did not make sense on its own. I had been given a long lecture in English grammar. But it had been a red herring. The name problem was soon forgotten and another vital bureau in the chain of approval left Beijing for a month on a fact-finding mission to Bangkok.

This time I needed to pin down Sun Xiaofeng, get him into a position where he couldn't back out. One word would be enough for me to launch *that's Beijing* and get away with it.

We chatted about his delegation, then I started directing the conversation where I wanted it.

'The *kanhao* Mr. Sun. You told me last month that it was ready. In fact we held back printing so we could use it for the first time.' That was not exactly true. We had only pretended to. 'We lost some advertising because of that.' Another gentle lie to put on the pressure.

'Now it is almost October,' I went on. 'As you know that means National Day, a traditional date for the launch of new projects, approvals to be given and so on. So are we going to get it? At last? You have been telling me that it was confirmed for ages. And as you know I've promised I won't launch *that's Beijing* until you have the *kanhao* for us. But our office up there is costing money. We need to start doing business.'

'Mark, Mark!' Sun Xiaofeng stopped me with a wave of his hand. 'It is confirmed. Please stop doubting me. Have I ever let you down?'

I smiled. Sun sat back in his chair like the chairman of the board about to declare a dividend. He left his hand out, palm towards me, then slowly twisted it to face upwards as he spoke. 'I can tell you now. We have the *kanhao*. I have it in my hand.' He bounced it gently up and down to add weight to his words.

'Why that's fantastic, Mr. Sun. Congratulations! And I must say my sincere thanks for all your hard work. When can we use it?'

'Ah,' he was smiling with the satisfaction of a man who has been proved right after years of doubt. 'There is still one small problem.'

When someone in China tells you there is a 'small problem' *xiao wenti,* the meaning is exactly the opposite. Imagine the Titanic hitting a 'small' iceberg. Whenever I heard *xiao wenti* my heart sank. This time I played along. The smile didn't leave my face.

Sun explained. 'Because of the national day holiday, GAPP is busy approving special anniversary issues of magazines and that sort of thing. They cannot put the final chop on our *kanhao* approval 'til straight afterwards. Just a formality. You wait and see. We'll have the *kanhao* in no time at all.'

I ignored the contradiction of what he had said a moment earlier and moved in for the strike.

'So we can launch *that's Beijing*. That really is great news. Thank you so much Mr. Sun. By the time the magazine appears we'll have the *kanhao* and no one can touch us!'

Sun thought for a moment then said exactly what I wanted to hear. 'Yes, I suppose we can.'

Got him.

Chapter Thirteen

Shanghai Glitter

I flew to Beijing in a fever of excitement. Preparations for the new magazine had carried on regardless of the Godot-like wait for a *kanhao*. I called Mike the minute Sun returned to his career planning with the provincial newsboys.

'We can print!' I shouted down the phone as if I had heard it from the man from del Monte. 'I'll be there as soon as I can.'

As soon as I got back to Shanghai I caught a flight to Beijing. When I walked into the office there the energy hit me in the face. So did the distinct smell of a joint; the spirit of the *Beijing Scene* still lingered. The staff had been notorious for working stoned. It was six in the evening on a Saturday and the whole team was there, along with the part-time proofreaders.

The place was a shambles. Cardboard coffee cups were balanced on the edge of desks. Crumpled brown bags that had contained takeaway food leant beside them, waiting for someone to brush past and knock the lot over a set of proofs. Questions were bouncing back and forth like ping-pong balls. 'Should this be in bold?' 'Do we leave a space here?' 'Do you italicize names of songs in music reviews or put them in quotes?' There was no time to look up the style sheet. They'd lost it anyway.

Mike, Jeremy and Shelley were fielding the finicky questions, and when I joined in I relished the last minute decisiveness, the urgency. The new designer was struggling to keep up with demand for pages. He had worked out the templates sent up from Shanghai and stuck to the rules and, I was impressed to see, done some great work on the features where he was given free rein. I was thrilled to see a magazine I recognized as my own with 'Beijing' written all over it. It was like the early days in Shanghai except this time everyone knew what they were doing. If they could keep up this level of dedication *that's Beijing* could not fail. We sent it to print at dawn on the Monday and I flew back to Shanghai. The magazine would be out in time for the holiday.

Now I felt like a publisher, a real one. Kathleen and I had created two magazines from scratch, learning from our mistakes. For *that's Beijing* I took a chunk of money and launched a magazine the way publishers do in the real world. I had found a market, come up with a plan, recruited a team and gone in, if not at the top, then half way up the ladder. I felt very grown up. All I had to do was make sure *that's Shanghai* earned enough to support *Beijing* until it broke even, which I was sure would happen within a year.

The next task was to pull the three magazines together. We could bundle advertising packages, share editorial content and make all the other economies of scale. I wanted every magazine instantly recognizable, the sections each in their allotted place, filled with their city's up-to-date information. I wanted a reader to see an open *that's* magazine anywhere in China and recognize it like an old friend.

Beijing had invigorated me. The work had been pure magazine making, no fighting with officials, searching out permits or setting up partnerships. Establishing a Beijing branch office for the consultancy had been as easy as booking a table at a restaurant, which is all it took. I invited a local *gongshang* official to lunch and explained my requirements. He mentioned he happened to own a 'service company' and for a modest fee everything was taken care of. We were legal, apart from the fact that our Beijing branch office was not allowed to publish or sell advertising. But there was nothing new or intimidating about that.

I knew the honeymoon would not last. There was sure to be trouble from competitors or the government soon but what the hell, I was going to enjoy it. Mike was prepared. We had the experience from Shanghai and Sun Xiaofeng had given the go-ahead, even if he hadn't meant it.

During my two-hour flight back from the capital I let myself go. I disappeared into the fantasyland of my media empire.

I landed in Shanghai and reality with a bump. October 2001 was an important month for the city. It was hosting the Asia Pacific Economic Conference, APEC, an annual gathering of the heads of state of every country with a stretch of beach on the Pacific Ocean. President Bush was due in, along with 19 other leaders and China's President Jiang Zemin.

Jiang had made his name as mayor of Shanghai. He was bound to want to show off his model city and *that's Shanghai* was happy to help, but while I had been preparing for the Beijing launch and running back and forth to Yangzhou to get Sun's support, yet another battle for survival had begun.

It started in early September with a notice from the Shanghai News Bureau. Yanghou's 'print number' that we had been using for years was no longer acceptable. We had to get a proper *kanhao* or stop the magazine. Sun Xiaofeng told the Shanghai News Bureau exactly what he told me: our *kanhao* was waiting for the ink to dry and any day now we would be legal.

While I might have had my doubts, the News Bureau knew for sure that Sun was making it up. It was their own lobbying, encouraged by the Shanghai News Office and the *Shanghai Daily*, that was obstructing Sun's application. My small-scale co-operation with the *Daily* on the classifieds had only gone so far to get them off our backs. They had been humouring me.

With the world media about to descend on the city, the Shanghai government was determined that its own English language media would be the one they read and praised. It was time once and for all to put a stop to this upstart foreign-run publication they found so embarrassing. They'd had enough of someone outside their control doing the job they were supposed to.

We had prepared an APEC special issue. We too wanted to show ourselves off to the world. We had been taking orders for extra copies from hotels, foreign chambers of commerce and consulates, who wanted them for their delegations. As usual for one of our crises, we had booked a record amount of advertising. And as usual, that made it a perfect opportunity to put the pressure on. The city government knew it, and took it.

Once again we set off on the hunt for a publisher, this time with the Yangzhou People's Government News Office in the same boat. Sun directed Shirley and me towards the Shanghai News Bureau Development Company, a commercial offshoot of the Bureau. The negotiations were straightforward and unusually brief. In return for monthly fee of 10,000 yuan, almost eight thousand pounds, and other unspecified benefits, the Development Company agreed to 'advise' us how to publish. They would also be given the right to check our content. We had two censors to deal with.

Immediately the vague contract was signed and fee paid, the Development Company gave us the name of a publisher and sat back. It was Shanghai Bai Jia 'One Hundred Families' Publishing House which, surprise surprise, was also closely related to the Shanghai News Bureau.

A Mr. Xu from the News Bureau proper agreed to accompany us to the first meeting with Bai Jia. In a sinister repeat of the meetings with the *Pictorial* and the Bureau in '98, he decided a western restaurant would be an auspicious setting for the launch of this cross cultural venture.

Mr. Wang Youbu represented the News Bureau Development Company and the man from Bai Jia was called Mr. Gu. The pair of them, along with Xu, sat opposite Shirley and myself.

It was a hot day so Mr. Xu rolled his trousers up over his knees, as you do in the countryside.

Wang got the conversation off to a cheerful start by telling the story of the banning of Mian Mian's — or Kika's — latest book. Mian Mian was a bad influence, with her talk of drugs, sex and rebellion. 'I have a lovely son,' he said. 'I want him to love his family, work hard, be respectful, be a patriot who loves China,' — and for good measure — 'and love nature.'

Wang liked the sound of his own voice. He spoke mellifluously, skipping from one subject to the next via impromptu juxtaposition. He moved onto the film director Zhang Yimou.

'Just as I disapprove of Kika's books, I don't like the effect of Zhang's films on foreigners. They make China look backward.' Zhang's films are often historical set pieces, so backwardness is part and parcel. Before I could get a word in Wang had segued onto our magazines and what he thought they could do to increase the appeal of China to the outside world.

'Mark, my colleague tells me you do a good editorial job with your publication. The writing and grammar are very correct. This is encouraging. But when you work with us we will have some requirements.'

I started to pay attention.

'For example, I am curious to know why you have an article about dancing in the October issue. What has dancing got to do with APEC? Dancing is an activity that comes under strict regulation by the government. Places for dancing must take stringent precautions against fire, and be hygienic.' He was referring to the rules that had been put in place since the blanket ban had been lifted. The best was yet to come.

'Of course,' Mr. Wang said with sincerity. 'Dancing at home is perfectly acceptable.'

I struggled not to laugh.

'Anyway,' Wang carried on, 'coming back to the story about dancing. You may run it but you must take out any mention of APEC. And we would like you to include details of the current regulations about dancing too.'

I murmured my stupefied assent and wondered how the hell we were ever going to produce a readable magazine with this Puritan dictating the content.

Wang had one more point to make. 'We are also curious to know why you have included a "Survivors Guide to APEC"? The word "survival" has a negative connotation. You survive *disasters*. Are you suggesting that APEC is a disaster? And why do you say you need a suit to survive? Surely a life jacket is what you need to survive a disaster. At sea at least.'

Wang sounded so well spoken and talked intelligently, with a crazy logic in there somewhere, but he was clearly a chopstick short of a full banquet.

Satisfied, not by my explanation of 'survival' as a joke in this context but with the conclusion of his mammoth speech, Wang sat back with a look of smug aloofness. The only comfort I could squeeze out of that nonsensical ramble was that it sounded like they were going to let us publish with Bai Jia's support. I was impatient to get on with that discussion.

The food arrived. I left mine untouched while I addressed Gu. 'So Mr. Gu, it seems you can help us publish. Shall we discuss how that co-operation might work?'

'Yes, let's,' he said. 'First of all, you must take the word "Shanghai" off the cover. We have been told by the News Bureau that the name Shanghai may only be used on publications by authorized representatives of the Shanghai Municipal Government.'

I was listening with concern but my eyes were fixed on Xu, the News Bureau official. He had picked up an entire steak on his fork. He brought it to his mouth and bit into it. He tugged. The meat did not come apart. He brought down his spare hand, which had been holding his knife and scratching his ear with its handle, placed the knife beside the plate and then used both hands on the fork. He ended up with a strip of gristle in his teeth. He spat it onto the plate and grinned.

'Next,' continued Gu, 'You must change the page size, remove all advertising, reduce the number of pictures and make it look like a book. You see, we can only give you a book licence. We have no *kanhao*. We are not a magazine publisher.'

Xu had taken a break from the battle with the steak and was spooning coffee with loud slurps, his mouth an inch from the lip of the cup. He was listening with patent enjoyment.

'But Mr. Gu, as you know, many magazines use book numbers.' I pulled a magazine out of my briefcase and laid it on the table. I had come prepared. 'Look at this one for example.' I flicked it open at the masthead. 'Published by Shanghai Bai Jia Publishing House'. Gu fell silent.

Xu put down his spoon and threw Gu a lifeline. 'Mr. Mark, you speak very good Chinese.'

'Thank you Mr. Xu,' I replied.

'But I bet you can't speak Shanghainese can you? Ha!' He laughed and dribbled a morsel of well-chewed steak, lowering his head until his mouth almost touched the plate.

'No, Mr. Xu,' I replied, looking him straight in the eye. 'You are quite right. I cannot speak Shanghainese. But then Shanghai is China's international city isn't it, and luckily for me, the world's international language, at least at the moment, is English. Can you speak English?'

Shirley kicked me under the table.

'Now Mr. Wang,' I thought he was my best shot. 'We have a thriving magazine business, we have a good reputation, and we are making money. Does Bai Jia, with the collaboration of your company, want to work with us and share the benefits or don't they?' I was getting tired of another farcical attempt to make our lives difficult.

Wang cut me dead. He turned to Gu and rattled off some Shanghainese behind Xu's back. Gu laughed.

'We're all friends here,' Gu turned back and grinned at me. 'Mr. Wang thinks it is a good idea for us to work together. We trust his company to inspect the content of this book. I will arrange for a publishing contract to be sent over to your office. OK?'

When I rushed back from launching *that's Beijing,* I was just in time to pay Bai Jia a couple of thousand US dollars for the book licence, and we came out with our October issue. There was no 'Shanghai' on the cover. And at the last minute we were told that the acronym APEC also required special authorisation from the News Bureau, which we were not going to get, so we had to take that off too. And there was no month because the magazine was no longer a periodical, it was a book. We kept the advertisements by pig-headed refusal to pay the fee if we could not run them. Apart from some anodyne changes to the content however, and a very tame article about dancing, the insides survived.

Later in October, when APEC came to town in a convoy of stretch limos, the *Shanghai Daily* shouted across its front page that it was the only official English language media for the APEC meeting. All publications like ours were banned from appearing anywhere near the venue.

But it was *that's Shanghai* the American APEC office called for a thousand extra copies to give to their delegates.

Thanks to the new magazine in Beijing, and the relentless, ever-spinning cycle of bullshit — to use a technical term — that I was dealing with in Shanghai, I was beginning to get fed up with the place, even if the skies were a beautiful blue because the government shut down all factories within a forty-mile radius for the duration of APEC. They also diverted all internet connections to the Pudong side of the river where the conference was being held, which slowed everyone else's access to a snail's pace. The tunnel under the river from Puxi to Pudong was sealed to all except official traffic and other roads closed for long periods in case a Pacific President had left his gift for Jiang Zemin back at the hotel. Prostitutes and kilt-wearers had been trucked off their patches again and all pirated goods disappeared. Shanghai did what it does best, it put on a good impression.

It was the same impression that had attracted us when we moved to the city in '98. Now I realized with the same clarity as those blue October skies, there was little more to Shanghai than just that, an impression. The city looked good and that was all the local government cared about, just as their citizens seemed to care only about clothes and cars, hairstyles and make-up, and their salaries at a safe white-collar job.

But it was worse than an obsession with looks. It went deeper. Even under a façade you should be able to find something of interest, some character, some spirit. Shanghai was a city of sixteen million people. There had to be someone doing something. Someone who stood for *something*. Damn it, there had to be something to the place.

I remembered a conversation I'd had with a foreign journalist, at the end of my first year in the city.

'Mark,' she said. 'I have been in Shanghai for two years. Why is it I can't get under the skin of the place?'

It was a party. She was attractive, and intelligent. I wanted to show some wit. 'You are under the skin,' I said. 'The trouble is; there's nothing there.' My off-the-cuff remark held more truth than I cared for.

We had come to Shanghai because it was a cosmopolitan city, packed with culture and energy. It was about to burst back into life after decades of stagnation. It was the number one city in China. In a few years it would be the financial centre of the Far East, the commercial centre, the economic driver of the whole region.

We had searched for culture high or low, from the back offices of the Concert Hall to the tiny bars on Mao Ming Road. We desperately wanted to find it. We desperately wanted to tell our readers, the world, about this resurgence.

In four years we found: one Shanghainese rock band, who hadn't recorded an album, one jazz singer; Coco, two women authors, half a dozen artists, one classical pianist who made his name in America and was enticed back once his star faded there, and who admitted when I interviewed him that Shanghai was a cultural desert, one modern dance choreographer, poached by the Shanghai Cultural Bureau from Beijing to take over the Shanghai modern dance troupe, who sacked half the dancers the day she arrived, one theatre with one playwright and two headline worthy actors who wrote and performed all the plays; rice bowl and laptop dramas about white collar life. That was it.

What culture there was in Shanghai, like so much in the city, was imported. The flashier it was, the more expensive, the better. Above all it had to be digestible for the local audience. Nothing adventurous or thought-provoking. Keep it familiar, safe, and bland.

Imagine a pop chart for lift music, or the West End showing one play a week, one night a week, and it's *Cats*, or your television choice limited to Brookside or Coronation Street.

An endless procession of second-rate ballet companies from the former Soviet Union trooped through town, thumping out barely distinguishable versions of *Swan Lake*. *that's Shanghai* kept count and couldn't help the sarcasm creeping into the listings as yet another Swan drooped to death in front of a chattering audience.

A gargantuan performance of *Aida* was put on at the city's sports stadium. You could barely see the singers and certainly not hear them for the incompetent sound engineering and the noise of the crowd. It would be wrong to call them an audience. They were there for the triumphal procession when thousands of extras supplied by the People's Liberation Army marched around the athletics track in a light drizzle, leading elephants and tigers in wheeled cages.

The Shanghai Cultural Bureau, which controlled and monopolized all artistic performance in the city, was ruled by an official named Gong Xueping. His nickname was 'Buzzcut' thanks to his close-cropped hair. He ran the bureau like a gangster runs his empire, even winning a mafia style turf war when he coerced the city government to merge the previously independent Radio and TV Bureau into his cultural one. He was respected because he got things done, like marching elephants into stadiums. Gong liked it big and brash.

During one of his bureau's rare departures from their norm, I attended a concert by a young violinist. I took a taxi to the office straight afterwards. Like a newspaperman rattling off a late night piece for the next day's edition, I had to get my disappointment onto paper as fast as I could. I would put it on our website the next day.

'Jin Li, 32... played to a half full Shanghai Concert Hall last night. What put the crowds off? The lack of publicity or promotion?

The fact that Jin is not a returnee Shanghainese but was brought up in Guangzhou and is of Korean ancestry? Or did those in the know anticipate correctly that Jin would play a standard (half)-crowd pleasing set of Paganini, Dvorak and then slip into bland film scores. Who decides the programmes for these concerts? There was nothing the audience could get stuck into, let alone Jin Li. And poor old Jin, known for his retiring presence, stuck on a chilly stage in front of a frosty audience, he could hardly be blamed for mucking up the Paganini... Music lovers of Shanghai, bear with it. One day we might get to hear something worth listening to, once talents like Jin Li are given a programme worth playing.'

Sixteen million people and they couldn't fill a concert hall for a one-night performance that might have held some promise, if the crowd-pleasing cultural authorities had let it. Culture in Shanghai catered to the lowest common denominator. And it was very low, and very common.

We tried to do something about it ourselves when we sponsored a performance of the latest pop band from Beijing, New Trousers. Their bright and cheerful tunes were being played all over China. The bar we chose would only give us a Sunday evening. The manager was concerned his business would suffer if we took a more popular evening. Then he asked that the band play cover tunes. He was frightened of putting off any of the few customers who might drop by. We kept control of the playlist and the small crowd loved the show. The band had charisma and rocked the house. A student at a Shanghai University — she was not Shanghainese — turned up early to secure a ticket, thinking they were bound to be sold out in minutes. If we filled the place, it was not packed, and we lost money. But that one student went a long way to making it worthwhile, and illustrated the lack of interest among Shanghainese for anything new or unfamiliar.

It was foreign cultural organizations and state art troupes who made the effort to bring something exciting to the city. Shanghai and Gong Xueping were happy to take the credit. 'See how international we are?' they said, without lifting a finger. And the public believed them.

One evening after a performance of *The Merchant of Venice* by the Royal Shakespeare Company, arranged by the British Council, I was accosted by a television reporter. She thrust a microphone at me and said in Chinese, 'So, how does this compare to theatre in your home country?'

'But that was from my home country.'

'He doesn't understand,' she said and turned away.

One of the biggest stories, and wildest myths, was the supposed 'return' of Shanghai to its previous elevated position as the capital of jazz in the Far East. The western media, and the expat rags, banged on about it for pages. I liked the idea, and I wanted to publish stories about it too, but it took minimal digging to find out that there had never been a Shanghainese jazz 'scene' in the first place. The famous Peace Hotel jazz band, on the Bund, were the most awful musicians I've ever heard. I tracked down and interviewed, myself, a trumpeter who used to play pre 1949 and was now playing for retirees in a hotel in the suburbs. I asked him about the bands. 'They were all from the Philippines,' he said. The bands, just as they are now, were all Filipinos, and the music they played the old-style equivalent of cover tunes in a Hilton hotel bar. Coco, for all his charms, was the only half original jazz musician in the city, and he was banned half the time.

In ten years in Shanghai, living at the heart of — and making a living out of it — the 'cultural' scene, I experienced two, just two, spontaneous, jazz-like, world-class sessions of the quality you'd find every night of the week in a suburb of Seattle. One was when Wang Lei, an outstanding musician I'd known in Guangzhou came through town, and the other was with Wynton Marsalis from New York.

Timidity in all things, including culture, seems to be a deeply ingrained Shanghainese characteristic. It makes sense when you remember that the Shanghainese were predominantly a population of refugees. During the city's boom years under foreign control, the countryside surrounding Shanghai was wracked with drought, flood, and famine and overrun by bandits, warlords, and rebellion. China in the early years of the twentieth century, which is when Shanghai took off, was a mess, and not a safe place. If the natural disasters did not get you then for sure a bandit would rob you or a warlord pressgang you into his private army. The peasants and rural townsfolk in the surrounding provinces of Anhui, Zhejiang and Jiangsu flooded into the haven the foreign powers had set up in Shanghai. Not only were they safe from all the threats outside, the foreigners gave them jobs and decent housing in those *nong tangs*. Fear is in the Shanghainese psyche. Fear is why they are Shanghainese.

That is not to deny that there were some gutsy Chinese who built business empires in Shanghai and faced down enormous risks to do so. It was those true entrepreneurs who would have founded modern Shanghai if they had been encouraged to stay. They were responsible for the cigarette and soap factories, business empires built on textiles and light consumer goods such as watches, electric goods, typewriters. But almost to a man they fled to Hong Kong when they saw the writing on the wall with the Communist take-over. Modern Hong Kong was founded by the Shanghai class of '49.

Left behind to greet the vengeful wrath of the Communists were the clerks and office workers who submitted to their fate, which was to be punished for having lived with and worked for foreign capitalists and enjoyed the benefits. They did not complain. They were refugees, not fighters.

The only time in the city's history when the Shanghainese made a go of something was during the Cultural Revolution in the 1960s and 70s. It was started in Shanghai, led by the Gang of Four, which included Mao's second wife, Jiang Qing, herself an adopted Shanghainese. At last the poor bullied Shanghainese could turn the tables. Jiang Qing exploited their sense of wrong to the full. Trainloads of Shanghainese Red Guards travelled to Beijing, where they fought street battles with the northerners. The country descended into chaos and for once the Shanghainese were not fleeing from it.

When the Cultural Revolution came to a dead stop with Mao's death in 1976, the Gang of Four were put in jail and the Shanghainese put firmly back in their box. As Deng Xiaoping sorted out the mess left by the Red Guards and opened China to the world he left Shanghai out in the cold. While special economic zones such as Shenzhen sprang up out of farmland in the south, Shanghai went nowhere.

The poor Shanghainese, they were always getting the wrong end of the stick, always being bossed about. No wonder they liked the quiet life.

As part of my attempt to find — and get to the feebly beating heart of — what little cultural life there was, I got involved myself.

My apartment on Anfu Road overlooked the garden of the office villa of the Shanghai People's Theatre and I was on chatting terms with the staff. One day the theatre manager asked me if I could act. I said I had done some amateur stuff. Why?

'We are looking for someone to play a stupid foreigner,' he said.

'I think I can do that.'

The play was called *Stock Luck*, and it was the third in a series inspired by Zhu Rongji, now Prime Minister, when he was mayor of Shanghai. The aim was to educate the masses about privatization and stocks and shares and other modern free-market ideas. I was to play a foreign expert at a textile factory that is about to be listed on the Shanghai Stock Exchange. My character was in fact quite clever. He had to invent a new textile to push the share price up. But he also made a hash of it every time he spoke Chinese, by mixing up his characters, which was unrealistic. Foreigner who can't speak Chinese certainly can't read it. And we mix up the tones. I used to do it myself for a joke in real life.

There was a novel and risky twist to the plot, a tiny *coup de theatre* for a Chinese instruct-the-masses play. I was to fall in love with the Chinese factory manager and she would reciprocate. The only concession to conservative correctness was the open-ended resolution, which left it unclear whether I 'got the girl'.

Gong Xueping, Buzzcut, came to watch the dress rehearsal. He would have final say on whether the play could be shown to the public.

Once we had made our bows to the empty auditorium, the stage manager shouted, 'Right, every member of the cast into the meeting room! Bureau Chief Gong will be giving us his opinion of the performance.'

I made my way towards the room on the side of the stage. I had been dying to meet this mythical figure in person.

An arm shot out across my front as I was about to step through the doorway.

'Not you foreigner,' an unfamiliar man said, avoiding my gaze.

I retreated and then returned to peek over the shoulders of a friendly lighting technician. By stretching my neck I could see Gong in the middle of the cast, holding court from a large sofa. The lead players were sitting around him, the rest standing in a respectful semi circle. It was hard to make out what he was saying. He spoke in sharp, short bursts. He looked serious, almost angry. No one made a sound in return. They only nodded their heads. The director was the chief target.

'He's pretty happy with the play,' my friend whispered over his shoulder. If this was happiness, what was it going to be like if the audience showed it the same way.

'Oh, hang on,' he turned back again, 'he's talking about you.' The lighting guy let me squeeze past so I could catch Gong's words.

'Now about the foreigner,' he said. 'I don't like him. He is on stage too much. He is too important to the story.'

He glared at the director. 'Get him on, get the laughs, and get him off.' He paused. 'And,' pointing his finger for emphasis. 'I DO NOT WANT HIM TO GET THE GIRL!' He shouted, and really did look angry.

My friend looked away in embarrassment.

The cast filed out silently. I accosted the director, an intelligent and kind woman in her fifties.

'So,' I asked. 'You going to cut my part?' I was enjoying my first and probably only ever job as a paid, part-time actor. It would be a shame to have it curtailed.

'Don't worry,' she said with a smile. 'We're not going to change a thing.' And she didn't.

So there were some gutsy Shanghainese who stuck around. I was wrong to generalize.

Chapter Fourteen

Shanghai Gold

For the September 2001 issue of *that's Shanghai,* the month before we launched in Beijing and the same month we faced the APEC-prompted attempt to shut us down in our 'home town', advertising revenue broke through a million yuan. That might only be 120,000 US dollars, which is hardly mega media corporation turnover, but from an investment of 20,000 US three years beforehand, it wasn't bad. And a million in whatever currency sounds good. It certainly made me feel good. Add up twelve month's and that put us at over a million dollars a year. For the first time in my life I was making decent money.

For all my disappointment in its shallowness and glitter, I couldn't deny Shanghai was a good place to earn a living.

We also seemed to have left our competitors standing. Earnshaw's *Shanghai Buzz,* which had become *Shanghai Today,* had disappeared without a trace. Ismay's *Shanghai Talk* and newly arrived imitators could only counter us by offering our clients bigger advertisements for less money. They were selling themselves short whilst we set the market and got the prices we wanted. We still received all of Virgin's print advertising for English language media. And we still wrote bad reviews if they were justified.

One evening I met up for a drink with Daniel Kohler, the American who had advertised the Yellow Pages in our second issue thanks to the Henry Restaurant review. He suggested we went to Face, a bar in the garden of H.E. Morris's old home, the

Ruijin Guesthouse, and one of the most popular drinking spots in Shanghai. It was an obligatory first stop for the western hacks, who were arriving every other day to write yet another story about Shanghai's rebirth, China's sexual revolution, and back-to-back interviews with Kika, Wei Hui or Coco.

We sat outside in the cool autumn evening. In front of us stretched the well-tended lawn, dominated by a large cedar and bounded on the far side by a bank of shrubbery. We could have been sitting outside a smart club on the rural River Thames but for the racket from the construction work on the office tower fifty metres to our left.

Daniel had given no reason for the meeting. Just a catch up, he said. His directory had appeared in a slim trial issue soon after his advertisement in '98. Now the full doorstopper edition was about to be launched, after years of problems not dissimilar to our own. I was happy to have a casual chat, if that's all he wanted. We were in the same business. By chance I had something for him.

'Daniel,' I said once we had got through the chitchat. 'I am about to do you a big favour, hope you don't mind.'

'What's that?'

'Well, it's funny we should be having a drink this evening because only today, in my office, I was saying it's time we got rid of all those lists of restaurants and bars, our directories. Did you know they were only fillers when we launched? We wanted to get the readers used to "listings". We couldn't find enough events for proper ones in those days. A true listings magazine lists events, and the addresses where those events are taking place. Repeating our directories every month is a waste of space. I know we're popular because of them, and I must admit it bugs the hell out of me, but now we have the *Bar and Restaurant Guide,* I want people to buy that, and I want to use that space in the magazine for more reviews of new places, better event coverage, that sort of thing. We're a magazine for Christ's sake, not a phone directory, that's what you do!

'So,' I carried on, 'No joke. This afternoon I told the team that next issue we're going to take them out, and I'm going to put in a blank page with a few words on it, dead centre. Want to know what they are going to say?'

'What?' Daniel looked interested.

'"Need a directory? Go find Yellow Pages!" We'll get the message across elsewhere in the magazine about how we're going to better use the resources we're wasting on the directories right now. Oh, and we'll promote our *Guide* of course. How's that for a gift?'

I had expected Daniel to be delighted. His face went pale.

'Mark, we're not ready yet,' he whispered, as if he did not want anyone else to hear. 'The new Yellow Pages won't be out till early next year.' He was silent for a moment and said, 'Can I pay you to put your directories back in?'

Whilst I had been honest about wanting to get rid of the directories, I still had reservations about doing so, and my sales director was dead against it. He saw them as useful for attracting advertisers. I decided not to tell Daniel. If I was not mistaken, I was about to be given a surprise gift, on a proverbial plate.

'I need you to keep them going for six months,' Daniel said. 'And it would be good if we could have some small ads scattered through them. Then when we're ready, you can pull them. How much?'

This was too good. I plucked a figure out of thin air. 'How about three and a half thousand US per issue? You become the sponsor of the bar and restaurant directories.' I held my breath.

Daniel thought for three seconds. I counted. 'Done,' he said.

'Oh,' I added, 'And if you don't mind, a month's deposit in advance, please. We need some security for a deal like this.' I gulped my beer to hide my nerves.

'No problem,' he said. I took another gulp, a large one. 'I'm flying to the States tomorrow. Write up a contract and read it to me over my mobile when I am in the taxi. If it's all OK, you can go round to my office and collect the cash tomorrow afternoon. I know you'll be good as your word.'

'I know you are too Daniel.' It was the only thing to say. We shook hands and drank.

The deal went through. I had made twenty one thousand US dollars over a beer and a handshake. Even if it had been a fluke, it was symptomatic. Once again a foreign company had thrown its advertising dollars at *that's Shanghai* — for the second time in the case of Yellow Pages.

And they kept coming. When the marketing managers saw the advertising working with the foreigners and then caught sight of a local Shanghainese with a copy of *that's Shanghai* under his or her arm, they stayed. We were reaching the clients' local market too, the honey pot they were here for. Our sales kept going up.

The profits were also going up, geographically, to Beijing, but there was still some to spare even with the fines we were paying. At last I started giving myself a decent salary, almost as much as I had once earned as a metal trader.

I could afford breaks like a long weekend in Phnom Penh, where I sat at sunset on the terrace of the Foreign Correspondent's Club above the slow moving muddy Mekong River, drinking cocktails and chatting to an old friend from student days in Beijing who was running his own business in Taiwan. I sheepishly enjoyed the sensation of success, being a self made man, and mixing with other entrepreneurs. I had never imagined joining those ranks. I enjoyed their amused smiles as I told stories of pinching KFC meals off a spoilt child in the early days, and eating bartered sushi. I flew to Hong Kong to talk business with international publishers, and splashed out on expensive meals for friends who had helped me out in my poorer days. On one trip back to the UK, I had dinner with two old school friends.

Justin and I had left on the same day, for the same reason: a dangerous sense of humour we shared, and the headmaster's lack of one. He started his entrepreneurial career almost immediately, selling roses and running nightclubs in Bristol, where he was supposed to be studying. Now he was running his own Internet business in London. Jason had made his career and money in Moscow property. The last time I had hung out with these two, I had been the square, the straightforward army officer, and junior metal trader. Then I had disappeared to China. Now I was coming back as one of them. I had never expected it to turn out that way.

Our conversation jumped from London to Moscow and on to China as we swapped tales of our adventures, compared the risks and rewards of our businesses and the places where we were engaged in them. Justin had access to funds that the financial markets made available in London but had to answer to boards of venture capitalists and bankers. Jason had to watch out for the Russian mafia. I chipped in with my stories of the government bureau raids. We faced different challenges, but we were all winning, or at least surviving. I felt like I was catching up with the pros, growing up.

When I got back to Shanghai after that trip I began to implement the systems and procedures that a maturing company needs. Top priority was a proper finance department to look after all the money. Until now, Shirley had been managing the accounts. I trusted her and was happy to let her run things, but I had begun to notice problems, such as important suppliers like our printers not being paid on time. I only discovered so because one month I called the printer to ask a favour. A national holiday was coming up and I was concerned that the magazine came out before it. Mr. Wang, not the original one, had been standoffish on the phone, almost frosty. Prompted by a nagging doubt I went over to the accounts department. Shirley was out. Our senior cashier told me that Shirley had specifically told her to postpone payment of the printer, for no reason. We had the money. I called Shirley. This could soon be a crisis.

'I just thought there was not need to pay them yet,' she explained. 'They haven't asked, so why worry?'

She being Chinese, I was amazed that Shirley did not appreciate that the printer felt it a matter of face and embarrassing to chase a big client as we had become.

I called Mr. Wang straight back, promised to make the transfer immediately and got the assurance I wanted for the next issue.

There were other undercurrents that started to reach the surface. With Shirley's approval and participation we recruited an experienced accountant, Englate Liu, fresh from an international firm. She was quite a catch, and not cheap. I had explained to Shirley we needed a formal accounting department, professional staff to run it, and that she should step back and let them get on with it. I had long ago realized that she had no real accounting experience, let alone qualification.

Englate was a breath of fresh air. She spoke excellent English, unlike Shirley who hardly spoke a word, and at last I started to receive clear financial reports, which if I did have any problem with, Englate could swiftly explain. I could concentrate more than ever on growth. Englate would keep count.

To help her we recruited a junior accountant, Lily Qin. Lily had respectable qualifications too but what most impressed me was her pleasant nature, her genuine way of speaking and a clear impression that she was more than just trustworthy. She had integrity and an obvious sense of right and wrong. I liked her. She was petite and pretty in a straightforward, rather un-Shanghainese way. She became popular in the office and even caught the eye of an American on the sales team, He was bitterly disappointed when he found out Lily was married.

Shirley and I were also disappointed by Lily when she told us she was pregnant, soon after she started work. For the first time we were going to have to pay for maternity leave. I was annoyed at the expense. But there's a first time for everything and we had to accept that as an established business we were going to have to shoulder it. I was quietly proud as well. We were behaving like a proper corporation.

Shirley coerced Lily into accepting much less than she was due by threatening to fire her on the grounds that Lily could have known she was pregnant when she joined us. Perhaps that was the case. This was a woman thing, as much a mystery to me as accounting. But it did not seem right, and painful though it was to pay up, I disapproved. I mounted my moral high horse but was powerless, even in my own company, to prevail on Shirley. She held control of the accounts and the bank-books.

The day before Lily's leave was to start, I took her into the meeting room and shut the door. She sat down on the new blue sofa and I pulled up a chair.

'This has nothing to do with the company whatsoever Lily,' I started. I paused awkwardly. 'I'm very sorry you are not going to be in the office for a while, but I'm delighted you're having a baby. I'm sure it's not cheap too, and I have an inkling that you don't have much money.' I tried to behave as unlike a boss as possible. I wanted to get this over with.

'I do at the moment.' I moved on, 'have some money that is. So here is a personal gift. Please accept it. And do not tell a soul, apart from your husband of course. This is between you and me, two friends.' I handed over an envelope stuffed with cash.

Lily's eyes had dampened as I was speaking. She took the envelope and put it into her bag, then brought a hand up to rub away the tears that were beginning to fall. 'Thank you,' is all she said.

I did not mention Shirley, maternity leave or anything remotely connected to the real situation. I was too embarrassed anyway. I was merely trying to do the decent thing in the quietest way possible. I was not short of cash.

I had no idea what a good investment I was making.

With Lily gone, Englate had her hands full. Next it was her turn to take me into the meeting room for a quiet chat.

'Mark, I am resigning,' she told me. I was devastated and it must have shown. 'I am very sorry but it is impossible for me to do my job here.'

'Why? How? Englate, you've been brilliant. You've helped me so much. You do a fantastic job.'

'Thanks for saying so, but the fact is: Shirley does not trust me. You cannot have an accountant you do not trust.' The choice of words, that 'you', stabbed me like a knife.

I had a horrid flashback to the old days, to the resignation letter from Neil in Guangzhou. Please, I begged silently, don't let it start all over again. Was this what Kathleen had warned me about with those last ominous words about Shirley? At least with Kathleen the fights had been out in the open. Was Shirley secretly doing things that obstructed our progress? The thought terrified me. What else was going on that I did not know about? The advertising company was in her name. I had given her twenty per cent of the Hong Kong company to reward and encourage her. She was my joint venture partner. I drove the worries from my mind. But I must talk to her soon, just to be sure.

I thanked Englate again for all she had done. We promised to keep in touch. Shirley took over the day-to-day accounting again.

There was one manager well placed within my staff who became a vital ally and supporter as I attempted to include Shirley in the management and development of the company — I was fast realizing she had even less business sense than accounting experience. That was Leo Zhou, a completely 'westernized' Shanghainese who became our national sales director.

Leo held an Australian passport. He was a classic example of the successful local. He was overseas educated, had a wife and child, and previous to *that's* magazines, he'd gained solid sales management experience with an international corporation. He had a house in Australia, apartment in Shanghai and a car. He dressed smartly, was immaculately groomed. He wanted to get ahead, in a small growing business where he could shine, and he liked the idea of media. He had been a perfect match.

At Leo's first sales meeting, held across the open plan office from where I was sitting, Andrew, our rampantly gay and highly effective local sales rep, had minced — he'd approve of the phrase — in half an hour late. The entire office loved him.

'Sorry darlings! Overslept. But that's OK. Where's the penalty box? I can afford it.' He slipped 150 yuan into the box where sales reps put five yuan for every minute they were late.

'Take that back,' Leo had ordered. Andrew looked surprised. Leo raised his voice. There was a frightening firmness in it. 'I don't want your fucking money. If I did I'd cancel your whole fucking commission. And I'd fire you. This is my sales meeting and I want you to fucking well be on time for it. You got that?'

There was a stunned silence. The sales team looked shocked and uncomfortable. Their eyes were glued to the table, like scolded school children. I was awed and delighted. Here was a Shanghainese with balls.

'Now,' Leo went on, the cold anger dissipating from his voice. 'Let's see how we can sell some advertising.'

Leo knew how to get a grip. Since that day he had driven the sales team with a textbook combination of carrot and stick. He also understood business and because it was he who brought in the money, and was Shanghainese, Shirley listened to him. And he listened to me. It was an unusual way to communicate with your business partner, but not an unusual one in a Chinese joint venture. Leo became something of a right hand man.

Between launching *that's Beijing* and saving *that's Shanghai,* and while the get-together of Pacific Ocean Presidents brought the city to a standstill, we moved office once again, into an empty villa owned by the Shanghai Beijing Opera Company. (That means a Shanghai company who performed Beijing style opera, in case you're wondering.) The Golden Magnolia had finally filled up.

The villa's gardens had long since disappeared but traces of the building's grandeur survived. The second floor — first by British reckoning — retained its parquet flooring. The ground floor had been tiled but the large rooms kept their original windows and leading. The bay windows of our meeting room, the old dining room, looked backwards into the blue plastic-roofed carport of the building behind us and frontwards into a shack that the previous tenants had used for storage, which is where we put our *aiyi,* the live-in office maid. She kept her toothbrushes in a mug on the outside of — inside for her — the windowsill. We asked her to remove it when we had important clients come to visit.

The finance department moved into the master bedroom. We put a small meeting table in the dressing room. I took a small upstairs conservatory, or glassed in balcony, for my own office. The terracotta patterned tiled floor was almost identical to my playroom in the Welsh farmhouse where I had been brought up. And here I was playing publisher.

We filled the outdoor balcony with garden furniture bought at a discount from an advertiser. There was still time before the weather turned cold to hold staff barbecues, like the ones I used to enjoy as an apprentice metal trader in a walled garden in Westminster. There the smell of sausages had wafted up the building and straight into the windows of the shipping department, who would invariably complain and hold their own barbecue the next day. In our Shanghai villa the rivalry for outdoor eating was between the sales and editorial departments, and I could join both.

We started taking interns. In fact we were overwhelmed by them. Not only were big businesses desperate to get into Shanghai, everyone who dreamt of being a businessman one day wanted to be there too, and the local English language media were a prime target. All you had to do was speak and write English, as I used to ask the editorial job candidates.

The *Shanghai Star* was giving gap year students the run of the editorial pages. We let them do the photocopying and light the barbecue, proper intern jobs, to the disappointment of the sandal-wearing directors of the British programmes that foisted their charges onto us.

It was with a real and undreamt of sense of achievement however that I sent some of our own Chinese editors to intern at *Time Out* in London. I had never imagined that one day I would help staff build a career. Now I was sending them overseas for training, the kind of thing multi-national corporations do, and when they came back I had positions to promote them into.

In my first private office I leaned back, put my feet on my desk, and indulged in even grander daydreams.

I recruited a manager, an American called Mike Cole, for *that's*

Shanghai so I could concentrate on the big picture. Mike joked that I should get out and play golf like other top executives, start networking at the nineteenth tee. I thought about it, then reminded myself, and told Mike, that I hated golf. So I set up Shanghai's first amateur fencing club — since 1949.

After the years of battling often faceless officials in fights that obeyed no rules, it was good to be back on the *piste*, fighting by rules I knew and understood and facing an opponent who if I couldn't see his face under the mask, at least I knew by name and would shake hands with afterwards.

Three times a week in the early morning I took a taxi to the Shanghai Sports Institute to train at the fencing *salle*. If I was going to run a club I had better get back on form. The coach, 'Old Bones', was a forty-something Cantonese suffering the effects of a professional sports career, hence the nickname. He made me welcome. The sessions began with a punishing warm up schedule and I began to get into shape again. I envied the students who did nothing but fence. If only I had had such a chance.

'Yeah Mark,' one of them said when I spoke up, quick as a flash, 'but you have a life.'

Sport in China is not for fun. It is for national glory.

The amateur club took off. For the first time ever I put a classified advertisement in my own magazine. I was flooded with replies. Within a week I had signed up several ex-international fencers as well as many keen amateurs, mostly foreigners. It surprised me how effective the advert was. No wonder Sun Xiaofeng was so worried about their impact.

Many of the founding members of the club were senior executives. I found that whipping a businessman with a sword was as useful for building contacts as whacking a ball around a landscaped garden, and more fun.

One day a feature writer from the *South China Morning Post* was waiting to interview me when I arrived at the office with my bag of fencing kit over my shoulder. She was Fionnuala McHugh, a charming and sharp-witted journalist from Northern Ireland. She latched straight onto the fencing analogy, writing how it prepared me for 'the cut and thrust of publishing in China.' I laughed it off but little did I know how apt it was. In that brief respite, the short period I enjoyed as a social sporting executive, and without realizing it, I was training for the next fight.

Another attack was coming, this time from a totally unexpected quarter.

Chapter Fifteen

The First Cut

That's Beijing survived unscathed for three months. I was out for lunch on a cold damp Friday in mid January when Mike Wester called. His voice had the ring of desperation of the last man standing, calling in to report he was surrounded.

The Beijing *gongshang* were raiding the office. It was vicious. They wanted the computers and financial records. Mike had slipped out two hard drives, including the vital Macintosh one with the next issue. The staff had been shocked by the ferocity of the onslaught. Mike let the juniors go home for the day. The others were putting up a fight. I could imagine them claiming to have lost files, that computers were broken, saying they had left their passports at home.

I told Mike to hold on and tried to call Sun Xiaofeng. He was flying back from Beijing to Nanjing, the nearest airport to Yangzhou. I had to wait for his plane to land.

I got back to Mike. He had more bad news. The *gongshang* had spotted we were signing advertising contracts with the Gao Bang consultancy company chop but issuing receipts from Shirley's advertising company.

What the hell was this? That was wrong and unnecessary and I knew it. I guessed Shirley must have given the instruction, to protect herself. She knew our consultancy couldn't issue contracts for advertising. But her company was taking the money. After many years of preparation, Shirley had emigrated to the States a month ago. She remained involved with the business, as well as being a shareholder. I reassured myself with the knowledge that Lily, who had become my chief financial manager, held Shirley's company chops. I needed to have words with Shirley again about her idea of how to protect ourselves and what was good for the company.

Now the *gongshang* wanted the chops too. Handing them over would mean unconditional surrender. Nothing happens in China, no business can run, without a chop. Giving them away would be like locking ourselves out of the office and throwing away the key, and giving the company cheque-book to the tramp on the doorstep on the way out.

Mike and I debated over the phone. Throw the chops out of the window and recover them later? Claim they were not in the office? Mike settled on the simplest option. He refused to hand them over. That took guts.

We tried to work out who had set the *gongshang* onto us. They were well informed. They knew of our past run-ins with the Shanghai authorities in surprising detail. How could they have got that information? It was possible our Shanghai enemies had stirred things up.

We had a new one too.

Gold Lion Advertising, who we had worked with for years in Shanghai, had pulled the plug on us. They started producing a brand new English language magazine of their own, *Shanghai Scene*, with the support of my old friends at the *Shanghai Daily*. They knew all our clients because they had copies of the contracts.

Shanghai Scene was launched almost the very day of the attack in Beijing, typical timing for a diversionary attack. The *Daily* itself had run a story with the nonsensical, confidence-inspiring line: '*Shanghai Scene* is the sole English-language magazine sponsored by the Shanghai Municipal Information Office.' The magazine was a transparent rip off of *that's Shanghai*, written in awful Chinglish and the design looked like a scrapbook.

I put my money on Gold Lion being the snitch to the Beijing *Gongshang*.

At last I got a ringtone on Sun's phone. He picked up. What was going on, I asked. We had found a publishing partner for the third issue of *that's Beijing* in December. They were *Chinaweek*, an English language magazine that belonged to the Communist Youth League, an important branch of the Party. *That's Beijing* was appearing as their supplement. The purpose of Sun's visit to Beijing had been to finalize some details with *Chinaweek*. We should have been safe as houses.

Sun was as lost as I was. He said let them take the computers. He would call *Chinaweek* and ask their help to get them back next Monday.

I slipped in a query. Had he paid *Chinaweek*? We had given him the money. If he hadn't passed it on they would be less likely to help, and us getting into trouble so soon in our partnership would hardly reassure them. 'Don't you worry about that,' he replied. 'It's all taken care of.' I hoped so.

Sun called me back after a few minutes. Good news. *Chinaweek* would stick up for us. Sit tight for the weekend. We'll get the computers and be back to work in no time.

The February issue of *that's Beijing* was produced in Mike's flat. Anyone on his staff with a laptop or old home computer moved it into his sitting room. The office had not been sealed by the bureau, but it was not safe to work there. They might make another raid. Mike changed output centres and printers. Meanwhile, our competitors in Beijing spread the story to our new and hard-won clients that we had been shut down. We were a flash in the pan, had bitten off more than we could chew. We should have stayed in Shanghai.

Mr. Sun joined in. It was all my fault, he said. I should have waited until he had given the go-ahead for Beijing.

'You know what? You're too stubborn Mark. You never listen,' he said, yet again. 'Now look what you have gone and done.' I listened patiently. There was no use in having a row. I needed him on side.

Then he recruited Shirley's self-righteous support from San Francisco. She joined in the blame game by email. When I asked her why she had left that gap in our defences in Beijing she replied, 'How can you blame me for that when you have made such a mess of things yourself?'

I raced from Shanghai to Beijing and back, then over to Yangzhou and on up to Beijing again. I barely stayed in one place more than a couple of days. I hauled in every *guanxi* I knew, and pulled up some new ones. The Chinese New Year was coming, which gave me an excuse to do the rounds of government offices with packets of expensive tea and bottles of brandy.

I called on the Editor-in-Chief of the *China Daily*, Zhu Yinghuang, right at the top of the English language publishing tree in China. He refused to accept the brandy so I left it with his secretary.

'Let's get in my deputy, Mr. Fang, and see what he thinks,' Zhu said. Then he added, 'He's the man who shut down the *Beijing Scene*.'

A grim-faced man came in and sat to one side. I explained our situation, dropping heavy hints that if *Chinaweek* could not get us out of this mess we would need a new partner. Despite Sun's assurance, nothing had happened for a month of 'next Mondays'. The computers were still with the *gongshang*.

Mr. Fang leered at me. 'Did you know Scott Savitt?' he asked, mentioning the name of the American behind *Beijing Scene*. 'We had a similar situation with him some years ago.'

'No, I never met him,' I replied, hoping we could skip that story.

'It was me who went round to his office and shut him down you know.' Fang leant forward. His eyes looked into mine like a psychotic criminal proud of his reputation for violence. 'I was there,' he growled, 'in his office. It was me who did it.'

'Mark,' Zhu interrupted with a smile. 'You know what I have always thought? Take over the *Shanghai Star*. You can have it. We need someone to make it work and you are perfect. Forget about *that's* magazines. You have seen how difficult it is. Drop it and come on board with us.'

I liked Mr. Zhu. We had met a couple of times. He was a jovial character, seemed to show genuine concern for my troubles, and was frank in his admiration of *that's*. It was a pity his right-hand man, whom I had never seen before, was a rabid anti-foreigner.

Zhu was offering me a poisoned chalice, in the nicest possible and probably genuine way. I laughed it away.

I retreated to Shanghai. Mike was coping in Beijing. At least *Chinaweek* would let us continue to publish under their name and use their chops for advertising contracts. But the *gongshang* problem, they made clear once they realized how difficult it was, had nothing to do with them.

I called Lily into my office. She had become a staunch and loyal confederate, my right hand woman. She was also turning out to be a competent financial manager.

'So,' I started, 'we can keep publishing in Beijing. We'll have to deal with the *gongshang* there in our own time, get the computers back and...'

'Pay the fine,' interjected Lily.

'Yup, the fine.' I tried not to think about that.

'They'll say we were doing business illegally. And you know

what that means.' Lily was not going to let me skip it: 'Confiscation of all illegal income.'

'Shit, do you have to Lily?'

'Sorry. But we need to prepare the funds.'

'You're right, as usual,' I paused. Lily let me move on from the unpleasant subject. 'Now, can you tell me what the situation is with the chops, particularly Shirley's company one?'

She nodded, and spoke slowly. 'Mark, there's some bad news. About those chops.'

'What is it?' I steeled myself.

'You know we had the chop here, and I kept it in my safe?'

'Yes.' I was guessing this was bad.

'Well, Shirley sent a friend round to borrow it. She said she needed it for something straightforward and it would be returned afterwards.' Lily was slowing down for the punch line.

'Go on.'

She hesitated, and came out with it. 'They did not return it. Shirley says she doesn't trust us with it anymore.'

'What?' I exploded. 'How the hell are we going to do business without the chop? It's the JV partner!'

'Shirley says we have to email or phone her in America when we need it, and tell her what for. If she agrees, she'll get her friend to come over. We chop whatever it is then give it back.'

'Lily,' I had been thinking. I kept my voice as level as possible. 'How much of the joint venture's money is in Shirley's company's account right now?' I was dreading the answer.

'That's the good news,' she smiled. 'Hardly any. I used it for Beijing's expenses.' Lily was smart.

'But we still have a problem,' she said. 'We need an advertising company in Shanghai, and Beijing too. We can still use Kaishenglin in Guangzhou. Shirley can't do anything awkward there because we are barely breaking even, in fact we are losing a bit.'

While Lily briefed me, in a thoroughly professional way, all I could think about was Shirley. What was going on with her? What was upsetting her? I had begun wondering a while ago, when the Beijing raid kicked off. I couldn't help suspecting that she and Sun Xiaofeng might be up to something. Had they secretly agreed I had gone too far when I launched in Beijing and decided to rein me in? But Shirley was a shareholder, and I was building the company. Sales were going up. We could afford to expand and she had agreed to *that's Beijing* before she left for America. All she had to do was sit back and wait for the profits, once Beijing broke even. Was Sun Xiaofeng prompting her, or was it the other way round?

I knew I had upset her by removing her name from the masthead, but she was patently not 'operations manager' anymore. She never had been, just as I had never been a 'planning manager'. Those were flags of convenience forced upon us years ago. There were a remarkable number of 'planning managers' appearing on Chinese magazine mastheads nowadays. We had started a trend.

Shirley was a partner in the Gao Bang JV and that was on the masthead, as I had explained to her. She had certainly helped when she was still in China but she had never been involved in the actual building of the business. She had lent us the use of the advertising company and sweet-talked our *guanxi*.

I thought some more, further back. If Shirley had set up a branch of her own company in Shanghai when we launched here that would have solved many of our problems. But she always arranged for us to work through local companies, which had hurt us when Gold Lion ditched us and held onto not a small sum of our money. And when we registered the JV, she had been happy to let me be the legal representative, in full control. For the first time it hit me: she had not done that out of deference, it was to keep herself safe. And yet she had obstructed my persistent efforts to set up a consultancy agreement with Yangzhou, which would have been legal and secure.

Shirley wanted to benefit from the business yet bear none of the risk: how very Shanghainese. Her naïve way of securing her interest was to use what power she had, with her company chops for example, but she was only forcing me to find an alternative. It also dawned on me, with dread, that she had no concept of the benefit I had tried to secure for her with the shares in Hong Kong.

Lily brought me back to the present. She was pressing me for an answer. How to operate in Shanghai without Kaishenglin, Shirley's company?

We decided to put small contracts, illegally, through the consultancy for a while. We could fudge the terms, make them look like consultancy agreements, and use that money to pay Gao Bang's expenses. Bigger contracts could go through *Chinaweek*, who were now supporting *that's Shanghai* as well as *that's Beijing*. In due course we could set up a new advertising company. I hoped that would not be necessary. All I wanted was a tight consultancy agreement with a publisher or Yangzhou.

'One last thing Mark,' said Lily before she left. 'Mr. Sun left this behind the other day. You want it? You could give it back to him.' She handed me a leather bound notebook.

I opened the book and flicked through the pages. They were covered in a dense web of handwritten Chinese, difficult to decipher. It was tempting. Very tempting. But even had I wanted to, it would have taken me ages. 'Integrity!' a voice in the back of my head shouted.

'No, I don't want it, thanks. You can give it to him.' I was about to hand it back to Lily when I looked down. I had left it open at the back cover. I noticed the edge of a photograph sticking out of the leather sleeve. This I could not resist. It was a picture of Sun Xiaofeng and Shirley, arm in arm in a park, probably the Slender West Lake in Yangzhou. Despite them looking like a couple, it was innocent enough. But it was obviously treasured by Sun Xiaofeng. I reinserted it in its hiding place and thought again about integrity.

'You keep it Lily.' I looked her in the eye. 'You know I could not read it anyway.' I stressed the first person very clearly.

Shirley flew to Shanghai from San Francisco a few weeks later. The main occasion was a happy one, my wedding. But to pay for it I needed the couple of hundred thousand yuan Shirley had been sitting on as the now redundant security deposit for the use of her company. I had let her keep the rest as a dividend.

Shirley dumped half of the amount due to me in cash, in a plastic bag, onto my desk with as much ill grace as she could muster. She gave no excuse, but promised to transfer the remainder once she got back to America. I had every reason to ask what she had done with it, but since she was going to be drinking my health in a couple of days, I chose to preserve the warm cosy feeling.

We held a snap board meeting in Shanghai, Sun Xiaofeng, Shirley and I, before I caught my flight for Guangzhou. I was marrying Joanna, the girl I had left in Guangzhou and stayed friends with, and over time one thing had led to another, and well… there you go.

'Now Mark,' Shirley said. 'You have no advertising company in Shanghai.' Thank you for stating the bloody obvious, I thought. 'What are your plans? I hear you are going to use Gao Bang to take advertising income. This is very dangerous, you know that don't you?'

Sun was looking neutral.

'Yes, I do.' I tried to keep the sarcasm out of my voice. 'But we have no choice and it will only be for a short while. I am sure we can get away with it.'

'By the way,' she said. 'Did you know that John Halo, our old employee, is back in China and has his own advertising company? His mother set it up for him.' Shirley was offering a solution.

'No I didn't.' The thought of that spoilt brat did not bring back fond memories. I remembered how at an office party he had threatened dear Iris Zheng with a broken bottle. No way was I going to trust him with our advertising income. His mother, thanks to her position at the tax bureau, was a potential threat, and I had no idea how close she had become with Shirley. I had to handle this carefully. It didn't take a sixth sense to work out there was something behind it.

'I don't think that will be necessary Shirley. Once we get a proper consultancy agreement between our company, that's yours and mine,' I emphasized, 'and Yangzhou, or a publisher,' I glanced at Sun Xiao Feng, 'we'll be fine.' He looked up and coughed.

'All right,' Shirley said. 'You do it your way. You always do. Don't say I didn't warn you. Bureau Chief Sun is my witness.' She looked disappointed.

And that was that. I had personal matters to attend to which distracted me from Shirley's threat. Surely no shareholder, director and JV partner would do something to damage their own company. The idea was ridiculous.

A fortnight later I returned from my honeymoon to be greeted by the Shanghai Municipal Tax Bureau. Our offence: using a consultancy company to receive illegal income from advertising. They had evidence, a surprising amount of it.

There was also a gloating email from Shirley: 'I told you so,' in so many words. She copied it to Sun Xiaofeng, with more criticism of my management of the business. This was no coincidence.

Lily briefed me on how she was dealing with the bureau. She had things under control but we were facing a massive fine, somewhere in the region of 400,000 yuan, approximately 50,000 US dollars. Word from Beijing was to expect a similar penalty from the *gong-shang* there too.

I was furious. Shirley had set up this latest attack, out of spite. She had emigrated to America, could not understand what I was doing for her, so to prove she was indispensable and to be reckoned with, she had stitched up her own company. For the first time I missed Kathleen.

And I was going to prove Shirley was behind the attack, if only to myself. The incredulity that a shareholder could do such a thing maddened me.

I called up my partner-in-law Bob Boyce. A year ago he had bought Kathleen out of her restaurant business. I needed some advice, or at least some sympathy.

'Mark, pay Shirley what she wants. She was the legal rep of Kathleen's and my company too and held the title. Buy her out. I know you might think it's painful but it is the best way to deal with her.'

'Thanks Bob.' Cold comfort.

I had made a mistake. Kathleen had warned me, of all the ironies. I had picked the wrong partner. Even worse, I had not asked for any commitment or investment from her. And to cap it all, if it could get worse, I could not change anything without her consent as a director of the JV, unless I went right back to scratch and started again, which would be an enormous task.

But first I wanted proof. I had an idea, a long shot. Integrity be damned.

I shut the door to my office, dug out a photocopy of Shirley's I.D. and placed it on my desk. Shirley's face stared up at me with the confident sweet smile of a woman in her early thirties. She looked like someone you could trust.

I logged onto the Internet, and tapped in the URL for her personal email.

'Username.'

I typed her email address.

'Password.'

I looked at her I.D. I held my breath, and typed in the digits of her birthday, starting with the year, then month, then day, the Chinese way.

'Welcome Shirley!' the screen flashed at me. I was in. Maybe I should have been a spy after all.

I clicked on the sent items folder. It was empty. Shirley was not saving her outgoing emails or she was covering her tracks. I went back to the inbox. There were a number of emails from Mr. Dai, a crony of Shirley's who lurked in our Guangzhou office, looking after her interests and upsetting the staff. I scrolled down. Then I found it.

It was an email from Jacky Luo, a cashier who used to work in our Shanghai accounts department. I had fired him not long after Shirley left.

I had once thought Jacky an excellent worker, and acquiesced to Shirley's unusual and sudden request that we double his salary. He often worked late and at the weekends. Then it had dawned on me that Jacky was not working for the magazines, and I realized why he never went home when I told him to. He was using our resources to help Shirley and Kathleen set up another restaurant. Kathleen was back in Shanghai by now, having declared she was done with China and the restaurant business. Once she had spent the money Bob and I had paid her, she had changed her mind.

Now it was made obvious to me how thick Jacky really was with Shirley. If I was behaving like a spy, that is exactly what he had been since Shirley left for the States.

In the thread beneath his email was one from her. 'How is the tax bureau investigation going? Is it true what I hear, that you yourself went and made an official complaint?'

It is difficult to extract the tone of voice from an email, but Shirley's sarcasm was all too apparent considering Jacky's reply above it.

'I would just like to say, if I had not discussed it with you beforehand, I would never have done such a thing. You have my absolute guarantee of that!'

So my own partner and significant shareholder had encouraged a cashier to grass on our own company to the tax bureau.

It is common for employees in China to stir up trouble if they think they have been unfairly dismissed. I remember firing our first ever HR manager because she failed to sort out the staff benefits required by law, the main job we gave her. So she went to the Labour Bureau and told them exactly that, that we were not giving the benefits, neglecting of course to mention it had been her job. It was almost funny.

This wasn't. I doubted the idea to go to the tax bureau had been Jacky's and indeed the emails made clear it was Shirley's decision to go ahead. I was stunned, but there was no way to use my proof except keep it to myself and prepare for the next act of suicidal treachery. Forewarned might be forearmed, but one of my own 'arms' was attacking me. I was going to have to be a contortionist to put up a defence. I needed every advantage.

Over the next few months I monitored Shirley's email. I excused myself on the grounds that I was employing her, which under the terms of the JV was the case, and I remembered reading somewhere that employers are allowed to check on staff correspondence. Not that it mattered. This was turning into a dirty war.

What I uncovered only upset me more. Shirley asked Jacky to

break into the office over a national holiday to download the company's financial files. Our *aiyi* scotched that one. She was no fool.

Shirley then asked him to persuade Douglas to pass on our distribution database to Kathleen so she could use it for direct marketing for her new restaurant.

And then there was the final confirmation, this time from John Halo himself: 'Dear Shirley, The Tax Bureau Internal Affairs department has started its investigation. The people who were helping Mark and Lily have been investigated and disciplined. Everything is ready, we are just waiting for the evidence. Jacky has to help with that. As a friend I have happily given you my help. I hope that what we have started will be completed. Please instruct Jacky accordingly.'

That's verbatim.

The woman was a frightening destructive force. Not only was she prepared to damage her own company, she was even ready to destroy the careers of junior tax officials. I was horrified at the machinations of someone I had once trusted so completely.

But Shirley had barely started. I looked on with a mixture of calm preparation for a fight and blood-simmering fury as she conceived a plan to transfer the entire business of *that's* magazines into her advertising company.

I felt like a spectator at my own execution. I could not intervene, only watch, and pray that one of the firing squad changed their minds or realized that to hit me they were going to have to fire a bullet through their own head.

Proposals flew across the Internet between Shirley, Mr. Dai in Guangzhou and Sun in Yangzhou. Her advertising company, headed by Mr. Dai, would take over the entire business operation of the magazines, Yangzhou would act as publisher, and Gao Bang, our only chance of extracting any profits from China, would be paid a fee for 'consulting with regard to the content of the magazines'. In other words, Shirley wanted to steal the business.

This was plain evil.

To my utter amazement, Kathleen reappeared online. She even pitched in with her own ideas.

One ex-partner who had been paid handsomely and one current partner who had been given a large share of the company for free were trying to steal the business from the person who built it, and the only one of us who had any financial stake in it. I know life can be unfair, but this was worse than the *Shanghai Daily*.

Then Shirley went too far. She upset Sun Xiaofeng. In fact it was Mr. Dai, who from the tone of his emails was not blessed with brains. He declared too soon to the Guangzhou office that he was taking complete control.

Sun Xiaofeng was livid. I smiled at the flurry of correspondence. Sun felt his authority was being undermined.

He copied me a letter he had sent to Dai and Shirley, which I had already read, putting Dai firmly in his place. 'The *that's Guangzhou* office reports to me and to the Shanghai office,' he declared. 'It is not independent and Mr. Dai is not the manager.'

I saw my opportunity. Sun changed sides of his own accord. He told me of Shirley's plan and forwarded me the latest draft, in confidence, and asked me what we should do. I was careful to sound surprised.

'This is awful, Mr. Sun. Not only is it an attack on your authority and my personal interests, it puts the magazines' survival at risk. You know what would happen if Shirley and Mr. Dai took control.' He did not need a prompt.

Having spent weeks preparing my counter move, I explained my plan to Sun as if it was just occurring to me. I pressed all the right buttons.

'The only direct influence Shirley has is in Guangzhou,' I told him. 'Let me set up a new advertising company there and move the business into it, with your approval. This way we can be rid of Mr. Dai' — I could picture Sun's face reddening — 'Will you support me? I'll take care of the details, and I promise you Shirley will have no legal basis to complain. Don't forget, she is a shareholder in the Hong Kong company.'

Sun thought for a long while. 'OK, I agree. But I prefer if this was done openly, with the prior approval of Shirley.'

That was impossible. But I could not tell Sun that, or how I knew.

I briefed the actual manager of our Guangzhou office, a bright girl called Katherine Zhao. She was delighted to hear that we were going to get shot of the irksome Mr. Dai, who had been making her life difficult.

By happy coincidence, Mike Wester in Beijing had recovered the computers from the *gongshang*. 'What do you want me to do with them? We've already replaced them.'

'Send them to Guangzhou,' I replied. And after a brief silence on the line, 'Don't ask.'

One Friday evening late in 2002 I flew down to Guangzhou. Only Katherine knew I was coming. I prepared myself for an unpleasant task. Katherine called the staff in for an emergency meeting. They were surprised to see me. I had made the tough decision not to include the accountant, a decent girl, but she was too close to Shirley and would be intimidated.

I made a short speech. I apologized, explained the situation and gave them the choice to come with me or try their luck with Mr. Dai. It helped that a day or so ago he had bullied them into signing new contracts with Kaishenglin Advertising. The contracts were one sided, and unluckily for dimwitted Dai, he had put everyone back onto a trial period that allowed them to leave with no notice. That was handy. And they had all been shown the irate letter from Mr. Sun telling them to answer to him, and the Shanghai office, which meant me, and not Mr. Dai. That was handy too.

I stifled a grateful sob when the ten of them agreed on the spot. Katherine backed me to the hilt. I was moved by their personal loyalty, something I never considered necessary in business. It was the company that counted, the company being the magazines.

'Right then,' I said. 'Pack your bags, personal belongings only, and come with me. The new office is round the corner.'

By midnight we had completed the move. I invited everyone for a late dinner.

Someone proposed a toast. 'Congratulations Mark! Here's to a new start, a new advertising company, and a prosperous and peaceful future for *that's Guangzhou*!' Everyone raised a glass.

'Please understand,' I replied. 'I am not proud about what we have just done. But I am proud of you guys. I know you care about the magazine. So let's drink to *that's Guangzhou*, which means you. And... Thank you.' I was emotionally and physically exhausted, and deep inside I was bitterly sad.

So was someone else. Not precisely sad, but definitely bitter.

It was the Monday morning and Mr. Dai had turned up to an empty office, an image I had savoured. Sun called me.

'Mark!' he shouted. 'I told you to try and work things out with Shirley before you made your move. I know I agreed to your plan but you have disobeyed me yet again. You and your damn stubbornness. When are you ever going to listen?'

'Bureau Chief Sun,' I replied, 'I am so, so sorry, truly.' I contemplated inventing an excuse but I was back in integrity mode. 'The situation was impossible. I had no choice but to act first.' I paused. 'And Mr. Sun, you can rest assured that the magazine will be all right. After all, that is all we care about isn't it?'

'Hmm, well yes, I suppose so.' I was getting away with it. He was still angry though. 'Guess who rang me just now?'

'Shirley of course. Sorry about that too. I'm sure she's mad. But please remind her she is still a shareholder of the company that is due all the profits from the magazines. I'll be in touch with her myself.' I already had a letter written.

'No, it wasn't Shirley. It was Kathleen!' His voice went up a pitch. 'I never want you to put me through that again. She was crying on the phone, screaming at me, calling me all sorts of names. I couldn't believe it! I am a government official damn it!'

I laughed. I couldn't help it. Sun giggled. 'It's not funny! I'm telling you. She was absolutely mad, a crazy woman.' I laughed again, this time with relief. I had done the right thing. I had Sun's support, and the magazines were safe.

'I'll come to Yangzhou as soon as I am done here, Sun Xiaofeng. We need to talk about the new publisher.'

'Yes, you better had.' He rung off.

The commercial operation of the magazines was secure. I had won a dirty fight with my own partner. It had been expensive, with the fine in Shanghai and the costs of setting up a new company and office in Guangzhou. At least the computers still worked after their incarceration in Beijing.

Our publishing licence problems looked to be coming to an end too. We had moved on from *Chinaweek* and started co-operating with China Intercontinental Press, a pet company of the State Council Information Office, the top authority in all media in China. Things were looking up.

Chapter Sixteen

The Dragon's Lair

Mr. Yuan Bao'an had a habit of pouting when listening and putting full stops on his sentences with polite coughs, hand over his mouth, when speaking. He wore glasses perched on the end of his nose. I put him in his mid fifties. I addressed him as Yuan *Laoshi,* Teacher Yuan. Like some schoolmasters he was gently patronizing and always ready, in his own time, with clever answers to my questions. The more direct the question, the more opaque the answer.

Mr. Yuan was my contact at China Intercontinental Press, Wuzhou Chuanbo Chubanshe. He never gave me a name card because he had no official position. He was a successful author and, as he explained: 'I am a consultant for Wuzhou. I have a certain amount of power to make decisions and execute them, and I am answerable to the *lingdao,* but I am also a free agent.'

He could dodge responsibility. If things got tricky, he could retreat behind the *lingdao*. If things went well, he could act like the boss and take the credit. These *lingdao* really were leaders, top government ones. They held positions in the State Council Information Office, a cabinet level body. They had serious power. I wondered if I would ever meet them.

Yuan lived in a large apartment that took almost half a floor of a block on the outskirts of Beijing, near the old Summer Palace, the one the foreign powers had burnt to the ground in 1860. Originally his home had been two apartments, maybe three. I never saw the full extent of it, but I was surprised by the private gym and the large book-lined study that I glimpsed at the end of a long corridor.

He also had a house in Qingdao, the seaside resort on the Shandong Peninsula, where he drove with his dog for regular long weekends. He boasted of the view of the sea from his rooftop garden.

Yuan was a consummate political operator. He knew many powerful people in the publishing world in Beijing, and he knew how to use them, please them, and most impressive and intimidating of all, play them off against each other.

I was wary of Mr. Yuan. In our meetings he could be petulant, patronizing, stubborn and then suddenly submissive, one minute a close friend, the next a haughty official. He was very different to Sun Xiaofeng, and he was infinitely smarter.

that's magazines had entered the lair of the dragon. Under Wuzhou's wing we were untouchable. The *Shanghai Daily* and our new enemies in Beijing bowed their heads and retreated. They knew that if they so much as took a jab at us, they would get burnt. The name 'Shanghai' made its way back onto the cover in Shanghai, as did the month of publication. I could concentrate on building the business and brand.

But our refuge had its hazards. At any moment the dragon could turn on us too, squeeze the life out of us, squash us, eat us up. Yuan made that plain in our first ever meeting.

'You need have no worries for the future Mark,' he had said. 'Now you are with Wuzhou you will always have a job.'

That was a bad choice of words.

It was matronly Madam Wu of Outgoing Propaganda who had introduced us. The partnership with *Chinaweek* had lasted six months, until they reinterpreted our agreement. There had been a nasty dispute that I was happy to let Sun Xiaofeng deal with. The boss of *Chinaweek* turned out to be a vicious and well-connected individual who, like one or two of our previous partners, thought he could steal our name and business. They had approached our clients direct, tried to engineer our shutdown and secretly applied for the trademark *'that's'*. They were also preparing a lawsuit against Yangzhou for what they considered to be our failure to fulfill our obligations: to pay three times more than agreed in 'administration fees'. The trademark application was obviously a trump card they meant to play when they needed it. I stumbled on it when the Trademark Bureau made public the application, as required by law.

Then the boss of *Chinaweek* was killed in a car crash along with his deputy and sidekick. They were driving back from a printing factory on the outskirts of Beijing, which they also happened to be suing, and were hit by a truck. Such accidents often happen in such situations. The man's name was put into a box on *Chinaweek*'s masthead. The only survivor of the crash was the managing editor, a decent guy, called Mr. Ma. I had met him a couple of times and liked him. His was the thankless task of producing an English language magazine with no native English speakers.

We sent flowers to *Chinaweek's* offices and when Ma got out of hospital I entered into quiet negotiations without Sun's knowledge to resolve the dispute and transfer the application for the trademark to Gao Bang. Ma agreed, happy to resolve a dispute he had inherited, get shot of a trademark he could not use, and make some cash. I slipped the trademark trump card up my sleeve. If Sun or Yuan found out I had it I had no doubt what would happen: 'Hand it over or we don't let you publish.' Or: 'Change the name.'

Yuan was careful how he set things up. Wuzhou would only deal with a government agency, he said, so we had to go through Yangzhou. That was fine by me, though not ideal. He added that Wuzhou would be applying for new *kanhaos* for us. When those were issued all agreements would be null and void and we would have to start afresh. This was cause for concern, but I would cross that bridge when we came to it. In the meantime I took the opportunity to pin down Sun Xiaofeng and got him to sign a detailed contract with Gao Bang that superseded the vague one he had with Shirley's company.

Sun was still annoyed with Shirley, and once we had sent a couple of drafts to each other, I made a one-day dash to and back from Yangzhou and got his chop before he changed his mind. I also drafted the agreement he would sign with Wuzhou. At last I had my paper trail linking the magazines all the way back to Klau and Benedict in Hong Kong. This was massive progress.

Shirley should have been pleased.

She was furious and did all she could do stop me getting the agreements signed. No matter how I explained that it was for her benefit, she kicked and screamed, and even threatened Sun Xiaofeng. He stuck with me.

Shortly afterwards an anonymous letter arrived on the desk of the General Administration of Press and Publications in Beijing. Once again it revealed details of our operation that could only come from inside knowledge. This one squarely pointed the finger at Sun Xiaofeng. He was a government official who was illegally employing foreigners. Worse than that, it went on, foreigners were taking advantage of him and using him. Only one person I knew had access to those details, and the knack for self-contradiction the letter betrayed.

For the first time in a while I tapped Shirley's birthday into my computer. This time there was nothing. I was only curious, not looking for proof that I would have to keep to myself. Yuan Bao'an had already dealt with the matter. Wuzhou was working.

They were also at work on the magazines' content. Despite their apparent invulnerability, Wuzhou was the most paranoid of all our publishers. It was explained to me that the more senior you are, the more careful you have to be.

A board of censors was appointed, including senior editors of state sponsored English language publications in Beijing. There was nothing we could do but hope they did not steal our content, which they did, but like gentlemen they refrained from using it in their print editions. Our articles began appearing on their websites instead, and only after we had published them.

I complained to Sun and Yuan.

It was Yuan who replied. 'Mark, there is nothing we can do. We cannot even complain. Those websites come under the authority of the State Council Information Office. We are colleagues.'

'But what about payment for the writers?' I asked. 'We are getting protests that their work is being stolen without their permission.' This was not true, though it should have been. Some of our contributors had complained in good humour, but they knew what was going on and that it was pointless to ask for compensation. They were actually sympathetic.

'I'll see what I can do,' Yuan said, and did nothing. Then he gave me an opportunity to stir things up.

We had been sent a review copy of a book called *Wild West China,* about Xinjiang Province, the Muslim autonomous region in northwest China where the government feared an Islamic insurrection was simmering below the surface. The book gave a comprehensive history of the chaos that had ruled the region for centuries.

In 1993, while still in the army, I spent two months in Xinjiang on a desert expedition. I knew a something of the region and the people. So I selected myself to write the review. I knew I had to be careful, but I couldn't avoid mentioning how the author sympathized with Uighurs. I sent a copy of the review to Yuan in advance. I knew it would raise concern and besides, I needed time to replace it if it was rejected, which it was, out of hand.

A journalist friend had recently started a tongue-in-cheek blog where he and a colleague were posting juicy stories about China that their agency would never go near. The blog was hosted overseas, out of reach of the censors.

'I've got this book review I can't publish,' I told him. 'You're welcome to it.'

It was up in a flash. At least it wasn't wasted.

It certainly did not get wasted. The very next day China Radio International, a government English language radio station with a website that made an art of plagiarism, had the review up in full. CRI was one of the content-pinching culprits whom Yuan had defended on the basis that they, and therefore we, were all in the same outfit. This was a chance not to be missed.

I sent a sardonic email to Yuan and Sun, with a link to the CRI webpage. 'Not only can you not protect the copyright of our material,' I wrote, 'you can't even protect the copyright of material we haven't published!' And for the hell of it: 'This proves I am right to be concerned about the confidentiality of our content inspectors. And may I ask why your — our — "colleagues" can publish this review when *that's* magazines can't?'

I sat back and waited for the reaction. It was spectacular. Sun Xiaofeng eventually tracked down the source and he must have guessed how it got onto the blog. It hardly took the brains of a government official to work that out. If he did, he never mentioned it, or accused me. I had my fun and made my point.

Tighter censorship was not the worst of my worries, even if our classified advertising now contained all the *frisson*-inducing excitement of a Halfords Manual and we were once again banned from using the adjective 'sexy' in any context whatsoever. What gave me sleepless nights was Wuzhou's attitude of ultimate ownership and control.

When our first issue appeared under their mocked-up magazine title, 'China City Series' in small print above '*that's*', and with a book number, unassailable this time thanks to their powerbase, I received a call from Yuan.

'Where are the 17,000 copies for nationwide distribution?' he asked.

'The what?'

'It was clear in our agreement,' he said. 'You are to help the government with the *deng xia liang* campaign.'

This was the first I had heard of it. I knew what the words meant, but not in this context: 'The light that shines downwards.'

'Please refer to the contract between the Yangzhou People's Government News Office and Wuzhou Chuanbo Chunbanshe,' he suggested helpfully. 'Clause 12.'

I pulled out my copy. I did remember some extremely weird wording that Wuzhou had slipped in and which Sun had attempted to explain, employing the metaphor of D-Day and the invasion of Europe in 1944. He had confused me so completely I concluded it was official nonsense and let it ride.

I checked the words again. 'Yangzhou agrees to provide free of charge, and to distribute, a number of magazines as required by the "Deng Xia Liang Project". The number of magazines, which will not exceed the current circulation (but if it does, then settlement of extra costs will be negotiated separately) is to be confirmed by Wuzhou 30 days in advance. Wuzhou will advise Yangzhou where to distribute the magazines.' I read it back over the phone to Yuan.

'You see?' he said. 'It clearly says you have to produce an edition for distribution all over China. This is the responsibility of Wuzhou Chuanbo Chubanshe. And now we are working together, it is your responsibility.'

I had long dreamt of going national with a magazine, but it would have to be very different from the city ones. I still had not worked out how. And here I was, two days too late, after we had started distributing an issue, being commanded to fulfill a dream I'd had for almost two years.

'I know what,' Yuan tried to sound helpful. 'Can you call back a few thousand of the Beijing magazine? You could take the covers off and replace them.' There was a moment of silence on the line. 'No, hang on, you don't even need to do that. Just cut out the word 'Beijing' or stick something over it.' He waited for my response. I was lost for words. So he carried on.

'Mark, you must understand. Wuzhou absolutely has to distribute these magazines to the national news offices. Our *lingdao* have been ordered to.'

Later on I worked out what was behind this. Wuzhou had been given a grant by the government. They had been paid to give the government 'face', at our expense. Not only at the expense of our own 'face', which a knocked-up national magazine would have been, making a mockery of our brand, but financially too. We were going to pay for a magazine that they had already been paid to produce. I will never know how much money Wuzhou was given by the government in return for their bright idea to publish *that's* magazines, though some clues did crop up later.

That was in the future. Right now I had to stop Yuan damaging our brand.

'All right Yuan *Laoshi*. If we have to produce a national magazine, please let me do it my way.'

Then I had a sudden idea, worth a try. 'By the way,' I tacked on as if it was an afterthought, 'Is there any chance of you contributing financially? It does say that in the agreement.'

'That could be arranged,' replied Yuan, the reluctance apparent in his voice. He stopped to think and came up with the perfect catch. 'But then we would want to insert our own pages into the magazine, after you have prepared yours and just before it went to the printers, you would have nothing to do with them...'

'...That's all right Yuan *Laoshi*, don't you worry!' He had got me and he knew it. 'We'll take care of everything.'

All of a sudden we had four magazines. I set to work to see how we could turn this to our advantage. I called up the Beijing office.

'Mike,' I said, 'You know how we edit and produce *that's Guangzhou* in Shanghai? How would you like another magazine in Beijing?'

'Sure, love to.'

I explained about the new national edition. We discussed how to create a brand new magazine in a week. All it would take was a little creative re-editing. We could do a proper job with the second issue.

'OK,' Mike was up for it. 'I can do this first one, but I'll need some extra staff for the next.'

Within ten days he had produced a national edition. If Yuan was impressed he did not show it. But he did pass on an official announcement from the State Council Information Office.

'As part of the *deng xia liang* campaign, initiated by the State Council Information Office, all regional news offices are instructed to ensure that the books published monthly by Wuzhou Chuanbo Chubanshe, under the name of *China City Series*, are distributed via your office to all places where the resident foreign community may find it, such as hotels, airports etc....' It went on a fair bit.

I was delighted. This was the first time ever that we were the ones issuing the decrees. We were at the heart of the propaganda system. We could produce a magazine and tell people, 'You WILL read this.' The tables had turned.

I faxed a copy up to Beijing and told Mike to send it to all the places that were to distribute *that's Nothing*, as we christened it. Yuan had made clear we could not call it *that's China*, yet.

Maybe later. So it was just *that's,* with an explanation of who was behind it in every issue. The official instruction from the Council Information Office would at least help us get into the state-run hotels across the country.

'What exactly is this *deng xia liang* thing?' Mike asked over the phone.

'Ah,' I said, 'It's a bit like D-Day. That's what Sun Xiaofeng told me, but he was talking utter bollocks. It took me a while to work it out.' I took a deep breath. 'Basically, the 'Outgoing' Propaganda Bureau, our dear friend Madame Wu... Remember her...?'

'Yup.'

'...Well she thinks they have the propaganda that goes overseas all sorted. Then they remembered there are heaps of foreigners living in China already, and they were worried they were overlooking them. You with me?'

'Yup.'

'So, think of the propaganda winging its way overseas as the light "shining out", got it?' Not difficult. 'Now they're keen to get the same message to the foreigners in China, and that is the "light shining down", like it does under a table lamp. It's quite neat in fact.'

Mike had been very patient. 'OK Mark, I understand. But what does this mean for us?'

The quip was out of my mouth before I could stop myself. 'Mike,' I said. 'This means the sun shines out of our arse. Or in other words, we are being told to do exactly what we have been doing for the past five years, promote life in China to the foreign community with an English language magazine! Seriously, enough sarcasm,' I remembered something. 'Apparently the *deng xia liang* campaign is still an internal Party matter, so we can't shout about it, that's what Yuan told me.'

'Mark, you just asked me to fax that notice to everyone!' Mike protested.

'Don't get logical with me Mike.' I really was turning into a propaganda bureau worker.

I let Mike get on with it. Although the national edition cost us money, we were getting our name out across China.

Let the light shine.

Chapter Seventeen

Watching Tigers Fight

There's a Chinese saying, one of the many: 'Sitting on the hill and watching the tigers fight.' It is self-explanatory.

In March 2004 the unbelievable happened. Something I never thought possible.

Brand spanking new *kanhao* were issued to *that's* magazines. One for each city. I was overjoyed. We had made it. We had disproved the doubters, shown it could be done. We were legal.

For the first time in seven years of publishing I was on the right side of the grey line that is media law in China. There were no more goal posts left for the authorities to move, no more ping-pong balls clipping the edge of the table. All I had to do was tweak the paper trail that led from the Hong Kong company to the actual business and I was home and dry. One day, some time in the future, I could reap my reward.

I should have learnt by now. Another round of trouble was about to begin.

To start with there was an extra *kanhao* for a magazine to be known as *that's China*.

We had relieved ourselves of our propaganda department duties on *that's Nothing* in January and replaced it with an English language travel magazine, *Voyage*, produced 'on behalf' of the Shanghai Tourism Bureau. At last I had made friends with them. The face of the vituperative official who had wished me dead years before was a picture when his *lingdao* welcomed me into their office. *Voyage* was working nicely. It was good to have an egg in another basket.

Yuan had seemed upset that we wanted to turn the 'light' off so soon, but he put up remarkably little fuss. Now I found out why. It was all a matter of timing. Wuzhou did not want us to produce *that's China*. They wanted to do it themselves.

I had picked up a hint when Mike Wester showed me a recruitment advertisement Yuan sent in to *that's Beijing*, 'Editors wanted for national English language magazine'. We made enquiries and were assured the project had nothing to do with *that's*, and would not conflict. Yuan had told us the name was to be *China Monthly* and its content quite different.

Then the signals started to get worrying. We planted job seekers, sent them to interviews, and listened with concern to their reports.

'Make it look just like *that's*.' The design candidate told us they had said.

I had used the imminent appearance of *China Monthly* to help me get out of *that's Nothing*. Now I realized I'd played right into Yuan's hands.

'I'm very sorry Mark,' he told me. 'The government insists we produce a national magazine. It is a condition of the *kanhao*. How can we have three city magazines and not a national one? And you didn't want to do it. You said so yourself in January.' I'd been caught again. At least I had made the switch to *Voyage* on my own terms.

We were in what I guessed was a yet another apartment of Yuan's. Property was the only place to put your money and expect a decent return, especially for government officials looking to hide money they had siphoned from the system, or their mistresses. I'm not suggesting Yuan Bao'an was one of those, but he did have a lot of apartments.

This one was near the Fragrant Hills. It was the 'villa style-living in an apartment complex' place I described at the beginning of this story.

The sitting room was barely furnished. A kitchen table sat in the middle surrounded by four chairs. A fax machine was perched on an old bedside table by the window. Some glass shelves held a collection of English and Chinese guidebooks.

Yuan made me a cup of instant coffee, the all-in-one, with powdered milk and sugar. It tasted sickly sweet and as cloying as Yuan's silvery excuses.

'But the name, Yuan *Laoshi*, you can't use our name like that.' I said. '*that's* is a brand we have built up over years.' This was still not the time to tell him I had recently secured the trademark from *Chinaweek*.

'Our *lingdao* told us that since we had such a well known name we must use it for the national magazine too,' he said. 'I understand how you feel Mark,' he slipped the sympathy in like an extra teaspoon of sugar, looking contrite.

'Then let us manage it,' I pleaded. 'You can't have two separate entities producing the same brand.'

'Out of the question. We have been clearly instructed to do this ourselves.'

Wuzhou had taken the credit for *that's* magazines to get our *kanhao*. The government had believed their bullshit. Even Wuzhou believed it. They thought they could produce a magazine because we had been paying them to let us do it for them. It was 'ability by association'. Nightmare scenarios began unfolding in my mind.

'Can we at least manage the advertising, supervise the content? Or else, can't you change the name? You know that English language names are not official for magazines.'

'Impossible,' he said. 'Mark, you do not have to worry. We are all one family now. We will work together.'

'All right,' I could play games too. 'How many copies are you going to publish?'

'I can't tell you that. It's a commercial secret.'

'Can I meet the person in charge of the project? We need to liaise at least.'

'Of course. But I do not have his number. We'll introduce you later.'

'How are you funding this?' I was battling to contain my anger, and I was wasting my breath. Wuzhou would have received a massive government propaganda handout, and Yuan would deny it.

'We are getting a little support, not much,' he lied.

My precious brand was going to be hijacked by its protectors. The dragon was flexing his wings. I could only hope the new *that's* magazine was going to be so cheap and awful that our readers would spot the rip off. It was unlikely they could produce something respectable, which I would have preferred immensely.

The first issues of *that's China* ran a series of long articles, six pages at a time, about a pork producer in South China. There were large portrait photographs of managers behind their desks and pictures of foreign businessmen shaking hands with Chinese ones across the top of a pigsty. It was classic commercial propaganda. Someone in Wuzhou was related to a pig farmer. The back cover was an advertisement for the same company. Images of sheep had been photo-shopped onto a golf course. 'Top quality pork!' the words said.

I bumped into an acquaintance on the street in Shanghai. He had a copy of *that's Shanghai* under his arm, on top was *that's China*.

'Congratulations Mark!' he shouted. 'Just picked up your new magazine!'

'Don't, please. It is hard to explain, but it has nothing to do with me.'

He looked perplexed.

'Please don't read it,' I whimpered.

'Mark, you OK?' He looked concerned. My face must have been a picture of confusion.

Now Yuan set in motion his plan to push Sun Xiaofeng and Yangzhou out of our circle. He made plain it was me who had to do the dirty work. With a cunning honed by years of shadowy politicking in Beijing, he took advantage of my desire to link the magazines as closely as possible to Gao Bang and the Hong Kong company.

I wanted to take care of Sun, in a good way. It was thanks to him we had survived all these years and I intended to reward him. I still held the vast majority of shares in the Hong Kong company. If I could secure its link to the magazines by a solid agreement between Gao Bang and Wuzhou, then I could offer Sun some of those shares and hopefully find a role that gave him the all important face.

That's your affair, Yuan told me. Sun had upset too many people in Beijing, he had to be disposed of. He was getting too big for his boots.

It was only because of Sun that we had made it into the shelter of Wuzhou. But Yuan was correct on one thing. Sun was throwing his weight around. He had just asked me to fire one of our best staff in the Beijing office.

He had asked Kitty, the office manager, to do something when she was busy for Mike. I had told Sun to go through the general managers or me. But he didn't understand western style management, reporting lines and all that other stuff that we had implemented over the years. He was a government official and assumed he could barge into our offices, get people to drop what they were doing and run his errands with a curt command.

We all had too much experience of officials barging into our offices, and Kitty had been trained to deal with them. She reported to Mike and no one else. Contribute her fiery temper, and that Sun Xiaofeng had once made a tipsy pass at Kitty at a company get-together, and you had all the ingredients for a one-girl mutiny.

Kitty told Sun Xiaofeng in no uncertain terms where to put his errand, in front of the entire staff.

Mike and I fought tooth and nail, but Sun had lost face. I never saw him so angry. Letters with government chops, faxes and emails flew from Yangzhou like volleys of Mongolian arrows. Mike and I replied, apologized, accepted liability, even told Sun it served him right, that we had warned him time and again to deal with the managers. It was no use. He threatened repercussions and even tried to delay us printing the next issue of the magazines until the matter was resolved.

Kitty had to be sacrificed. It was painful, and wrong. Our only grounds for her dismissal was that she had stood up to a government official, something she had seen Mike and I do countless times.

As the petty argument played out, Sun asked Yuan to support him. Yuan turned him down and sat back to watch, like a man sitting on a hill watching tigers fight. Once Kitty was gone, Yuan threw down another bone. Visas.

For years we had put all visas for foreign staff through Yangzhou. The Yangzhou People's Government News Office could arrange the hard-to-come-by residence permits with ease. The hitch was all our foreign staff, for official purposes, lived in Yangzhou.

Whilst we could pretend if necessary that the Shanghai foreigners were making daily business trips to the bigger city, that did not wash for Beijing. Yangzhou is hardly Slough to Beijing's London. And the regulations for foreigners' living arrangements in Beijing were tighter than Shanghai's. Mike was constantly fielding complaints that staff could not get tax rebates on rent, licences for motorbikes, or even register with the local police as required by law, because they officially lived in a city at the other end of the country.

Although he denied it, Sun Xiaofeng knew that by registering us in Yangzhou his control over us was strengthened. In the worst case, he could get us thrown out of the country. In the meantime he could genuinely say we worked for him. If I was going to get closer to Wuzhou, I had to move house from Yangzhou. I prepared for a showdown. Yuan, fully aware of the potential for a spectacle, went back up his hill.

Shanghai was easily taken care of. One by one as foreign staff moved on we put their replacements on work visas from the Gao Bang joint venture. Eventually there was only me left. My young daughter was also a Yangzhou resident. That was a little scary. My old friends Entry and Exit Shanghai took care of us.

that's Beijing foreigners were not turning over so fast. With a little foresight, and a small risk, we had put some new staff onto tourist or business visas. They were vulnerable.

Sun was the first to stretch out a claw. Irked by my manoeuvre in Shanghai, he flew to Beijing and demanded that all foreigners in the office sign new employment contracts directly with him, on the spot. Neither Mike nor I were given any warning. We prevaricated, I made up some excuses to delay, and Mike rushed round to the Beijing Entry and Exit Bureau.

The pressure from Yangzhou increased. Sun declared that I would never get visas for the staff because they were editors not consultants, and reminded me with a thinly veiled threat that he knew several were on the wrong visas entirely and risked being thrown out of the country.

That Christmas, 2003, again on the very day itself, I had a call from Yuan. I had to sort out the argument with Sun who had been complaining bitterly or else, guess what, we could not go to print with the January issue. It was futile to remind him he had asked me to do his dirty work in the first place. After another round of calls we designed a temporary compromise and got the magazine out. Yuan sat back to watch the next round.

A few days before the Chinese New Year a month later, Mike called. There was panic in his voice again. The Entry and Exit Bureau had raided the office. All foreigners without work visas had been given four days to leave the country. This was dramatic. The jokes that I would get thrown out of China had grown stale over the years. I hovered between fatalistic acceptance and the satisfaction of at last reaching this dizzy height of official disapprobation. It certainly made a good story. My sardonic telling of it was tempered by the fact that Mike was one of the illegal aliens.

I flew to Beijing and met the deportees at Starbucks. Of the half dozen, most were phlegmatic. We had dealt with worse.

I was surprised however by the reaction of the new American editor, Christiaan. He and I had been friends for years, and he had perfected the Old China Hand nothing-shocks-me-anymore attitude since his days as a news wire reporter. If anyone should have taken this in his stride it was him. But he started a mutiny.

They say never employ friends. That was difficult in China, and employees soon become friends anyway. Now I had the theory proved.

As we huddled round a small table by the window of the coffee shop, our faces as grim as the dark and rainy evening that was developing outside, Christiaan let rip.

'This whole thing sucks,' he shouted. 'You and your fucking magazines Mark. You're always getting into trouble, getting your staff into shit with you. When are you going to sort your mess out and look after people?'

He made a painful allusion to the Kitty incident. I was grateful he did not refer to it directly. Mike looked at me with sympathy, but this was my mutiny now, not his. Christiaan had already had a go at him.

'And the magazine's shit too. You'll never repeat the success of the *Scene*.' Christiaan had been involved in the *Beijing Scene*, back in the day. 'You're just not cool.'

One of the sub editors mumbled his assent, another young American who I had down as the impressionable type. It was impossible to tell what the others were thinking. My old friend Jamie Wilson was there. His face was blank but he looked like he was waiting for me to take charge. That was encouraging.

Christiaan hadn't finished. 'You have no idea what's really going on in Beijing, in arts, music, theatre. You're just producing another expat rag like all the other rubbish out there.' That hurt. And I was thinking, hang on a second Christiaan. You're the editor. That's your job. I didn't want to get involved in an argument about the magazine. Not now. I let him carry on.

'The whole thing is a waste of time. I'm wasting my fucking time. I've got better things to do than edit your fucking rag. This fucking meeting is a waste of time. I can fucking well take care of myself.'

He had given me my opening, and a chance to carry on where he left off.

Before he could say it, I interrupted. He had put the words in my mouth. 'If that's the case Christiaan. Then why don't you fuck off right now?'

'Yeah, I will.'

'Good.'

The tension left with him. We got down to solving the problem. Everyone being thrown out, apart from Christiaan, was to go to Hong Kong and return with formal employment invitation visas from Gao Bang Beijing. We would do things by the book. Mike could deal with the Entry and Exit Bureau for the paperwork and at the same time switch the Yangzhou staff over to Gao Bang. He faced a massive challenge. It would be all but impossible to get the staff away from Yangzhou without a chop from Sun.

Jamie asked a question. 'Mark, our competition are already talking to our clients, telling them we are in trouble again. You know what that means.' I did. Funny how these stories got out so fast. 'What are we going to tell them?'

I thought and smiled. 'Fight bullshit with bullshit. I know it's daft, but stupider things can happen. Tell the clients I arranged the bust because I wanted to get rid of Christiaan. I had some staff kicked out and only allowed the ones I wanted back in. Saved me a fortune in termination packages.'

'You serious?' asked Jamie.

'Absolutely.'

Within a month we had all the foreign staff on Gao Bang visas. They even said 'editor' on the editors' ones. Mike had pulled it off without any of the necessary documents from Yangzhou. Even he could barely believe his luck. He had caught a clerk at the Entry and Exit Bureau when she was struggling with a translation into English and helped her out.

Sun seethed with fury. Yuan had watched the show impassively. As part of my strategy to get the staff out of Yangzhou's grasp, I had offered him the chance to put the editorial staff onto Wuzhou's books, knowing full well he could never do it. A call to a mole on the staff of *that's China* had confirmed that.

The game was going well again. I had secured my team and I had my own offices in Shanghai and Beijing. I had three domestic advertising agencies, one in Joanna's name in Guangzhou, in Lily's in Shanghai, and Mike Wester's fiancée Toni had done us the same favour in Beijing. I hoped the agencies would soon be superfluous, but they might be useful, depending on the terms of the agreement I was going to make with Wuzhou. All the pieces on the board were in place.

Now all I had to do was get the agreement between Gao Bang and Wuzhou. I turned my back on bloodied Sun Xiaofeng. I'd patch him up later. And walked up the hill to negotiate with Yuan.

'There is something you must understand Mark, before we start this next step,' Yuan told me over the kitchen table.

I waited as he let his severity sink in.

This was the moment I had been waiting for, fighting for, over seven long years. At last, having often wondered if it would ever be possible, my exit plan for the business was in sight. I was going to secure the prize for all my hard work, see my investment turn into the promise of a real financial reward. It was for this that I had ploughed all the profits back into the business, held onto my shares, fought off competitors and my own partners. Maybe those partners, Shirley and Sun, would at last realize what I had been trying to do, for them too, and we could all be friends again.

Yuan knew my position. I had repeated it often enough, and I knew his. Wuzhou's official remit was to promote China to the resident international community. *that's* magazines did that. I wanted to build a media business and secure my interest in it. I was fully aware of the delicacy of the situation, thanks to the half-formed Chinese media industry regulations. I knew there would be charades to play, that it would have to appear as if we were under Wuzhou's control. 'I am happy to be used, Mr Yuan,' I once told him, 'so long as I get my just reward.' He had expressed understanding.

He cleared his throat, looked straight at me and asked me the question. That question. 'Do you want to co-operate?

'Yes please Yuan *Laoshi*. Yes I do.'

Yuan Bao'an left his eyes on me as he sat back, one hand on the table. There was no indication that he was happy or even relieved to hear my answer. He knew he held all the cards.

One by one he laid them on the table, starting with an ace.

'Mark, you must understand something first: this will not be a negotiation between equals.' There was no hostility in his voice. If anything there was patience. 'We can discuss terms and conditions, and guarantees and all the other things one covers in a negotiation, but I must make very clear, at the end of the day, that what we, Wuzhou decide, will be final.'

I kept quiet. OK I thought, it's not the first time I have heard this from an official in China. And I had dealt with it too. They negotiate from a position of political power, using intimidation, I use my commercial strength, and wits.

'There's something else,' Yuan said. 'I put the matter to my *lingdao,* and they do not agree to make a deal with Gao Bang. It must be made directly with the advertising companies.'

This was bad. A nasty surprise. Yuan had let me believe he would work with Gao Bang and used that promise to convince me to get rid of Sun Xiaofeng, and satisfy my hope to make Sun happy afterwards. Although I controlled the advertising companies, they were not in my name.

'Yuan *Laoshi,*' I said. 'You know perfectly well why the contract must be with Gao Bang. We had a perfectly satisfactory consultancy agreement with Yangzhou. All we have to do is transfer that to Wuzhou.'

'Wuzhou is not allowed to enter into a consultancy agreement for publishing,' he said.

'What do you mean, 'not allowed to'?' I asked as calmly as I could. 'Consultancy agreements are perfectly normal and legal.'

'We are part of the government. It is illegal for us to enter into an agreement with a foreign consultancy company.'

'That's rubbish Yuan *Laoshi,*' I could not help myself. 'Yangzhou is also part of the government and government at all levels in China uses all sorts of consultancy companies. Why just the other day, KPMG, a massive foreign consultancy, came to me on behalf of a Shanghai district government to ask me to help produce a brochure for them.'

I had riled him. He fixed his stare across the table at me, his eyes cold and stern. After a moment for effect, he said with an icy ferocity. 'Mark, if I say something is illegal, it is illegal.'

This was bullshit. The sickening sensation that I was about to be taken advantage of was sinking in.

'Now, shall we get back to the agenda?' He softened again.

The best thing I could do was shut up and listen. I needed time to find a way out of this.

As I sat in silence, my mind spinning, Yuan went through his list of demands. I scribbled them down in my notebook, assessing my chances of countering them:

'Wuzhou is now the publisher and de facto owner of *that's* magazines because Wuzhou holds the *kanhao*. Up until now, *that's* magazines have been illegal. Now that Wuzhou has taken over and secured the *kanhao,* they are legal.'

I loved the irony of that last bit, especially since Wuzhou had been publishing us for two years with book numbers. I fully expected Yuan to think he owned us, and was happy to let him think so, but I was going to make sure I kept control of the business. Oh, and I had the name. But I wasn't going to tell him that.

'Wuzhou will have complete control of editorial content.'

No surprise there.

'The editorial department will 'belong' to Wuzhou.'

I'd catch him out on the visa problem later. I knew he couldn't get visas for foreign editors because he hadn't for the ones at *that's China*. He didn't know I knew that.

'Wuzhou will have first rights and final say on any supplementary editions, such as guides, or special issue magazines for other cities, for example Qingdao.'

I guessed he wanted to work from his holiday home.

'Wuzhou is only willing to sign agreements with the three advertising agencies. However, the business will continue to be run exactly as it is at the moment.'

That was a contradiction, but it was obviously me who had to work it out. And if the deal really did have to be with the agencies, I'd better start working out how to link them to Gao Bang.

Yuan again: 'Since we will be using proper *kanhao*, the fees will increase. The figure will be decided later.'

Hang on, I thought, you now 'own' the magazines, and you just said nothing will change, but we are going to pay more for the privilege of doing your job for you, which you have probably received a massive government grant for. This is unfair... One more thought though: we could retail the magazines now they had *kanhao*. Maybe a way to make more money and pay for higher fees... next?

'All "internal contradictions" with Yangzhou and Shirley Li must be resolved by Mark Kitto before any contract is signed.'

So I got to finish the dirty work, thanks, and if Wuzhou 'owned' the magazines now, how come the 'internal contradictions' as Yuan so quaintly put it, were my problem?

'Wuzhou will have no commercial liability or responsibility for the magazines. It is Mark Kitto's responsibility to manage the business.'

The hypocrisy was fine by me. No change there, though it would all depend on the agreements.

'that's China however, remains fully under control of Wuzhou and will operate independently yet in co-ordination with the three city magazines.'

Farce. I got responsibility for the money-making magazines' success, which was based heavily on our brand name, and paid for the privilege, whilst he got to play havoc with that same brand name. No. This was going to be my key sticking point and negotiating card when we got down it.

He was getting to the bottom of the list.

'Wuzhou will nominate a Chinese editor for each magazine (only Chinese nationals can be editors-in-chief) and supervisory personnel in the accounts departments of each office. Salaries for these people will be paid by Mark Kitto.'

So the censors moved into our offices. We could deal with that. Might even help a bit if we got to know them better. But let them 'supervise' the accounts, when we were responsible for the financial success of the magazines, and paying a set fee? He must be joking.

Finally. 'There might be a possibility of forming a joint venture with *that's China* if Mark Kitto is willing to invest, but this will not be possible for the city magazines because Wuzhou does not have the staff or resources necessary.'

That really was taking the piss. I *might* be offered the opportunity to bale out a loss making pig-farming manual, but was denied the opportunity to lock in my interests in the profitable magazines I had built. He had just made clear what he was really after.

'Thank you Yuan *Laoshi*.' I put down my pen when he had finished. 'I clearly understand your position. If it is all right by you I will go away and work out how to accommodate it, and how to protect my commercial interests in whatever agreement we sign. I am sure you appreciate the need for that don't you?'

'But of course Mark.' He smiled, like an indulgent executioner permitting the condemned to write his last letter.

'Shall we meet again tomorrow?' I asked. 'I don't need much time.'

I locked myself up in my hotel room. I opened my notebook at the latest page and turned on my laptop. Despite the ominous demands, the underlying threats, the clear attempt Yuan was making to take over the business, I relished the situation. With a perverse sense of enjoyment I sat down to tackle his issues one by one. I had got out of similar situations in the past. And I was driven by the knowledge that once this one was resolved I would be running three magazines with their very own *kanhaos*. There was plenty of opportunity, once again, to turn a disadvantage to an advantage. This was my last big challenge. It was me against Yuan. In my opinion we were evenly matched. I began to type.

I faxed over my proposal the next morning then followed in person once Yuan had read through it. He objected on the spot to a couple of points, but his reception was otherwise warm.

'Let me speak to my *lingdao*,' he said. 'I'll get back to you.'

Over the next few weeks Yuan gradually chipped away, one by one, at every level of protection I had worked into the proposal bearing in mind his *lingdao's* likely objections. I thought my wording was a masterpiece that would please the officials yet also contained a subtext of commercial practicality.

I was wrong. He cut it, paragraph by paragraph, all the protection, block by block, until I was left with no foundation, let alone the framework, for a real business. He stonewalled. My walls came crumbling down.

So I took up my sticking point and laid into Yuan about *that's China*, which had begun approaching our advertising clients, offering ridiculously cheap deals, or free introductory offers, whilst it continued to churn out vapid articles about Chinese folk customs, quaint minority peoples, and the health benefits of pork. It had also started pinching wholesale from our bar and restaurant directories, but because they were trying to squeeze in three cities' worth they only reprinted the lists from the letter A to a quarter of the way through the alphabet. It was a small comfort that our readers had cottoned on that the magazine was a cheap imitation. Distribution points were commonly chucking it into the bin when it arrived in ever decreasing numbers.

'Yuan *Laoshi*, how can I sign these agreements which make me responsible for the business of the city magazines, and liable to pay you a large fee,' which had been set an astronomical 100,000 yuan per month, 'whilst you are allowing *that's China* to damage our business like this?'

'How can we be damaging your business?' he replied. 'We are not making any money from *that's China*. How can we affect your sales when we are selling so cheaply? Surely, if we were charging more, then we would be damaging your business.'

The commercial naivety, no, the plain stupidity, was unbelievable. 'That's precisely my point!' I shouted down the phone. 'I would actually be happy if you were getting more money! Can't you understand that?' I sighed in frustration as I hung up.

I was beginning to run down again. I had single-handedly re-launched *Voyage* and over the same months been bouncing back and forth between lawyers, cities, and publishing partners, trying to solve the conundrum of how to work with Wuzhou. To keep me distracted Shirley, from wherever she was in the world, had launched a spiteful campaign of slander, sending letters from her personal lawyers to all and sundry. I played along and got her to make a full retraction, but it was a waste of time and precious energy. She lobbied and exasperated Yuan and Sun in turn, trying to insinuate her advertising company, Klau and Benedict Hong

Kong's joint venture partner, back into control of the magazines' operation, all the while expecting me to buy out her shares in the Hong Kong company. Talk about 'internal contradiction'.

More depressing and spirit sapping was the gradual realisation, growing clearer every drawn out day, that quite the opposite of helping me get closer to my goal, Wuzhou was pushing me further from it. I had turned to the electronic score box beside the fencing *piste*, convinced I had made a hit, and the wrong light was shining.

It looked like I had met my match at last. These guys were powerful, commercially ignorant and potentially harmful, and determined to get their own way. They did not talk sense, they did not obey any rules. They made them up.

I remembered something else Yuan had said a while ago. 'Mark, now you are working with Wuzhou, you know there is nowhere else you can go. We are the State Council Information Office. We are the top of the ladder.'

I had run up against the very heart of the old school Party propaganda system. It was beating strongly even if it had been on a life support machine since the day it was born. Whilst on the periphery there might be signs of self-sustaining life that eked out a precarious existence, at the system's centre the outdated, deluded, expensive and embarrassingly bad — if only they could see it through the eyes of the people they thought they were impressing — Chinese centrally controlled media had not changed for decades.

I had hoped to make a difference, believed my own delusion that I could. I had tried to beat the system, do something useful, and make an honest fortune. How stupid. But I still wasn't finished.

Chapter Eighteen

Calling Major Tom

'Well, Mark, you're fucked.'

I was with an Australian lawyer, a friend with long experience in China, and a habit of straight talking despite, or maybe encouraged by, his distinguished reputation. He had agreed to look over the final draft of the Wuzhou agreements with the advertising companies, over lunch.

'Then again,' he said. 'You're not entirely fucked. These agreements leave you in control of the business, just, and for as long as things go smoothly. You could basically run it and milk it for all you can get. You might make some decent cash. But in the end you are well and truly fucked. You'll never walk away with anything like the value you deserve, or hope for.'

I had reached the same conclusion. It was not comforting to have it confirmed.

'Can't you find someone else to look after you?' he asked, meaning another government department.

'No. We're at the very top. There is nowhere else to go,' I said. 'These guys control everyone who moves, who writes, who distributes, who does anything on paper in Chinese media. They could ban this menu if they wanted.' I laid my palm on the plastic folder between us. He smiled at my feeble joke.

'What about Hong Kong? Have you thought of that?'

I was thinking about it, back to the time when Asia City Publishing, smart people with well-run city magazines in Hong

Kong, Singapore and Bangkok, had approached me immediately after I bought out Kathleen in 2000. They offered a fair share swap. I described the massive risks in China media and confessed I didn't even own *that's* magazines. No one did. I simply had a company linked to them by a slender thread and personally controlled their day-to-day operation. Still they wanted a deal. It was an attractive offer but I turned it down. I had just secured full control of my baby and I wanted to raise it myself. That opportunity had long since passed. There was no one else I could think of who would be interested, let alone have the influence to see off Wuzhou.

Then quite by chance, I met someone who was interested and possibly did have the influence.

It was at an awards gala organized by *New Weekly*, a Chinese language glossy magazine. I was invited to present an award. If nothing else, I had made it onto the B list.

The schmoozefest was held in the grand ballroom of the Shanghai Hyatt in the Jinmao Tower, the hotel I had upset with my joke about the mile high club, back in our early issues. New Weekly was based in Guangzhou and run by some lively Cantonese editors, which endeared me to it, plus there was an interview with me they had run some years ago. Joanna came along to help me spot the right people, some of whom she had known in Guangzhou.

We were shown to a top table by the stage. Flora Zhang, a former Miss Hong Kong, now successful fashion designer, and her regular Shanghai companion Mi Qiu, the Shanghai modern artist who had featured in our first ever issue of *Ish*, were already there. I air kissed both.

There was another Hong Kong Chinese I did not recognize at the table. He was wearing a tailor-made suit and his long hair was swept back to where it touched the back of his collar. He was tall, a little overweight and looked sophisticated, confident. I marked him down for a banker. He stood up and introduced himself in perfect, lazy toned, public school English.

'How do you do, I'm Anthony. From Tom Group. I've heard about you Mark. You've done a good job with *that's* magazines. I read it every time I'm in town.' I thanked him.

I knew something of Tom Group too. It was an acquisitive media company owned by Li Ka Shing, Hong Kong's biggest businessman. Tom had started out as a dot.com and then switched the money that flooded in from investors into print media. An IPO connected to Li has no trouble raising funds. They still had a major 'online presence' as the lingo put it, but the money, and expansion, was going into print and television.

I wanted, I needed, very much, to talk to this guy. Tom Group might be the perfect saviour for *that's* magazines. They were influential, powerful even thanks to Li. He had built the massive Oriental Plaza development in the very heart of Beijing. And they were commercial, corporate. They were real businessmen. How could I make an overture? My mind raced.

We sat across the table from Anthony. Throughout the dinner, while the small talk crossed back and forth and we clapped as the procession of awardees trooped onto the stage, I sized him up out of the corner of my eye. I was on tenterhooks. He looked about the same age as me. I was careful to impress, as subtly as possible.

The only time I made a fool of myself was on the stage. I noticed none of my fellow presenters were saying much. Surely that was wrong. I had seen these shows on TV. We had to sing for our supper didn't we? I remembered the introduction to the interview I had given *New Weekly*. I had never forgotten it, because my Chinese staff teased me about it. When my turn came to present my award, I was prepared.

'Ladies and gentlemen,' I hunched down to the microphone and spoke in Chinese. 'You must forgive my pronunciation as I read out the name of the recipient of this award, but then, as loyal readers of *New Weekly*, as all of us here tonight are...' the gentle sarcasm did not raise even a snigger, I carried on regardless, '... You might recall the first lines of an interview I gave the magazine a few years ago. They read,' I paused dramatically before the quote, upping the pitch of my voice slightly, ' "Mark Kitto, in his atrociously accented Mandarin, said..."' I paused again, for the self-deprecatory joke to sink in.

It did sink, like a stone. No one even smiled. I remembered too late that in China you do not take the mickey out of yourself. Such an idea is utterly alien to a culture obsessed with face. I broke the stunned silence I had created.

'So without further ado,' I stuttered, 'the award for best-dressed-in-his-spare-time actor, singer and restaurant owner of the year,' or whatever it was for, 'goes to...' I read out the name with as much élan as I had left, which wasn't much.

The compere stepped up to the mike. 'We're sorry to say that so-and-so cannot be with us tonight to accept his award.' He spoke clearly and professionally into the microphone, which was at perfect height for him, 'So I will accept it for him.' Laughs all round.

I slunk back to the table. Everyone was too polite or confused to say anything about my *faux pas*.

'They probably thought you really were upset at the magazine,' Joanna whispered, 'and that you were getting your own back.'

'Oh hell,' I replied. 'That's the last time I try to make a joke in public in China. My staff love it when I goof around in my speeches at our parties.'

'That's because they're your staff.' Joanna delivered the crushing put-down, a wife's privilege.

'Enough!' I hissed.

As the party broke up, Anthony came over.

'We must have a chat Mark. Meet up for a beer sometime. I'd love to hear about *that's*.'

'And I'd love to hear about Tom, and your plans for mainland China.'

'I'll call you,' he said, and left. I said a quiet prayer.

I turned to Joanna as I watched his retreating back, 'That guy is my only hope.' She squeezed my hand.

It was not long before I got the call. I tried to keep my expectations in check. I felt like a drowning man. I had to keep calm. We met at T8, an expensive fusion restaurant. We went through the British ritual of first acquaintance. Schools were slipped into the conversation after the places where we were brought up, university, army — his brother had been both a Para and Royal Marine, an interesting history and entrée to five minutes of gentle probing back and forth — and our professional careers. Anthony had been a banker. I had guessed right.

Then he started pumping me for information. How had I set up the magazines? What was the secret of our success? What was our structure? What did I think of the Chinese language market? In return he gave me a lesson in Hong Kong corporate speak using words I knew from the back pages of *The Economist*. He also described, in terms I could understand, Tom's plans for the mainland.

Tom was a corporate beast. Nothing wrong with that, but their trajectory had been very different from my experience of pulling myself up by the bootstraps, sustained by free sushi. They expanded by acquisition. They did deals over expensive dinners. They had purchased some of the best magazines in Taiwan, leaving the management in place. The idea was to bring them over to the mainland one by one, and use them and their experience to build a print media empire in China. They had recently established a landmark joint venture with a major Chinese publisher, more symbolic than practical. It brought them into the complicated inner circle of the Chinese publishing world. They were building some serious *guanxi* at high levels. It sounded impressive.

Now for the bad news. Tom was not interested in foreign language media. I felt the water closing over my head. Then I remembered what Anthony had said about buying decent-sized media companies that were profitable. I might not have a proper company as such, but my business was profitable. There was a straw. I grasped for it.

'Yes, well, we just passed the three million a year mark,' I threw in when money came round again. 'Not bad considering where we started.'

'Profit?' asked Anthony. Damn.

'No, turnover I'm afraid.' He looked less interested.

'Yuan?'

'Oh no, US.'

His interest perked up again. We talked more about how *that's* magazines worked, where the money went and why. Then I made my pitch.

'Anthony, let me explain why I'm keen to talk to you guys.' Over the past few days I had thought through what I was going to say.

'It's like this. I have a successful business but it's not safe. I am operating in a way so grey it is black. My future certainly looks black with my current publishing partner.'

He was paying attention.

'I have held on tight to the majority share of my company, and complete control of the business, and fought off God knows how many people, because I have always hoped that one day I'd find a safe home for it, an exit plan, which was impossible to put in place when we started.'

I took a deep breath and crossed my fingers under the table.

'If I can find a company, or someone, who can offer me a safe haven for my business, I will give in return, for free, a major stake in it. I am prepared to sacrifice a large amount of what I have put in, built and held onto, in return for security and the chance to keep growing and one day benefit in real terms.'

'What do you mean exactly?' Anthony asked.

'All right,' I leant over the table. 'Say Tom was interested in my business. I think Tom has the ability, thanks to Li Kai Shing's influence, and your expansion plans for China, which means you know the right people, to provide a secure way to publish *that's* magazines and protect them from the attacks that I have faced, and will continue to face when I walk away from Wuzhou. If you can offer that security, I will give you a large share of the business.'

Anthony looked confused. In his corporate world it was not normal to be offered a big stake in a profitable business for no money, not even a request for buy back options or share swaps or some other complicated financial scheme that I knew nothing about, and had no interest in. After seven years of fighting I wanted peace. I wanted someone else to face down the goons. I wanted to get on with publishing. I knew there would be a nasty fight with Wuzhou. I would have to explain that to Tom, and how I was confident of dealing with it. First I had to get them interested.

'I know it sounds crazy,' I finished off, 'But that's what I am offering. Shares in a profitable media business in return for a safe home for it. Simple as that.'

Anthony rested his chin on his hands and thought hard. Then he looked up and said with the air of a London banker who's had an idea over a pint in a Chelsea pub: 'I think you should have a chat with our new CEO of Tom Group China. Let me give you his number.'

After that dinner I walked for a couple of blocks to let my excitement calm down. It didn't work, so I dropped into a bar for a quiet whisky. I sat up at the bar, lost in my own world as the rowdiness of any weeknight in Shanghai swirled around me.

This might work.

Christ.

There was going to be one hell of a fight with Wuzhou. The mother of all fights. But what choice was there? Watch my creation slowly die the death of a thousand cuts? I smiled at the *double entendre*. I must be in a good mood if I was making puns with myself. How many 'cuts' had they made to our content already? Enough 'sexual' references to make even a bar girl blush. Would certainly confuse her. I laughed quietly into the rim of the glass, my elbows splayed low across the wooden bar top.

Or give it one last shot? No, not the whisky. I was over that. No way I could get drunk tonight even if I tried. Too much to think about. One last shot at saving my business with Tom.

I needed to see what they could offer. How strong were they really? How brave? They better have good enough *guanxi* to put Wuzhou back in their box when they went crazy.

The first of the 'suits' came to my office a week later. Ekkehard Rathgeber was wearing it. Tall and immaculately turned out, the CEO of Tom China brought with him an energy and can-do spirit that had me on the edge of my seat and the pair of us firing off ideas like school boys who have dreamt up a wicked prank.

We had a lot in common. Ekkehard had set up the German publishing giant Bertelsmann's operation in China. Blocked by tight laws governing book distribution, he invented a 'book club' that now covered the whole country. The story was legendary.

Like me, Ekkehard had fought and clawed his way to success, making up the rules where there weren't any, apologizing when the authorities caught up with him and pushing his way round them as they invented new regulations. But he had been working in a much grander scheme of things, with a big name behind him. He had met and dealt with the biggest names in the publishing authorities too. Best of all, we shared a belief — although mine was a little worse for wear just then — that anything could be done in China. There was always a way.

I started the serious talk with the all-important word: *kanhao*.

'Absolutely no problem,' Ekkehard said in his word perfect, clipped German English. 'They cannot stop us. We make an arrangement with a publisher, they rent us a *kanhao*, we put their name on the cover like all the other magazines do, and there you go.'

'But,' I hated having to say this. It was best to get it out in the open. 'Wuzhou are going to fight like mad, and they are powerful.'

'Who are these guys?' Ekkehard waved a hand. 'For sure, they are publishers yes? You don't want to work with them but you do with us and another publisher? So what? What can they do?'

'Well, according to them they can decide if something is illegal,' I suggested.

'Illegal? How could they say we are illegal if we are simply doing what everyone else does,' he paused for a split second, 'and they themselves have been doing with you in the first place. For how long did you say? Come on Mark. Do not worry. We can deal with them.'

I did worry. But I could not help being affected by Ekkehard's enthusiasm. I was beginning to feel better than I had for a couple of months. He was stirring my will, for fighting and publishing, especially the publishing.

'Now, what sort of deal are we talking?' Ekkehard was getting down to business.

I couched my proposal in open-ended terms. It was basically

what I had said to Anthony.

'Tom will only be interested in a controlling stake.' Ekkehard was point blank on that.

'If that means 51 per cent and I can manage my company with reasonable autonomy, I can consider it,' I replied.

'Yah, for sure,' Ekkehard was quick to comfort me. 'We have seen what you have done. We would not want to interfere.' I believed him. 'Now what about the price?'

Again I repeated what I had said to Anthony. Safety in return for shares.

'Mark,' Ekkehard sat forward, suddenly earnest, 'may I give you some advice?' He was a year older than me and experienced in a similar but different way. I had tried to hide the sense of helplessness that had been eating me since Wuzhou had slammed the door in my face. This man held the key to my escape. I was not ashamed to show it. I would be tough if the situation required, but I still had a bit of bouncing back to do.

He spoke softly, with experience, 'Mark, do not undervalue yourself. For sure,' that was his catchphrase, his icebreaker for every other pronouncement, 'we are business people at Tom. You must behave like one too. I understand your situation and your feelings, but don't give yourself away. You must get something up front. Think of what you have put in.'

'Thank you Ekkehard.' I was humbled. 'I'll have a think.'

'You do that,' he sat back. 'Let's get some basic ideas worked out. Then I can report back to my board and we'll take it from there.'

We got stuck in. My mood swung higher as we discussed how to move the operation into Tom, how to find a publisher, and how to do so with the least impact to our sales. Now I was confident I could trust this slick, compassionate, suit wearing CEO, I revealed my master plan, as I thought of it.

Wuzhou was going to come after us. No question. They sincerely believed they owned *that's* magazines outright. If I produced a facsimile of the magazines with anyone else, no matter how powerful, there'd be a dust-up of such epic proportions, China could invade Taiwan and no one would notice.

So, I explained, let's leave them with *that's* magazines. Ekkehard looked concerned. Hardly surprising. He thought he was going to buy them.

I went into more detail. Although the brand name was undeniably a massive asset and I owned it, what I valued more was ability to produce the magazines. That meant the team, the operation, the client base and all our knowledge, skill and reputation.

'Look,' I said. 'Wuzhou has already started destroying the brand's value with *that's China*.'

I repeated a homemade maxim: 'It is not the value of your business in China that counts. It is your ability to do business.' I was not talking about business ability as in physical ability or skill, I was talking about the licences, the opportunity to do business. He understood.

We could build the value once we were safe with Tom. *that's* would disappear anyway or even better perhaps, at least just as good: Wuzhou would beg us to keep them going.

'But then how do we compete? How do we build a new brand?' Ekkehard said.

'There's the catch, the beauty of this.' I was excited to be telling someone the idea I had been sitting on since the quiet whisky after my meeting with Anthony.

'First of all we go weekly.' I watched for his reaction. He nodded, waiting for more. I was thrilled by the idea of a true events magazine, an end to those bar and restaurant directories. We could run reviews of events that were ongoing. No more: 'If you go to this it might be like this.' We could say: 'Last night we saw this, and it was awful/good/brilliant, and this is why. Now go see it tomorrow.' I couldn't wait. No need to go into those details yet with Ekkehard. I gave him what he wanted to hear.

'Generally, though costs increase, but there are clever ways to control that, your monthly revenues double when you go weekly from monthly.'

'Can you give me a spreadsheet on that?'

'Of course.'

'What's next?'

'The clients. Any existing clients get offered ads in the weekly for as many months as their existing contract. Then they switch to the weekly rates. *that's* will have disappeared, at least as everyone knows it. They will have no alternative and it will be obvious to them that we are the *that's* team producing the weeklies'

'How?'

'No one else can produce the quality we do.'

'For sure, but what about the name?'

'This is the best bit.' I felt like I was in a sales meeting with a client. 'We're already using it, and half of our readers know the magazine by it.' He perked up.

'It's our unofficial Chinese name. Sounds catchy in English too.'

I had not meant to tell Ekkehard. Only two people knew I had applied for the trademark, Lily and a lawyer. It looked like Ekkehard needed a final confidence boost.

'Zai.' I said it. Pronounced 'ds' and an 'i' as in 'eye'. In Chinese it means 'at'. We had been known as *Zai Shanghai, Zai Guangzhou,* and *Zai Beijing* by our Chinese audience and partners since the day each magazine launched. Even *Clueless in Guangzhou* had been *Zai Guangzhou.* And if we were to be the top English language city magazine in China, selectively given away for free but also sold on newsstands, my ultimate aim and the final step in creating a real city magazine, then we needed a Chinese name that also worked in English. *Zai* would work for anyone who spoke even the most basic Chinese and any tourist with a copy of the Lonely Planet China Guide who had once asked where the lavatory was. *'Cesuo zai nali?'*

I showed it to Ekkehard in its Chinese character on the cover of our latest annual Shanghai guide. I think that was the clincher. I had shown him I had a plan that involved expansion, particularly towards the Chinese market. He looked impressed.

If we continued to produce *that's* for Wuzhou it would be under our terms. In our own time we'd take the clients over to the new weeklies and let *that's* die a peaceful death, or languish under the auspices of Yuan. It was going to be sad, and difficult to explain to people whose opinion I valued, but my goal was to produce real magazines, which made a difference and money. We would still do that. We were going to do it even better than before.

I waited nervously to hear back from Ekkehard. To me we seemed the perfect match. I couldn't help daydreaming. Once I had got my existing business safely wrapped up in Tom's corporate packaging there was so much more that could be done. I longed to do a decent Chinese version of *that's*. The market was wide open.

When it came, only a week later, the response from Tom's board was positive. Then almost as quickly they changed their minds. Ekkehard came over in person to apologize. I was touched by his decency. We weren't a big enough fish. I understood, but I was gutted. I resigned myself to making the best of the short business life left to me by Wuzhou.

Then Ekkehard called again. He had spent a long international flight beside his boss. We were back on. They wanted to start due diligence as soon as possible. I made my offer. Three hundred thousand US for me, three million yuan loan at nominal interest to help tide over the new company that I would set up and retain 49 per cent of and would own the new magazines. They accepted.

'Own the magazines'. Those three words meant the world to me. With their legal and corporate expertise, Tom was going to make me a shareholder in the business I had invested in and given my heart and soul to, which I had built to four offices, 120 staff and almost a hundred thousand copies of magazines a month. I guessed the business, if all the regulatory and political problems could be solved, was worth about ten million US dollars. I like to think that was conservative. I was sacrificing 51 per cent, giving it away.

I was more than happy, I was deliriously happy. I could escape from Wuzhou's slow strangulation. We were safe. My team that had worked incredibly hard was safe. I could pass on shares as bonuses or options to the senior managers, the ones who had stood by me through thick and thin, like Lily, and Mike Wester, or Leo who had driven the sales ever higher. Real shares in a real and profitable company. This was a dream come true.

Lily and Leo knew of my plans and the basics of the negotiations with Tom. Now I briefed the general managers. They would all be involved in the due diligence but more important, they had to understand what I was doing, why we needed to do it, and how it would affect them.

There were reservations. Although I had tried to explain to them all, when I saw us heading inexorably into the jaws of Wuzhou, that we were Gao Bang Ltd, a magazine making company, like a king maker, everyone thought of themselves as an employee of *that's*. It was one of the keys to our success. We all believed in *that's* as a brand and what it stood for. Me more than anyone. Now the boss, one of the two creators, was telling them to demolish it.

I smiled as I remembered one of Kathleen's tirades. 'I started this, so I can destroy it!' she had screamed. She had started *Clueless*, no question. But at the time of the outburst she was talking about our fifty-fifty partnership. I was going to carry out the threat myself. I was going to destroy *that's* in order to save it.

It was difficult and delicate work. I spoke to the managers individually. Mike Wester in Beijing took the most convincing, not because he saw any future with Wuzhou. He had been in the frontline of our skirmishes so he knew how life was going to turn out if we stayed with them. His problem was that he had personally created a *that's* magazine, and did not want to see it disappear.

Mike Cole in Shanghai played along without hesitation. In no time he had produced a plan for a weekly. He was good at plans. I was only just discovering he was not so good at managing.

From the head office a couple of blocks away I was uncovering some unpleasant details of what had been going on in the Shanghai office under Cole's stewardship. Worst was the culture of small-minded divisiveness he had encouraged between the Shanghai staff and the other magazines. Where I had once praised good ideas that could be passed from magazine to magazine, he encouraged the search for mistakes and opportunities to criticise. Not my idea of constructive in-house competition or collaboration. In fact it sickened me.

As we talked about the set up with Tom, Mike Cole kept returning to the question of where he fitted in. He liked to look after himself. I had discovered that early on when he got me over a barrel on his appointment as general manager. He knew I was stuck at the time. I had been paying him a small fortune for a year of housekeeping and some doorstep gossip. I decided he was not going to fit in with Tom. He would find out when his contract was not renewed.

Lily and Leo had different issues. They were both Shanghainese. They did not like Hong Kongers and true to the spirit of their native city, they did not like fights they thought could be avoided.

Lily had been through every battle by my side, more often than not right in the thick of it, sometimes on her own whilst I was away. It was she who dealt with the tax bureau attack set up by Shirley and then endured Shirley's bitter invective in an email barrage copied to Sun and Yuan. Sun Xiaofeng had rounded on her when he could not get his way with me. And there were countless other occasions when she had taken my flak.

She deserved a break more than anyone. But Lily's main worry was she was not up to standard as an accountant for Tom. She was right. I did not want to tell her before it was all confirmed that I was arranging for her to go on a proper accountancy course, at the expense of the new company. In the meantime she asked me why could we not stay with Wuzhou? We had the *kanhaos* and were making money. Why rock the boat again?

I asked her back, 'Lily, hypothetically, which would you prefer if you had to choose: a slow painful death or a sudden and quick end?'

'I would rather put it off,' she replied.

'You mean the slow painful death?'

'I suppose so, yes.'

Leo was thinking along similar lines, but his concern was losing sales in the chaos of the changeover. That would affect his personal income. He was regularly earning the highest salary of all of us, and deserved it. Annual sales were on their way to four million US dollars by the end of the year.

I joked with him. 'Leo, you know that once we've pulled this off you and the other managers will be getting shares in a real company that is going to own the business we have created. I will be giving them as bonuses, or options, or making people pay for them, like any normal private company. Here's how it works for you. I have already explained how we bring the clients with us.

The less you lose along the way, the cheaper the shares for you. You keep the temporary loss, temporary mind, to the minimum, I'll bloody well give you shares for free!'

'I see,' he said.

I had one last problem to clear up: Shirley, who still owned 20 per cent of Klau and Benedict Hong Kong, our shelf company that was going to disappear forever back into the shadows.

I had taken Bob Boyce's advice almost a year ago, and agreed to pay Shirley off. It was the only way to close the matter. After some petty to'ing and fro'ing on the price a deal had been struck. The transfer certificates were prepared, I signed them and sent them on to her in San Francisco.

Then she had started playing games again. She put the price up by fifty per cent based on an irrelevant technicality. I refused point blank. Over the year I tried to rescue the peace deal, but all I received in return was a volley of vicious emails, copied to anyone she could think of, calling me a 'scoundrel, and a rascal', 'treacherous and deceitful', and 'a thief wearing a gentleman's hat'.

I made one last offer to settle with her. There was no need. I was in a perfect position to default. And Tom had no concerns about my 'internal contradictions' like Yuan Bao'an. The original price, which I was sticking to, was not equal to 20 per cent of the money I was going to receive from the deal with Tom, but bearing in mind that she had been given the shares, and then done everything she could to destroy their value, I had a clear conscience. She did not reply.

So all was set for one last showdown. The deal with Tom was signed. They had almost completed due diligence. The procession of suits in and out of our head office reached a peak. I wondered if mine had survived eight years in mothballs. I might be needing them. A powerful publisher was lined up in Beijing, with equal weight to Wuzhou. The plans were all in place for the weeklies.

With a heavy heart, I prepared to say farewell to the brand I had built over seven long years.

'That's that then,' I resigned myself. The next few months were going to be difficult, very difficult, but once I got through them I was on my way. The fortune I had built in China would be secure.

Chapter Nineteen

Coup

On the second of September 2004, a Thursday, I sat at my desk in the small Shanghai apartment that was the new, national head office for *that's* magazines. Across the hallway was the marketing department. Next to it was Lily's small office. Inside, in a wardrobe, were the safe and the chops for the consultancy and Lily's advertising company. In the reception room, the new *Voyage* team was squeezed in beside the finance department. We had outgrown the apartment the day we moved in. Leo sat in the dining room, with large windows that overlooked the busy junction of Yong Jia Road and Tai Yuan Road directly below. Workmen had been digging up the road for the entire time we had been here.

I liked my quiet space in the back. I had a view across the complex's central garden and could look over a tall pine tree onto the green lawns of the villas next door. Sometimes a gardener marched up and down them with a lawnmower. The hum and rattle brought back memories of English summers. If the wind was right I could smell the fresh cut grass from my balcony. Children came out to play after school. Their excited shouts and screams rising to my open window prompted me to pack up for the day and return to my own family. My daughter had just had her second birthday. Joanna was due to give birth to our son in a few weeks' time.

I was waiting for a fax from Tom's head office in Hong Kong. Ekkehard had called in advance. Somehow Wuzhou had found out about our plans. Yuan Bao'an had written to Ekkehard's boss.

The text was intimidating, openly threatening. 'Mark works for Wuzhou,' it said, paraphrased by Ekkehard. 'He has been a bad boy. He belongs to us and will be punished. He has no right to talk to anyone about the business of *that's* magazines.' It had gone on for two pages. It closed with a direct and menacing warning to Tom: 'We know that Tom Group has plans and is eager for expansion into media in mainland China. But the mainland's publishing industry has still not completely opened up. There is no foreign company entering publishing on the mainland who does not have a chink in its armour somewhere. We are sure your company has considered this.'

One of the assistants from the finance department brought in the fax. Her face looked grave. She had noticed the letterhead. She handed it over without a word and left me alone.

How had Wuzhou found out? One of my own staff? I had been extremely careful. Barely five people knew of the Tom deal. Someone in Tom? That's what Yuan said to Tom but I imagined it was part of the intimidation. Or were our emails and phones really being tapped, as Sun Xiaofeng himself had often warned me? I would find out one day. The pressing problem was how to deal with Yuan. I only had one option. For a change I was going to have to apologize in advance. I picked up the phone.

'Mark, you must come to Beijing at once,' Yuan said. 'This is an extremely serious problem. You have acted illegally. My *lingdao* wish to speak to you. You are in very serious trouble.'

'Yuan *Laoshi,*' I replied. 'My wife is due to give birth any day now. I can't leave Shanghai. I have to wait.'

'I am warning you,' he ignored my plea. 'If you do not come to Beijing there will be nothing I can do to help you.'

'Yuan *Laoshi,* let me explain please, on the phone. What I am planning with Tom will not affect *that's* magazines. My company is entering into a commercial partnership with Tom. May I remind you that you have barred my company from dealing with Wuzhou? What I do with it is my affair. I have always told you that I am a businessman and you have sympathized with that position. You will still have *that's* magazines.' I was not telling a lie, but Yuan was not stupid. Why then had I fought so hard for them? It was a question I did not want him to ask.

I asked Joanna if it was OK that I made a dash to Beijing. We settled on the following Monday, there and back in a day. Yuan promised to arrange the meeting with his *lingdao*. I was confident I could explain myself in person.

On the Friday I could not go into work. I was physically sick with worry. That evening, Lily and Leo requested a meeting.

'Come on over,' I said.

I dragged myself from bed and pulled out a bottle of whisky. The first sip made me feel better. Leo joined me with a glass. I huddled in a dressing gown on an armchair and faced their severe faces.

They wanted me to go through the move to Tom and why we were doing it one more time. I went back to the beginning. By the time I finished I was invigorated, my confidence completely genuine. If we stuck together we would make it, like we always had.

They came back to their personal benefits. I explained again. I did not make any concrete promises. I was in no position to. I stressed how they would be looked after, particularly to Lily. They had trusted me for so many years and I had never let them down. I looked at her, searching for a sign of faith.

'We understand,' they said in unison and left me to my lonely weekend.

It passed quietly. On the Sunday I joined some friends from Beijing days who were in town for a wedding. They had come from various parts of South East Asia whence they had scattered over the years. We met for lunch at the Ding Xiang Garden, a popular weekend *dim sum* spot.

I told them how I had stumbled on the place when it opened and written one of our first restaurant reviews about it. It was in the wing of a retired cadres' rest home, surrounded by beautiful gardens that used to be open to all. I had spent many weekend afternoons in a pagoda beside the lake with a good book. Then the restaurant took off, perhaps thanks to my review I joked, and the gardens were closed to all but the old cadres to save them from being overrun.

I scarcely thought about my morning flight to Beijing the next day. I was amongst old friends. It was when they praised my success, told me how impressed they were that I had stuck it out in China, that I remembered how fragile it was.

I was settling down at home to pass on the lunchtime gossip to Joanna when Mike Wester called from Beijing.

'Mark, I am in a very difficult position.' He sounded like he was fumbling for the right words.

'What is it Mike? Tell me.'

'I... I... don't know. There's something... something, going on. I feel I should tell you, but...' He got a grip, and spoke more evenly now he had made his start. 'Mark, if I tell you, then I will be breaking a confidence. And I don't want to do that. But I think you should know. I don't know myself exactly what it all means.'

'In other words, you too are not being told the full details? Seems an odd confidence to want to keep, Mike.' I had a horrible, gut wrenching feeling about where this conversation was going, but I would be damned if I did not seem to be in charge.

'Yeah, you're right, but I feel caught in the middle, so I would rather not say it out loud, you know what I mean?' He paused.

'Mark,' he spoke very deliberately, 'there are senior people in our company talking about what you are doing with Tom. And they don't like it. And they are in a position to screw it up. And I am not going to tell you their names, but...'

'Lily and Leo?'

'Yes. I did not say it. Lily has been up here in Beijing recently, and I don't think she was doing what you sent her to do. She spent a long time talking to my fiancée Toni, about the advertising companies and what would happen to them if we go to Tom.'

'That's OK Mike, I'm not surprised. It doesn't necessarily mean...'

'Mark, I haven't finished. I have been told that either I side with them, and we keep the magazines with Wuzhou, or else. It is as plain as that. I don't know who else is involved, but you can assume that someone senior in the Shanghai office is, probably Mike Cole, and someone they trust in the Guangzhou office.'

That did stop me. I felt hollow, empty. My brain went blank. It was as if my whole mind had shut down. For several seconds I dumbly existed.

I came out of it and spoke quietly. 'Mike, is there anything like a timetable, or plan?'

'No,' he replied and I believed him. 'I don't think they trust me entirely. I didn't give them a very straight answer.'

'Is it possible they are only checking their options? Sounding you and others out should they think it necessary to pull off a coup some time soon? I mean, I had a meeting with both Leo and Lily in my flat on Friday. I went over the whole thing again with them from start to finish.'

'And what did they say?'

'That they understood.'

'Could be taken two ways couldn't it Mark?'

'I suppose so, now you mention it.'

I refused to believe that Lily and Leo would betray me, at least not without giving me a chance. Not them. I had given those two so much, and most of all my trust. Lily was my CFO, the legal rep of the advertising company. She controlled the cornerstone of the whole business. We had an agreement in writing giving me control of her company, but that had been a formality and it was not legally binding anyway. We had been through so much together.

No, not Lily. Leo I had to admit was a bit of an office politician. In the process of looking into Mike Cole's management I had unearthed some silly games Leo was playing between different departments in Shanghai. Nothing serious, or so I thought.

Besides, hadn't Lily and Leo worked so hard to build the business? They surely couldn't think we would be better off with Wuzhou than Tom?

And they had been in my home two days ago. In front of my pregnant wife and child they had listened as I explained how what we were about to do was for the safety of us all. I could not be that blind. They could not be so heartless.

'Mike.' I pulled myself together. 'I'm coming to Beijing tomorrow as you know. I am going to meet Yuan and his *lingdao*. I'm prepared. I know how to handle them. You and I have already discussed how we could carry on *that's* at the same time as the new magazine. They have forced the issue before I am completely ready. But we'll deal with it. Tom is right behind us. Please believe me. I'll come and see you straight afterwards.'

The next morning I arrived at the airport in good time for the eight o'clock flight. I was carrying a briefcase with a notebook in it, nothing else.

It was a bright and clear morning, the sun rising on an Indian summer's day. I paused outside the terminal. I had plenty of time. I looked at my reflection in the glass wall. I was a dark silhouette against the bright blue sky. I leant in close to study my face.

'Are you ready Mark? You know what you're doing? Can handle this one? Sure you're not out of your depth?'

'I don't know,' I answered myself truthfully. 'For the first time, I really don't know. I feel alone.'

'You are mate,' my image smirked back at me. 'Totally alone. Why don't you have a cigarette and a think?'

I turned around and squatted down on the raised concrete curb that ran along the wall. It was just broad enough for my backside. I lit a cigarette and squinted into the low sun, rising over the city to the east. I was afraid. Wuzhou, Yuan Bao'an, the *lingdao*, they scared me.

Once I had flicked the butt away, I stood up and brushed the seat of my trousers. There was no turning back now. I marched up to the check-in counter. There was no queue. I took my boarding pass. The deserted hall increased my sense of unreality, the distance from what was going on around me.

'Gate number 16. No rush sir,' the young man on the desk said.

Then I'll go outside for another smoke.

Back in the sunshine, I thought again. No more pep talk with a pane of glass. Time to get serious.

'When do people strike when they are mounting a coup? When is the ideal moment?' asked the voice of China experience.

'When the person they are taking over from has his back turned. Or is away from his power base.'

'Quite. Who are your enemies?'

'Wuzhou. Yuan Bao'an.'

'Where do you think he is right now? Waiting for you in Beijing? Why are you going to Beijing anyway?'

'Because he asked me to. Because he wants me out of the way.' It was dawning on me like the sun rising over the horizon.

Well, I hope you win this one, whatever it's about. Wanna coffee?'

'Thanks Mark, but I need to get on.' I was having trouble holding back from blurting out my story. Mark had always been a rock. 'And Mark,' I kept it short. 'This really might be the last one.' I turned away to hide the emotion screwing up my face, and walked out of his door.

Back on the street I paused to take stock. Now where? It was too early to find Lily or Leo. But I wanted to talk to someone.

Simone, the *that's Shanghai* sales manager. She was always up early. Something about her cats I remembered. And she was a good friend.

'Mark?' she sounded surprised when she answered her mobile. 'I thought you were on a plane to Beijing.' How did she know about that?

'I'm not. I changed my mind.' She did not ask. 'Simone, I know I can be straight with you. Can I ask you please, is something going to happen in the office today?'

She spoke carefully. 'Actually, I am there now. And yes, we have been told there will be a meeting this morning. It will be held by Lily and Leo. Everyone has been told to attend.' The sound of her strong German voice made me feel better. 'Mark,' she went on. 'Is it possible to see you, now? I would like to tell you about something, something that happened over the weekend.'

We agreed to meet at a coffee shop halfway between the office and the street where I was standing. I walked. It helped me think.

The pavements were busy with commuters rushing to their offices a little after nine o'clock. Buses with squealing brakes pulled up at their stops, the doors snapped open and ejected passengers like lotus seeds popping out of a pod. The junction of Changshu Road and Huaihai Road was backed up as usual by a scrum of taxis, pushing and shoving their way across the lanes. Traffic wardens blew their whistles and with their tiny tour leader pennants waved cyclists onto the pavement. The Tibetan trinket sellers had already spread their multi-coloured blankets covered by their wares on the grass verges, like flowerbeds.

I felt detached from day to day life. I looked at the thronging streets as if for the first time, or the last time.

Simone was waiting for me deep inside the Camphor Garden Coffee Shop, away from the street side windows and the chance that someone might spot us. I felt pale, if I did not look it, as I sat down.

'You OK Mark?' she asked.

'I think so.' We both lit cigarettes. I had smoked half a packet already. 'Can you tell me what's happening Sim?'

'I'm not sure,' she said, 'but over the weekend Leo called me. He asked some very unusual questions, for example what I thought of you, and your management of *that's*. Then he asked about Michael Cole too, same sort of questions. It was very odd. And he's been speaking to my sales staff, late last week, one by one. And now there is this meeting today, at 10 o'clock.' She thought for a moment. 'Oh, and another thing. Did you know Michael Cole went to Beijing last week? Just for one day.'

'No I didn't. But I remember looking for him last Thursday, and thinking it odd no one knew where he was. It was then I suppose.'

Simone was looking at me with a mixture of sympathy and just a little approbation. Maybe I was imagining it but I could not help thinking that she held me responsible for letting this situation develop and for losing my grip on Mike Cole, whom she had never liked. If she did feel that way she was right. I was responsible.

Simone and I walked back to the Shanghai magazine office. Staff were drifting in. Nothing seemed amiss. Then I found Lily in the finance department. Her surprise was obvious. She did not ask why I was not on a plane. I asked her to come outside to the small anteroom. We sat side by side on the same blue sofa that she had cried on when she left to have her baby.

There was a massive lump in my throat. I struggled to get the words past it. Her face was devoid of any emotion, pure blankness yet with a clear hint of inside, superior knowledge.

'Lily. You're fired.' I had to say it. It was the only way to find out, to be sure.

She did not flinch. Her tone patronizing, she said straight back to me, 'Mark, it is not that simple.'

I was right.

'Where's Leo?' I asked. I felt myself falling through space, like in a dream.

'I don't know.'

'He's going to be fired too. If I can't find him, I'll call him and tell him over the phone.' I stood up. It took a supreme effort. I felt utterly drained of energy.

'Mark,' Lily looked up and spoke again. 'It's too late.'

I walked over to the head office. I was drifting in and out of shock. I called Leo's mobile on the way.

'I just fired Lily, and you're fired too.' I felt in control as I said it.

'No I am not Mark.'

'Yes you fucking well are. Come and see me in my office, now!' I shouted and hung up. And I slipped back into my swirling dream world.

As I was about to enter the lift, Simone called. 'Mark, they're all here. The meeting is about to start.' I turned and strode back the way I had come. My sense of purpose returned. I was building a sweat.

It always happens to someone else, never you. You hear the stories and joke about them over a beer with your friends: when

I got back to the *that's Shanghai* office, I was locked out.

The security guard stared at me from inside the metal grill and glass door, his face set in a mask of determination. He didn't say a word, just shook his head. *Aiyi*, the housekeeper and cleaner we'd had for years and who Mark Secchia once caught cutting her toenails on my desk, looked out from the door of her shack and clucked something in Shanghainese. She indicated I was welcome to sit in her lean-to until the door opened. I waved her away.

Simone and Samz, the Malaysian Chinese art director, appeared in the reception area. They looked agonized.

'I'll get my key.' It was Samz. He dashed up the stairs and down again to open the door. He glared at the security guard, who was twice his size but stepped back.

'Thanks Samz,' I walked inside. 'They're in the meeting room?'

'Yes. We refused to take part. They locked us out too.'

I tried the door handle. It was locked. I slumped down onto a sofa and tried to smile. I was numb. I knew I had to do something, get in there and say something. But what? Samz and Simone stood beside me. Their presence helped a fraction. They were good people. Behind that door were some bad ones.

I stared at it. It was the door to my private hell. When it opened, I had to go in there.

At last the handle turned. I leapt to my feet and caught the first of the staff, their faces a mixture of confusion and embarrassment when they saw me.

'Please could everyone go back inside.' I had to try.

Most of them were standing. There were only ten chairs around the table. I looked around the sea of faces, all directed at me. The ones I knew well seemed to be trying to show some sympathy, and helplessness. Those I was not so familiar with struggled to look blank, or at the floor. Mike Cole was absent, which I thought odd.

At the head of the table there was enough room for three people to sit abreast. In between Lily and Leo was Yuan Bao'an.

'So we're obviously not meeting in Beijing today Mr. Yuan.'

It was Leo who spoke. 'Mark, it is done. We are taking over.' His voice was strong and clear. 'You are no longer in charge of *that's* magazines. Mr. Yuan is here to give his approval and support. Wuzhou is the publisher. Everyone in this room understands and will be working for us now.'

One of the young foreign editors, who I had penciled in for editor-in-chief of the Shanghai weekly, was standing right beside me. His eyes were trying to say something. I knew he meant well. He was a decent guy. No one broke the silence. I had to speak.

'What has happened here today,' I was choking with emotion, 'is a horrible thing. Horrible.'

Now what? I was stumbling over my words. 'But what I have been trying to do over the past months is something very good for us. Very good.' So that's it, I thought, I am going prattle about good and evil. Hardly save-the-day at the last minute inspiration.

'I have been working hard on a plan to save this business, this magazine, from the slow death it faces with Wuzhou, with Mr. Yuan.' I pointed at him. 'That plan still exists and can still work. There is a good company who want to work with us and can look after us.' Yuan smirked at me. No one noticed. They were looking at me.

'You wait,' I spoke up. The tears were close. 'Just wait. I'll sort things out and I'll take care of you all.'

I stepped back. I had run out of things to say. The staff filed past me. Some of them touched me on the arm, out of sight. Yuan stayed at the head of the table. I ignored him. Leo and Lily made to pass me too.

'You can bloody well sit down. Now!' They sat. I shut the door and moved round the table and took a chair facing them.

'How could you betray me like this?' I shouted. 'You knew what I was doing. You came to my own house and had me explain it to you again, a few days ago. You knew what had to be done and you know bloody well that Wuzhou is going to destroy this business! And in case you forget, it is my business that I paid for and built over seven years of damned hard work.'

'Exactly Mark, it was at your house I realized you betrayed me,' it was Leo, putting on a show of anger too, 'when you told me I must buy shares if I did not keep all the clients. How could you do that to me?'

'Leo, you stupid bastard. For one thing that was a lighthearted attempt to encourage you, and secondly there is nothing treacherous about inviting staff to buy shares in a private company. You idiot.'

'But Mark, you've fired me. If you had not fired me, I would not have done this.'

'You what!? You mean to say that in the five minutes after I called you, you got Yuan Bao'an down from Beijing,' I pointed at him, listening smugly to my every word. I knew he understood perfectly, even though he pretended he could barely speak a word of English, 'called a meeting of all the staff and organized a takeover, the theft, of my business? Don't be so fucking stupid to expect me to believe that.' I wished I had been a boxer, not a fencer. 'I know you've been planning this for some time.'

'That's not true Mark,' Leo was trying to look like he had been falsely accused. 'It was not us, I promise. We were forced into it. We are not the ones who betrayed you.'

'Save your bullshit, Leo. And get the hell out of my office. Now! This is Gao Bang's property, and you have been fired.'

'No it's not.' It was Lily, in a quiet voice. 'This office now belongs to my company. I transferred it.'

Of course, she had the chops of both companies. I shouldn't have been surprised and I wasn't.

I spoke evenly, trying to keep the anxiety out of my voice. 'What about the bank accounts Lily?'

'Don't worry. We will not steal Gao Bang's money.' The irony would have been hilarious, if they had not just stolen everything else from me. I knew I had no legal title to it but in a few weeks I would have done, thanks to Tom. They had caught me at the last minute.

'And you'll be paid your salary for August,' Lily continued. As if I cared a hoot.

'What about our agreement for the use of your company?' I asked her. 'You're going to cancel that I suppose.' It was a pointless question but her answer gave me a clue to her motivation.

'You already cancelled it Mark when you told me it would be taken over by Tom.'

'That was for your own good, you silly… oh, what's the use?' I trailed off.

'Don't worry, you'll be taken care of Mark,' Leo again.

The impulse to tell the lying, scheming, two-faced treacherous bastard to go fuck himself was overwhelming. I despised the sight of him. I felt sick. How dare he make such a transparent lie to my face.

'Well,' I wanted to get out of there. 'You've done it. You're going to destroy *that's* magazines, with Wuzhou's help. You have no future. You know it. You've stolen my creation and you're no doubt going to milk it for all its worth before it dies.'

'But Mark, you said yourself we were going to lose *that's* when we went to Tom.'

'You're forgetting two things,' I stood up. 'One: I built it, and two: I had a future for us, all of us, and the spirit of *that's* and all it stands for. Together we could have rebuilt it, in no time at all in fact, and all have benefited.'

I walked out without looking at Yuan.

I followed the street back to the head office. I felt like a tragic, defeated hero. It wasn't that bad a feeling.

The fight was over. I had lost. I had fought with honour and I had been betrayed. I held my head high. The world looked different, and it was, my world at least. It looked happier. It was as if I had been spat out from a maelstrom. I could go home and rest, defeated, but alive. It was almost a relief.

If nothing else the years struggling against all those odds, the government, the partners, the officials, the raids, the deportations, they had inured me to defeat. They had made me tough, even if there had been some terrible low points. Above all I knew, I was sure, I had done something good. And I was not finished forever.

Then again, I had to admit this was pretty final. I had lost a fortune the minute that I was about to get my hands on it, and my magazines. They had been my whole life, at least until I married Joanna.

I sat for a long time at my desk, in the special leather executive chair that Lizzie, our marketing and event manager who had left almost a year ago had surprised me with when she reorganized the meeting room.

'You're bloody executive geezer now aren't you,' she'd said as she wheeled out the cheap seat that I had sat in since I could remember. Lizzie was 'geezer this' and 'geezer that'. She'd even got the Chinese staff using the word. She was as English as cheddar cheese, even though she had hardly lived there. She came up from Hong Kong to work for us. 'I want to work in media in China and you're top of my list,' she had said when we met for an interview, which finished in a nightclub at three in the morning.

I thought of all the other good people I had employed over

the years. Shelley Yip, married and moving back to Canada. Iris Zheng, married and emigrated to California. Meady Tang, one of the *Time Out* interns, married and living in London. Neil Gough, my favourite managing editor in Guangzhou: Time magazine Hong Kong. JR, the water ballet maestro: running his own publication back in Manila. Carol Lu, intern at *Clueless in Guangzhou*, then managing editor, then arts and entertainment in Beijing, then Guides editor in Shanghai, now running art galleries. Sam Ailwood, sales then editorial in Shanghai, then Beijing, then managing editor of *that's Nothing*. So many people. So much we had done. So much we had all been through. So much they had done for me.

And I had gone and lost it.

I went home and let myself into our apartment. Our family *aiyi* was giving our daughter her lunch. Joanna followed me into our bedroom. I sat on a chair and pulled her towards me. I put my arms around her waist and laid my head against her pregnant tummy. Our son was in there. I spoke to him as much as to Joanna.

'Honey, they've stolen my business. I have lost everything. I've let you down. It was for you, for Isabel, and him,' I touched her stomach, 'that I did all this. And I have lost it, all of it.'

And then I sobbed. I had held myself together all morning, too preoccupied by anger and ideas how to save something from the disaster to let in any emotion. Suddenly it all flooded out. My shoulders heaved and the tears poured down my cheeks. In between gushes I told Joanna the basic facts of the day's events. The betrayal of Lily and Leo had hurt me more than I realized. Now it broke my heart.

'Don't worry. We'll be OK.' Joanna said the words of comfort. 'You've got us. We'll always be here for you.'

I sobbed some more.

Chapter Twenty
Retreat

My China publishing career did not end that horrible September day. It lasted a few months more. Over the course of the following week I did everything I could to rescue something from the wreckage. Ekkehard and Tom Group were supportive. They tried to salvage our deal but the publisher they'd lined up was threatened by Wuzhou's *lingdao* in the State Council and backed out. That scuppered the city weeklies.

'Mark, we still want to work with you, but you need a product,'Ekkehard told me. 'What have you got?'

'The travel magazine?' I said. 'I can probably rescue that.'

'Can you make it work? And for how much? Can you give me a budget, something under a couple of million yuan?'

Time was short. I had to act fast to rescue not only the magazine but the staff to run it. I spent the week in the boardroom of Tom's new Shanghai office, struggling through excel files, and I uncovered more details about the takeover.

Mike Cole had indeed flown to Beijing to meet Yuan Bao'an as Simone had said. He told Yuan what I was planning with Tom Group and put himself forward as the person to work with once Yuan got rid of me. Yuan had called Leo, and Lily. He would prefer to work with Chinese. Leo and Lily had either believed his threats, were scared by his power — it's that Shanghainese thing again — or made the decision to help Yuan push me out and run the business themselves. Cole would have to go too.

While I understood Lily and Leo's motivation, and fear, I was sickened by the way Mike Cole had played along, lying to my face, pretending to be supportive,while the chaos he had unleashed destroyed my life.

Yuan had gone to see him in Shanghai first thing on the morning of the takeover, to sound him out again, and decided it was better to stick with the devils he knew, Leo and Lily.

Next shocker: I discovered Cole had been preparing all along to set up his own weekly magazine anyway, with staff he'd have taken from me. That was why he'd done bugger all to make a difference to *that's Shanghai*. When he failed to steal it, he offered staff jobs with his new venture that was ready to go. He even had financial backers. I was right to want to fire him.

Tom approved my numbers and told me to bring the staff. I summoned a meeting on the top floor of a bar and restaurant that had been one of our longest standing clients. They threw in the drinks and food for free.

Thirty of the key editorial and marketing staff had hung on, resisting the pressure from Yuan and Leo to sign up with them and telling Mike Cole to wait. It was an emotional meeting. I could only take twenty. There were tears, protests and grim-faced acceptance, followed by hugs and handshakes. The people I couldn't accommodate at Tom went to work for Mike Cole. That meant Leo and Lily were left without an editorial department, so they invited Kathleen and Shirley back to help. Shirley insisted they would do so only if Lily paid her the money I had agreed to pay a year ago for her shares. Lily paid. I did not get the shares. Of course not. Shirley slapped on a 'consultancy fee' and rounded the amount Lily and Leo had to pay in total for her and Kathleen's help up to one million yuan, payable in advance.

Kathleen and Shirley threw a party at Kathleen's new restaurant on the top floor of the Shanghai Art Museum, to celebrate what they thought of as their regaining control of *that's* magazines. They invited everyone in Shanghai who had ever had anything to do with the magazines, except me. Sun Xiaofeng was there, even Mr. Wang from the News Bureau Development Company. I was told the officials and Kathleen and Shirley made grand speeches.

The next issue of *that's Shanghai* could have been retitled *that's Kathleen*. Her restaurant appeared throughout the listings and extracts from a rambling 'how-to' book for expats she had written and published privately about living in Shanghai appeared in the features, followed by a reader's quiz about the same book. I forced myself to read through it and remembered with morbid satisfaction what Kathleen had said all those years ago, when we dreamt up *Ish*. This is what she meant by 'deep and meaningful' features.

According to old friends in the *that's Shanghai* office, Shirley spent her time photocopying every internal document she could find that might be useful for her campaign to make my life miserable. I didn't read the gloating email she sent me.

I assume it was gloating.

After a couple of issues Leo and Lily got rid of Kathleen and Shirley and recruited a young team of foreign editors. Shirley tried to sue them, and asked me to be a witness on her behalf.

Up in Beijing Mike Wester was caught in the crossfire. I heard that Toni, his fiancée and the legal rep of my advertising company in Beijing, was threatened by Yuan in person. 'If you do not do what we say, we will withdraw the *kanhao* from *that's Beijing*. The magazine will not appear, nor will the advertising, and the clients your company has made contracts with will sue you. We will make sure of that. We will also make sure that the strictest penalty is enforced. That might mean jail.' Poor Mike. He was just about to get married. He had a team to look after, a business he had built, even if it was with my money and template. I encouraged him to take care of himself and his staff. We remained friends though our relationship was tricky. Of the three city magazines, *that's Beijing* was always my favourite. It had character, and attitude, like Beijing itself.

In 2008, a month before the Olympics, Yuan and Wuzhou kicked Mike out, put in their own team and in one issue destroyed the magazine. Mike put his experience he had learnt to good use. He moved his staff back into his apartment and came out with *The Beijinger,* with another publisher. It's still going.

Tom took good care of me, while they could. They put up the money to turn *Voyage* from a side project into a full on glossy travel magazine. Getting stuck back into making a magazine kept me busy. I loved the work. The team, considering what they had just been through, were brilliant.

Then Shirley complained to the Shanghai News Bureau, in person, and presented them with a copy of the old Gao Bang, our joint venture, consultancy contract with the Tourism Bureau to produce *Voyage*. We had been using a book number for Voyage without any problem since I started the project, nine months before. The arrangement had been passed on to Tom. Shirley asked Yuan Bao'an to help, and we lost the publisher.

Through intermediaries I made clear to Yuan Bao'an that all I wanted was to get on with my life. The travel magazine was no threat to him or *that's*. The message came back that he understood and would not interfere. He proceeded to make our lives hell. Our printer was threatened with jail.

Tom found another publisher to replace the original one I'd used for *Voyage,* but Yuan Bao'an called the General Administration of Press and Publications in Beijing. In turn they told our new publishing partner, also using a book number, to drop us. That publisher had good *guanxi* of his own at GAPP too. I called up Yuan, using the *that's* trademark licence agreement which we had just started negotiating as an excuse for the call and also a bargaining chip. I slipped in the name of our publisher's friend at GAPP.

'Give him a call,' I suggested. 'Withdraw your complaints about *Voyage* and I'll be nice about licensing you my trademark.' It was bold but it was worth a try.

The next day I had a call from our publisher. His *guanxi* in GAPP had been accused by Yuan of taking bribes from us and he was hopping mad. Yuan had stuck another knife in.

I was all the way back to square one, searching for publishing partners and building a magazine. I had the Tourism Bureau on side and Tom paying the bills. At last we found a perfect partner, way down south in Guangxi Province, who was publishing a Chinese language travel magazine. In March we came out with the first issue of *Voyage* with their support. For once the agreement was completely legal, the ping-pong ball in the middle of the table. Not a single loophole. I relaxed. Now I could get on with business. I was enjoying the work with Voyage more than I expected. I always liked travel.

Ten days later the Guangxi publisher's Shanghai agent called my mobile. She was hysterical.

'Mark! I know you said there might be trouble but you didn't tell us it would be this bad.' I had indeed warned her to look out. And I'd said it might be bad.

She was frantic with worry. 'All hell has broken loose. My boss has been summoned to Beijing by the State Council Information Office. It looks like our own magazine is going to be shut down, he might lose his position…'

'Slow down,' I said. 'What trouble are you talking about?'

'That you are a supporter of independence for Xinjiang!'

'What?'

She spoke slowly. 'The *lingdao* in Beijing have told us we are working with a Muslim separatist sympathizer. Mark, if you were Chinese, you'd be in jail. They say you're a terrorist!'

'That's ridiculous. Besides, what has it to do with the magazine? It's produced between Tom and your guys.'

'Oh yes, the magazine. Funny that. They said that the arrangement between us is perfectly legal. It's working with you *that's* the problem.'

So Yuan got me back at last for that book review stunt I pulled. I had to admire his cunning. He had me on paper, quoting someone who sympathized with the Xinjiang Uighurs, Muslims.

I resigned from Tom and *Voyage*. Wherever I went I would be hounded by Wuzhou and they would use all their power, the full weight of their *lingdao* in the State Council to destroy any attempt I made to work in media in China. And they would use that power in their special way, to attack anyone who came into contact with me. I was a pariah. Ekkehard was sorry. But the only chance *Voyage* had was if I stepped away from it.

Yuan Bao'an called Tom and demanded that the next issue of *Voyage* carried a full-page announcement making clear that I had nothing to do with the magazine anymore. The person I handed it over to disguised the notice as a brief response to a reader's letter.

I tried to work out why Yuan was so determined to destroy my working life in China. Was he afraid of me, as some people suggested? There is the theory that if you knock someone down, be sure to finish them off completely or they will come back for revenge.

I did not want revenge. How could I get it anyway? My only hope for any redress was my trademark, and that would be a commercial negotiation, so I hoped. Yuan held the *kanhao*. I could never publish with them again. The licenses had been issued with the official name *'Chengshimanbu'*, *City Walker* in English. *'that's'*, because it was an English word, could only be an unofficial title.

Or was Yuan worried I might turn *Voyage* into a competitor? Knowing his complete lack of commercial sense, that was possible. But we were already co-operating with *that's Beijing,* much to Yuan's fury, as I heard from Mike Wester. Did he think I held some secret that could harm him, like the payments made into his personal account in the early days of our co-operation? We had accepted his excuse that he would pay the money on to the censors. But I had no evidence. I wasn't interested in looking for it either. Most likely it was the trademark. That had been a nasty surprise for him. Perhaps Lily and Leo had been too embarrassed, or afraid, to tell him about it.

My last ever publishing partner had added a word about the trademark at the end of her hysterical phone call. 'One more thing,' she had said. 'The *lingdao* from the State Council Information Office said something very weird when my boss was leaving his office. He literally called him back as he was going through the door. It was: "And you can tell him we're going to get his trademark too." What's that all about?'

The legal battle for the *that's* trademark would drag on for two years, but my mind was already turning to what I could do next; a fresh start. After seven years in the cut-throat, back-stabbing world of Chinese state-dominated media I wanted to get back to a different, happier China — the one that I had fallen in love with all those years ago as a student.

Joanna and I had a weekend hideaway in a small village built in the early 1900s by foreign missionaries as a heat retreat, on the top of the first mountain you come to, due west of Shanghai. Its name is Moganshan. After a long, yet — compared to what I was used to — gentle battle with the government agencies who control the place, we had secured a ten-year lease on a derelict stone house and restored it to something like its former glory. We furnished it with the basics for a summer weekend hideaway and installed a fireplace and chimney so we could use it in winter too. To get to it, once you'd found your way across the Zhejiang plain on the old B-roads, round the shambolic suburbs of Hangzhou and along the country lanes, and up the mountain itself, you still had to climb two hundred steps from the nearest tiny road. It really was a hideaway.

We decided to move our young family up there. Our daughter Isabel was two years old, and Tristan, our son, had arrived the week after the takeover. (He had been born in the Ruijin Hospital, across the road from the H.E. Morris's old home, the Ruijin Guesthouse. It was a difficult, nightlong birth, and I had stumbled out of the hospital in search of breakfast. As if led by a whimsical sprite I found myself in the old building of the hotel, the original Morris family home. There I was, right back where I started in Shanghai, in the home of my British predecessor whose grandson I had bragged to, seven years ago. Now I might have a grandson, with my name, one day. And he could say almost exactly the same thing as Morris had to me.)

But unlike Morris's grandfather I didn't have to leave China, not yet. Joanna and I established a small coffee shop on our mountain. I went into the kitchen, she ran front of house. Our children spent the first decade of their lives running through bamboo forests, learning characters by rote in local schools, and how to swim in mountain reservoirs with no shallow end. We could walk for miles and bump into an old lady picking wild tea who would look up, call them by name, and tell them which of their school mate's great grandmother she was.

When I wasn't needed in the coffee shop I sat on the terrace outside our house, looking out over the hills and down to the plain, glass of whisky in hand — smaller than the ones I used to knock myself out with in Shanghai — nursing my wounds. I went all the way back to where I had been before I fell in with Kathleen: a young Englishman in China who had wanted to be a writer. And I at last became one. The Hong Kong-based Asian Literary Review — the 'Granta of Asia' — published one of my short stories. I became a columnist for a prestigious British magazine. 'Illustrate the big picture of China with anecdotes about life there' was the brief. When my first book came out, which was supposed to be the sequel to this one, the sense of achievement, of having done something useful and permanent in China, at last, was immense. And it had my name on it, as an author. I didn't have to hide behind a made-up job title of convenience: like planning manager.

Over the years, on the mountain, the pain faded and I was able to look back with pride at what *that's* magazines had achieved. I know we helped when Shanghai won its bid for the World Expo in 2010. Not only had we designed and edited the bid materials but the Shanghai mayor had taken our magazines to Paris to show how international and sophisticated his city was. One of his secretaries had come to the office to collect the copies. We helped with the Olympic bid too. That Yuan Bao'an re-took control of *that's Beijing* before the event itself is cast-iron proof.

And we helped to bring people together. I treasured the memory of how a journalist friend told me he noticed, and appreciated, how we never used the word 'Chinese' or 'expat' — 'foreigner' even — in the magazines.

I must admit to developing mixed feelings about China and

the Chinese however, that have nothing to do with my magazine business and how it ended. Life is good. I am over it. But I regret what the country has become. It is nothing like the China I fell in love with as a student in the nineteen eighties. The obsession with money and personal power that the Chinese Communist Party has bred into society has filtered down to every level.

The Chinese have always set great store in personal wealth, but never to the extent they do today, and never without some sort of check or balance, like religion, or a tradition of government officials either exiled or who resigned in protest to become the conscience of a nation, expressed through literature, particularly poetry.

The Chinese deserve better. They are better.

Mao Zedong famously said, or is reputed to have said, in Tian'anmen Square when he announced the founding of the People's Republic of China on the first of October, 1949: 'The people of China have stood up.'

One day soon perhaps they'll walk too, along a path they'll choose for themselves.

I hope so.

www.fortysix.tv